COOKING WITH
Bon Appétit

COOKING WITH
Bon Appétit

Recipe Yearbook 1988

Editors' Choice of Recipes from 1987

THE KNAPP PRESS
Publishers
Los Angeles

Copyright © 1988 by Knapp Communications Corporation

Published by The Knapp Press
5900 Wilshire Boulevard, Los Angeles, California 90036

Library of Congress Cataloging-in-Publication Data

Recipe yearbook 1988.

   (Cooking with Bon appétit)
   Includes index.
   1. Cookery, International.   I. Bon appétit.   II. Series.
TX725.A1R4233   1988   641.5   87-22610
ISBN 0-89535-195-1

Bon Appétit Books offers cookbook stands. For details on ordering please write:
   Bon Appétit Books
   Premium Department
   Sherman Turnpike
   Danbury, CT 06816

On the Cover: *Fresh Tuna with Piquant Sauce. Photographed by Irwin Horowitz.*

Printed and bound in the United States of America
10   9   8   7   6   5   4   3   2   1

❧ Contents

❦ *Foreword*

In this, our second annual collection of recipes from *Bon Appétit* magazine, you will find an exciting mix of food styles, from the exotic to the homey; from spicy and unusual flavor blends to familiar and comforting tastes and textures. Some of the country's finest restaurants and cooks have contributed to the 200-plus recipes here, selected by the editors to represent important trends of the year.

A major influence from last year, Southwestern cooking is still going strong, with its distinctive spices and emphasis on grilling. The grill has become an essential cooking tool, and you will find it used many ways in this book, from smoky grilled pizzas to skewered vegetables basted with cumin butter. Another highly spiced regional cuisine, Creole cooking, is still making its mark as well, flavoring dishes from poached eggs and fettuccine to a Thanksgiving turkey with Jambalaya stuffing.

What was the start of a trend last year is now a full-blown fact of culinary life: Home cooking is being boldly celebrated at dinner parties and in elegant restaurants across the country. All-American favorites—stews and Sunday roasts, bread puddings and old-fashioned layer cakes, even humble macaroni and cheese and meat loaf—can be seen on the menus of fashionable restaurants everywhere.

Also continuing is the popularity of a lighter, more informal kind of dining-out. Bistros encourage diners to savor and linger. The fare ranges from wholesome country favorites like stews and casseroles, to antipasti, innovative pastas and main-dish salads. Some of this year's most creative and delicious cooking has come from these chic cafes and restaurants.

In October the magazine introduced a new column that answered the needs and requests of many readers. In the belief that food that tastes good can also be good for you, "Cooking Healthy" offers ideas for food that is not only nutritious but also delicious, uncomplicated and attractive. Besides this column, recipes throughout the magazine are reflecting this important trend.

In another growing trend, people are eating breakfast and brunch more often. Whether it's a business-oriented "power breakfast" or a leisurely weekend party, the morning meal is a great opportunity to start off the day with something easy, light and healthful, or to experiment with exciting new menu choices. *Bon Appétit*'s definition of breakfast foods includes the traditional, from homemade hot cereal to cottage cheese griddle cakes, as well as the unusual, such as spicy eggs with tortillas, salsa and cheese or an English-style creamed rice pilaf with fish, ham and egg. Whatever your personal preference for the morning meal, you will find a variety of ideas here.

Variety—and a devotion to quality—has been the unifying theme for the diverse foods presented in this volume. Throughout the year, whether the cooking is Southwestern, Creole, Italian, Chinese or straightforward American, the emphasis is on traditional flavors and recipes that have been refined, lightened and updated with innovative techniques and the best locally available ingredients. The result: a "sophisticated freshness" and contemporary appeal.

To round out our review of trends, we've included at the back of this book a section called "News '87—The Year of Food and Entertaining in Review." Consisting of brief notes on products and services, restaurants and people, travel tips and diet news, "News '87" tracks some of the more important developments of the year. For your current use, all prices, addresses and other information have been updated as of this yearbook's publication date.

1 ❦ Appetizers

Appetizers, hors d'oeuvres, antipasti, tapas or dim sum—whatever you call them, these savory tidbits are among the most popular recipes in the magazine. Often, some of the best come from favorite restaurants: Grilled Caponata (page 3), an unusual blend of grilled eggplant and red onion with a touch of unsweetened cocoa powder added to the tomato base for extra flavor; Suppli di Riso (page 5), crisp fried balls of saffron rice and cheese, served with a tangy tomato sauce; and Hoisin Barbecued Spareribs (page 9), crisp yet succulent pork lightly smoked with tea leaves and covered with a sweet and spicy glaze.

As is true of many of the recipes this year, good spicing and bold flavors are definitely a trademark of these tasty openers. Hot and crunchy Peppered Pecans (page 2) and down-home Louisiana Hot Chicken Wings (page 9) provide a zippy, satisfying welcome. Variations on more traditional appetizers include a surprisingly easy Caviar Pâté (page 4), herb-flecked Four-Pepper Ceviche (page 3) and Pork Rumaki (page 10).

Peppered Pecans

8 servings

1 tablespoon olive oil
1 teaspoon freshly ground black
  pepper
1 teaspoon freshly ground white
  pepper
1 teaspoon cayenne pepper
1/2 teaspoon dried thyme, crumbled

2 egg whites
1 tablespoon Worcestershire sauce
1 teaspoon hot pepper sauce
1 teaspoon salt
4 1/4 cups pecan halves (about
  1 pound)

Position rack in upper third of oven and preheat to 375°F. Brush heavy large baking pan with oil. Mix black and white pepper, cayenne pepper and thyme in small bowl. Whisk egg whites in medium bowl until foamy. Whisk in Worcestershire, hot pepper sauce and salt. Add pecans and toss to coat. Sift pepper mixture over pecans, tossing pecans quickly.

Spread pecan mixture evenly in prepared pan. Bake 5 minutes. Stir nuts, breaking up any clumps. Bake until crisp and deep golden brown, stirring twice and watching carefully to prevent burning, about 7 minutes more. Transfer to bowl. Cool completely. (*Can be prepared 4 days ahead. Store in airtight container.*)

Fennel and Celery Sticks with Olive Oil-Mustard Dip

Makes 2 2/3 cups

4 egg yolks
6 tablespoons coarse-grained Dijon
  mustard
1/4 cup fresh lemon juice
2 cups olive oil

6 tablespoons freshly grated
  Parmesan cheese
Fennel sticks
Celery sticks

Combine yolks, mustard and lemon juice in medium bowl. Whisk in oil in thin stream. Stir in Parmesan. Serve with fennel and celery sticks.

Chinese Nachos

8 servings

1 cup plum jelly
1/2 cup mango chutney
1 1/2 tablespoons red wine vinegar
1 teaspoon dry mustard
1/4 teaspoon hot pepper sauce

1 14-ounce package won ton skins
  Vegetable oil (for deep frying)

Chopped green onions

Combine first 5 ingredients in heavy small saucepan. Stir over medium heat until thoroughly blended and bubbly.

Cut won ton skins in half on diagonal. Heat oil in deep fryer or deep skillet to 365°F. Add won ton skins in batches and fry until golden brown and blistered, 2 minutes. Drain on paper towels.

Spoon sauce into bowl. Garnish with green onions. Serve hot or at room temperature with fried won ton skins.

Curried Cheese Spread

Makes about 1½ cups

2 3-ounce packages cream cheese, room temperature
1 cup grated sharp cheddar cheese
¼ cup minced onions
1 tablespoon dry Sherry

1 teaspoon curry powder
¼ teaspoon salt
2 tablespoons mango chutney, chopped

Blend cream cheese with cheddar in medium bowl. Mix in onions, Sherry, curry powder and salt. Stir in chutney. Serve at room temperature with crackers or toast. (*Can be prepared 2 days ahead. Cover tightly and refrigerate.*)

Grilled Caponata

Grilling the eggplant and onion adds a fine smoky nuance to this traditional Italian appetizer.

Makes about 1 quart

2 tablespoons dried currants
2 8½-inch-long eggplants (unpeeled), cut into ⅝-inch-thick slices
1 large red onion (unpeeled), cut into ⅝-inch-thick rounds
Extra-virgin olive oil

1 16-ounce can Italian plum tomatoes, drained and chopped
2 teaspoons unsweetened cocoa powder

20 capers (preferably packed in salt)
10 pitted green olives, sliced
8 Kalamata olives, pitted and quartered
3 tablespoons chopped fresh Italian parsley
¼ cup balsamic vinegar
¼ cup extra-virgin olive oil
Salt and freshly ground pepper

Soak currants in hot water 30 minutes.

Prepare barbecue grill (medium heat). Brush eggplant and onion with oil on both sides. Grill eggplant until soft, about 5 minutes per side. Grill onion until lightly charred and cooked through, about 8 minutes per side. Cool slightly.

Mix tomatoes and cocoa in large bowl until cocoa dissolves. Drain currants and add. Mix in capers, olives and parsley. Peel onions. Coarsely chop eggplant and onions and fold into tomato mixture. Stir in vinegar and ¼ cup oil. Season with salt and pepper. Let stand at least 30 minutes before serving. (*Can be prepared 4 days ahead and chilled. Bring to room temperature before serving.*)

Four-Pepper Ceviche

Crunchy and colorful appetizer fare. Use any leftovers the next day.

10 servings

2 pounds yellowtail, sea bass or red snapper fillets, cut into ¾-inch cubes
1¼ cups fresh lime juice

3 medium tomatoes, chopped
1 medium red bell pepper, cored, seeded and diced
1 medium green bell pepper, cored, seeded and diced
1 medium yellow bell pepper, cored, seeded and diced

6 green onions, minced
10 to 12 small bird chilies,* diced or ¼ teaspoon dried red pepper flakes
4¼ tablespoons olive oil
2 tablespoons chopped fresh cilantro
¼ teaspoon dried oregano, crumbled
Salt
Fresh cilantro sprigs or bell pepper strips

Arrange fish in glass container. Pour lime juice over. Cover and refrigerate 2 hours, stirring once or twice.

Combine next 9 ingredients. Stir mixture into fish. Cover and refrigerate 1 hour, stirring occasionally.

Season ceviche with salt. Garnish with cilantro sprigs or bell pepper strips.

*Available at Latin American markets.

Caviar Pâté

8 servings

3 hard-cooked eggs, halved
3/4 cup sour cream
1/4 cup chopped onion
3 tablespoons mayonnaise
2 teaspoons fresh lemon juice
1 teaspoon salt
1/2 teaspoon Worcestershire sauce
1/4 teaspoon freshly ground white pepper
2 to 3 drops hot pepper sauce

1 1/2 teaspoons unflavored gelatin
2 tablespoons cold water
3 ounces salmon caviar
1/2 cup minced fresh parsley
1 tablespoon chopped fresh dill

Additional caviar
Thinly sliced pumpernickel

Mix first 9 ingredients in processor or blender until smooth. Refrigerate.

Sprinkle gelatin over cold water in small bowl. Set in pan of simmering water and stir until dissolved. Stir into sour cream mixture. Fold in 3 ounces caviar, parsley and dill. Pack into 2-cup loaf pan or decorative mold. Cover and refrigerate at least 3 hours.

To serve, unmold pâté onto platter. Garnish with additional caviar. Serve with thinly sliced pumpernickel.

Liver Pâté on Apple Rounds

8 servings

6 tablespoons (3/4 stick) butter
1/4 pound chicken livers, finely diced

1 1/2 cups half and half
3 tablespoons all purpose flour
1/2 teaspoon salt
1/8 teaspoon freshly ground pepper
Pinch of freshly grated nutmeg

1 egg yolk, beaten to blend
1/2 cup coarsely grated Swiss cheese

5 to 6 tart green apples, cored and sliced into 1/8-inch rounds

Melt 1 tablespoon butter in heavy small skillet over medium-high heat. Add livers and sauté until firm and browned but still pink within.

Bring half and half to boil. Melt 3 tablespoons butter in heavy medium saucepan over low heat. Whisk in flour and cook 3 minutes. Whisk in boiling half and half, salt, pepper and nutmeg and boil until very thick, stirring constantly, about 3 minutes. Remove from heat. Stir some of sauce into yolk. Whisk back into sauce. Stir in sautéed livers, cheese, then remaining butter. Adjust seasoning to taste.

Preheat broiler. Spread mixture on apples. Broil until bubbly and browned.

Suppli di Riso

These crisp rice and cheese fritters, a traditional treat in Italy, are served with a tangy tomato sauce.

8 servings

Sauce
- 1 tablespoon olive oil
- 1/2 cup finely chopped onions
- 3 tablespoons minced peeled carrots
- 2 cups diced canned Italian tomatoes (liquid reserved)
- 2 tablespoons dry white wine
- 1 tablespoon red wine vinegar
- 1 tablespoon minced fresh Italian parsley
- 1 teaspoon minced fresh thyme
- 1 teaspoon minced fresh oregano
- 1/2 teaspoon salt
  Pinch of cayenne pepper
  Freshly ground pepper

Fritters
- 3 tablespoons butter
- 1 cup chopped onions
- 3 garlic cloves, minced (about 1 tablespoon)
- 1 1/4 cups Arborio rice*
- 1 teaspoon salt
- 1/4 teaspoon freshly ground white pepper
- 1/8 teaspoon saffron threads, crushed
- 2 1/2 cups water
- 1/3 cup whipping cream
- 1/3 cup freshly grated Parmesan cheese

- 1 egg, beaten to blend
- 1 1/2 ounces mozzarella cheese, cut into sixteen 1/2-inch cubes
- 1 1/2 ounces Gorgonzola cheese, cut into sixteen 1/2-inch cubes
- 1 1/2 cups fine dried breadcrumbs

  Vegetable oil (for deep frying)

For sauce: Heat oil in heavy medium saucepan over low heat. Add onions and carrots and cook until tender, stirring occasionally, about 10 minutes. Add tomatoes with liquid, wine, vinegar, parsley, thyme, oregano, salt, cayenne and pepper. Bring to boil. Reduce heat, cover and simmer 30 minutes. Puree in blender or food processor until smooth. (*Sauce can be prepared 1 day ahead. Cover and refrigerate.*)

For fritters: Melt butter in heavy medium saucepan over low heat. Add onions and cook until translucent, stirring occasionally, about 10 minutes. Add garlic and cook 2 minutes. Stir in rice, 1/2 teaspoon salt, pepper and saffron. Add water and bring to boil. Reduce heat, cover and simmer until rice is tender, about 20 minutes. Remove from heat and let stand covered 5 minutes. Stir in cream and Parmesan cheese. Cool.

Stir egg into rice mixture. Add remaining 1/2 teaspoon salt. Separate rice into 16 portions using about 3 tablespoons for each. Moisten hands with ice water. Roll each portion between palms into round ball. Press 1 cube mozzarella and 1 cube Gorgonzola into center of each. Roll in breadcrumbs. (*Can be prepared 1 day ahead. Cover and refrigerate. Bring to room temperature before frying.*)

Heat oil in deep fryer or heavy large skillet to 375°F. Add fritters in batches and fry until golden brown, turning occasionally, about 5 minutes. Remove with slotted spoon and drain on paper towels.

Rewarm sauce over low heat. Coat bottom of each plate with 1/4 cup sauce. Arrange 2 fritters on each. Serve immediately.

*Available at Italian markets and most specialty foods stores.

Vegetable Fritters

Makes 12

1½ cups shredded unpeeled baking
    potatoes
¾ cup shredded unpeeled zucchini
½ cup shredded peeled carrots
¼ cup grated onions
2 eggs, beaten to blend
¼ cup all purpose flour

1 tablespoon dried parsley flakes
1 teaspoon dried chives
1 teaspoon salt
½ teaspoon freshly ground pepper
½ teaspoon garlic powder
2 tablespoons vegetable oil

Preheat oven to 200°F. Combine potatoes, zucchini, carrots and onions in colander; squeeze dry. Transfer to medium bowl. Stir in next 7 ingredients. Heat oil in heavy medium skillet over medium-high heat. Add vegetable mixture in batches, using ¼ cup for each fritter and mixing batter frequently. Cook fritters until crisp and browned, 4 to 5 minutes. Turn and cook until browned, 3 to 4 minutes. Drain on paper towels. Serve hot.

Curry Triangles

Makes about 22

Filling
¾ pound skinned and boned chicken
    breast, minced
1 tablespoon oriental sesame oil
1 tablespoon soy sauce
1 tablespoon Chinese rice wine
1 tablespoon cornstarch
1 teaspoon sugar
1 teaspoon finely minced peeled
    fresh ginger
1 garlic clove, minced

Dough
2½ cups all purpose flour
½ teaspoon salt
⅔ cup solid vegetable shortening
½ cup ice water

2 tablespoons (¼ stick) butter,
    softened

2 tablespoons vegetable oil
2 teaspoons curry powder
2 tablespoons oyster sauce*
½ teaspoon sugar
2 tablespoons Chinese rice wine
1 tablespoon cornstarch dissolved in
    ⅓ cup chicken stock
1 egg beaten with 1 teaspoon water
    (glaze)

For filling: Toss chicken with next 7 ingredients in nonaluminum pan. Let filling stand 2 hours at room temperature, or refrigerate overnight.

For dough: Combine 1½ cups flour and salt in large bowl. Cut in ⅓ cup shortening until mixture resembles coarse meal. Gradually add ice water, stirring until dough forms ball. Turn dough out onto lightly floured surface and knead until smooth, about 2 minutes; dough will be very soft.

Place remaining 1 cup flour in bowl. Cut in remaining ⅓ cup shortening until ball forms. Turn dough out onto lightly floured surface and knead until smooth, about 3 minutes.

Roll first dough out on lightly floured surface into ⅛-inch-thick rectangle. Pat second dough out into ⅛-inch-thick rectangle. Set second dough atop first dough. Press gently with rolling pin to seal dough together. Using hands, roll dough up as for jelly roll. Roll dough out into ⅛-inch-thick rectangle. Spread top of dough with butter. Using hands, roll dough up as for jelly roll. Refrigerate at least 1 hour; dough will be very sticky.

Roll dough out into ³/₈-inch-thick rectangle. Using hands, roll dough up as for jelly roll. Refrigerate 30 minutes.

To assemble: Preheat oven to 375°F. Heat wok over high heat. Add oil. Add chicken and stir until opaque. Stir in remaining ingredients, except cornstarch and glaze, in order given. Add dissolved cornstarch and bring to boil. (*Can be prepared 1 day ahead. Cool completely. Cover and refrigerate.*) Roll dough out to ³/₈-inch-thick sheet. Cut out 2-inch rounds. Roll each round into 3¹/₂-inch circle. Gather and layer scraps; roll and cut additional rounds if necessary. Place 1 scant tablespoon filling in center of each round. Using thumb and index finger, pinch 3 sides of dough up and together, forming triangle and leaving space in center. Brush with glaze. Set triangles on baking sheet. Bake until golden brown, 20 to 25 minutes. Serve immediately.

*Available at oriental markets.

New Orleans Oyster Tartlets

Makes 24

Creole Mustard Dough
3 cups unbleached all purpose flour
¹/₄ teaspoon salt
³/₄ cup (1¹/₂ sticks) well-chilled unsalted butter, cut into pieces
¹/₄ cup well-chilled solid vegetable shortening, cut into pieces
¹/₄ cup plus 2 tablespoons (about) ice water
¹/₃ cup Creole or other mild whole-grain mustard

Oyster Filling
2 cups dry white wine
24 large shucked oysters (juices reserved)

3 tablespoons minced shallots

1 cup (2 sticks) well-chilled unsalted butter, cut into 16 pieces
2 tablespoons Pernod
¹/₂ teaspoon freshly ground white pepper
Salt

Fresh chives

For dough: Mix flour and salt in large bowl. Cut in butter and shortening until mixture resembles oatmeal. Mix ¹/₄ cup water and mustard in small bowl. Add to flour mixture and stir just until combined. Mix in enough of remaining water 1 tablespoon at a time to bind dough. Shape dough into ball. Divide in half. Flatten each piece into 1-inch-thick round. Wrap in plastic and refrigerate until well chilled. (*Can be prepared 3 days ahead.*)

Roll 1 dough piece out on lightly floured surface to thickness of ¹/₈ inch. Cut into 4-inch rounds using cookie cutter. Fit rounds into 3-inch round tartlet molds; trim edges. Repeat with remaining dough. Gather scraps, reroll dough and cut out additional tartlets, if necessary. Arrange tartlets on large baking sheet. Refrigerate at least 30 minutes. (*Can be prepared 2 days ahead.*)

Position rack in center of oven and preheat to 375°F. Pierce pastry with fork. Bake until golden brown, 12 to 14 minutes. Cool slightly on rack. Unmold tartlets and cool completely on rack. (*Can be prepared 1 day ahead. Store at room temperature in airtight container.*)

For filling: Bring wine to simmer in heavy medium nonaluminum saucepan. Add oysters and reserved liquor and cook until oyster edges just begin to ruffle, about 1 minute. Transfer oysters to medium bowl using slotted spoon. Add shallots to wine and bring to boil. Reduce heat and simmer until liquid becomes syrupy, about 30 minutes.

Strain shallot mixture into heavy small nonaluminum saucepan. (*Can be prepared 8 hours ahead. Refrigerate oysters and poaching liquid separately.*)

Preheat oven to 200°F. Rewarm oyster poaching liquid over low heat. Off heat, whisk in 2 tablespoons butter. Set pan over low heat and whisk in remaining butter 1 tablespoon at a time, removing pan from heat briefly if drops of melted butter appear. (If sauce breaks down at any time, remove from heat and whisk in 2 tablespoons butter.) Whisk in Pernod and freshly ground white pepper. Season with salt if desired. Add oysters to sauce. Cover pan and remove from heat. Let stand 5 minutes.

Warm tartlets 5 minutes. Arrange 3 tartlets each on 8 plates. Spoon 1 oyster into each. Spoon sauce over. Garnish with chives. Serve immediately.

Shrimp with Cilantro and Tequila

4 servings

3 tablespoons butter
2 large red bell peppers, cored and cut julienne
2 large green bell peppers, cored and cut julienne
2 large yellow bell peppers, cored and cut julienne

¾ cup LaVilla Butter*

16 uncooked large shrimp, peeled and deveined
½ teaspoon minced shallot
½ cup tequila
1½ cups whipping cream
¼ cup minced fresh cilantro
Salt and freshly ground pepper

Melt 3 tablespoons butter in heavy large skillet over medium heat. Add bell peppers and cook until just tender, stirring frequently, about 5 minutes. Set aside.

Melt ¾ cup LaVilla Butter in another heavy large skillet over medium-high heat. Add shrimp and shallot and stir until shrimp are opaque, about 3 minutes. Add tequila and heat briefly. Remove from heat and ignite with match. When flames subside, remove shrimp using slotted spoon. Add cream to skillet and boil until thickened. Return shrimp to skillet. Add bell peppers and cilantro. Season with salt and pepper. Serve immediately.

*LaVilla Butter

Makes about 1 cup

6 tablespoons (¾ stick) butter, room temperature
6 tablespoons margarine, room temperature
4 teaspoons dry white wine
1 tablespoon diced green bell pepper

1 tablespoon diced red bell pepper
2 teaspoons fresh lemon juice
1½ teaspoons freshly ground pepper
1 teaspoon Worcestershire sauce
1 teaspoon minced garlic
¼ teaspoon salt

Using electric mixer, beat butter and margarine until increased in volume by a third. Stir remaining ingredients into butter mixture. Cover and refrigerate until ready to use. (*Can be prepared 1 day ahead.*)

Louisiana Hot Chicken Wings

6 to 8 servings

2 cups (4 sticks) butter
6 tablespoons Crystal Hot Sauce
¼ cup fresh lemon juice
2 tablespoons hot pepper sauce
2 teaspoons dried oregano, crumbled
1 teaspoon dried basil, crumbled
½ teaspoon dried marjoram, crumbled

½ teaspoon garlic salt
½ teaspoon dried rosemary, crumbled
½ teaspoon dried thyme, crumbled

24 chicken wings, cut in half at joint

Melt butter in heavy medium saucepan. Add remaining ingredients except chicken and simmer 1 hour, stirring occasionally.

Preheat oven to 400°F. Arrange chicken wings in ovenproof glass baking dish. Brush generously with sauce. Bake 15 minutes. Brush generously with sauce. Continue baking until crisp, 15 to 20 minutes. Reheat sauce. Serve chicken wings immediately, passing remaining sauce separately.

Hoisin Barbecued Spareribs

A mild smoking occurs as the rib drippings moisten a layer of tea leaves during the final cooking—one of the secrets to this exceptional dish.

6 to 8 servings

3¼ pounds pork spareribs
¼ cup plus 1 tablespoon honey
¼ cup hoisin sauce
¼ cup soy sauce
1 tablespoon plus ½ teaspoon catsup
1 tablespoon minced peeled ginger
1 tablespoon minced garlic
1½ teaspoons ground bean sauce*
¼ teaspoon hot pepper sauce
¼ teaspoon liquid smoke flavoring

¼ teaspoon freshly ground pepper
¼ teaspoon freshly ground white pepper
¼ teaspoon cayenne pepper
¼ teaspoon onion powder
¼ teaspoon garlic powder

½ cup black tea leaves
¼ cup firmly packed dark brown sugar
2 tablespoons five-spice powder*

Using sharp knife, cut halfway down between each rib to separate slightly. Score underside of ribs with knife. Transfer to large baking pan. Mix next 9 ingredients in bowl. Blend next 5 ingredients in another bowl. Gradually whisk spices into honey mixture to blend. Pour over ribs, turning to coat. Cover and refrigerate overnight, turning ribs over occasionally.

Preheat oven to 375°F. Drain ribs, reserving marinade. Set rack in large roasting pan. Arrange ribs on rack. Bake until well browned, about 45 minutes, turning ribs twice and basting with some of reserved marinade every 10 minutes. Remove pan from oven.

Increase oven temperature to 500°F. Remove rack with ribs from pan. Combine tea leaves, brown sugar and five-spice powder. Sprinkle over bottom of roasting pan. Set rack with ribs over tea mixture. Continue baking until ribs are crisp, about 5 minutes. Cut into individual ribs. Brush with remaining marinade. Transfer to platter.

*Available at oriental markets.

Pork Rumaki

Use meaty bacon without a lot of excess fat; trim if necessary.

Makes about 36

1 ounce dried shiitake mushrooms
¹/₂ pound ground pork
¹/₃ cup finely chopped peeled fresh water chestnuts* or canned water chestnuts
¹/₃ cup finely chopped onions
3 tablespoons finely chopped snow peas

2 tablespoons soy sauce
1 egg, beaten to blend
¹/₄ teaspoon freshly ground pepper

18 (about) bacon strips, halved widthwise

Vegetable oil (for frying)

Soak mushrooms in hot water to cover until softened, about 30 minutes. Drain; cut off tough stems and discard. Finely chop mushrooms. Transfer to large bowl. Mix in pork, water chestnuts, onions, snow peas, soy sauce, egg and pepper. Cover pork mixture and refrigerate 2 hours.

Shape mixture into 1-inch balls. Wrap each with bacon slice and secure with toothpick. Set on baking sheet. Refrigerate 30 minutes.

Heat oil in deep fryer or heavy skillet to 375°F. Add pork in batches (do not crowd) and fry until golden brown, turning occasionally, about 3 minutes. Remove using slotted spoon and drain on paper towels. Serve immediately.

*Available at oriental markets.

2 ❦ Soups and Salads

The soups in this chapter seem to be custom-made for light and nutritious eating. There are plenty of fragrant broths with fresh vegetables and herbs added for color and flavor, such as Mess o' Greens Soup with Garlic and Lemon (page 13), Double Chicken Consommé with Shrimp, Corn and Cilantro (page 14), and Mestizo Gazpacho (page 12), an extra-light version of the classic (serve it with a shot of tequila).

Other recipes include creamy vegetable soups that use pureed vegetables more than cream for a smooth consistency: Creamy Greens Soup (page 16), a blend of zucchini, spinach, parsley and split peas, and Butternut Squash Bisque (page 17), spiked with rum and lime and served with curried whipped cream. On the heartier side, there are Five-Bean Soup (page 18), a wholesome stew of protein-rich legumes, and Greek Fish and Fresh Vegetable Soup (page 19), a variation of bouillabaisse.

For exciting salad openers, there are some wonderful new ideas for greens-and-dressing combinations, as well as a few surprises. Fresh spicy greens such as escarole, radicchio and arugula are tossed with toasted breadcrumbs and basil vinaigrette (page 20) in a typically French bistro salad. Jicama-Sunchoke Salad with Mustard Dressing (page 21), crunchy and full of texture, is the ideal do-ahead dish, as its flavor improves with age. Everyone's choice on the dinner buffet table will be our Molded Cranberry Salad (page 21), flavored with pink grapefruit juice and served with a honey mayonnaise.

Main-dish salads are always a great favorite. Our offerings range from the light to the hearty: Hot Beef Satay on Kale and Romaine (page 23), served with a spicy peanut dressing; Farmer's Market Turkey and Lentil Salad (page 24), dressed with piquant sun-dried tomatoes; and a refreshing Smoked Salmon, Beet and Cucumber Pasta Salad (page 25), tossed with dilled sour cream and mayonnaise.

 Soups

Mestizo Gazpacho

A light version of the classic gazpacho. Serve this refreshing soup accompanied with a shot of tequila.

4 servings

4 large evenly shaped jicama (about 2 pounds each)
2½ pounds tomatoes (about 9 medium), quartered
1 large cucumber, peeled, seeded and diced (about 1¼ cups)
2 medium tomatoes, peeled, seeded and diced (about ½ cup)
½ cup minced green onions (about 4 small)
2 tablespoons strained fresh lime juice

1 serrano chili, seeded, deveined and minced
½ teaspoon minced garlic
½ teaspoon Worcestershire sauce
½ teaspoon salt
Freshly ground pepper

2 tablespoons minced fresh cilantro, parsley or chives
Minced, seeded and deveined serrano chilies
4 fluted lime slices

Peel jicama using potato peeler or paring knife. Using melon baller and paring knife, hollow out each jicama to form "soup bowl" with about 1-cup capacity. Dice enough of scooped-out jicama to measure 2 cups. Transfer to large bowl. Reserve remaining jicama for another use. Cut scalloped edge on jicama bowls and carve decoratively if desired. Trim bottom to flatten, if necessary. Wrap jicama bowls in plastic. Refrigerate 8 hours or overnight.

Puree 2½ pounds tomatoes in processor. Strain through fine sieve into large bowl to eliminate seeds. Add chopped jicama, cucumber, diced tomato, green onions, lime juice, chili, garlic, Worcestershire and salt to puree. Season with pepper. Cover and refrigerate at least 8 hours or overnight. (If preparing 1 day ahead, do not add garlic and green onion more than 8 hours before serving.)

Taste and adjust seasoning. Pour soup into jicama bowls. Sprinkle with cilantro and chilies. Garnish with lime.

Chilled Red Bell Pepper-Tomato Soup with Corn Salsa

6 servings

2 tablespoons olive oil
1½ cups coarsely chopped white onions
1 garlic clove, coarsely chopped
3 pounds tomatoes, coarsely chopped
1 tablespoon minced fresh basil
1 teaspoon salt

⅛ teaspoon freshly ground pepper

2 pounds red bell peppers, roasted* and quartered (juices reserved)

Corn Salsa**
Crème fraîche or sour cream

Heat oil in heavy large saucepan over low heat. Add onions, cover and cook until translucent, stirring occasionally, about 10 minutes. Add garlic, cover and cook 5 minutes, stirring occasionally. Add tomatoes, basil, salt and pepper. Increase heat and bring to simmer. Reduce heat to low, cover and cook 15 minutes, stirring occasionally.

Cut 1 bell pepper into ¼ × 1½-inch strips and reserve. Add remaining peppers and pepper juices to tomato mixture. Puree in processor in batches until smooth. Strain through fine sieve, pressing with back of spoon. Add bell pepper strips. Refrigerate until well chilled. (*Can be prepared 1 day ahead.*)

Taste soup and adjust seasoning. Ladle into bowls. Serve, passing salsa and crème fraîche separately.

*How to Roast Bell Peppers

Preheat broiler. Char peppers 3 inches from heat source until blackened on all sides. Wrap in paper bag and let stand 10 minutes to steam. Peel off skins; do not rinse. (Rinsing tends to strip the peppers of flavor and juices.) Work over sieve set in large bowl to catch juices. Cut peppers in half lengthwise, then remove seeds and cut out ribs. (*Can be prepared 2 days ahead, covered and refrigerated.*)

**Corn Salsa

Makes about 2 cups

1 cup fresh corn kernels (from about 2 medium ears)
1 medium tomato, seeded and finely chopped
¼ cup finely chopped red bell pepper
¼ cup finely chopped green bell pepper
¼ cup diced red onion
¼ cup diced, peeled and seeded cucumber
2 tablespoons olive oil
1 tablespoon fresh lime juice
1 tablespoon fresh basil julienne
1 teaspoon finely chopped seeded jalapeño chili
¼ teaspoon salt
¼ teaspoon freshly ground pepper

Combine all ingredients in large bowl. Toss well. (*Can be prepared 6 hours ahead. Cover and refrigerate.*)

Mess o' Greens Soup with Garlic and Lemon

The lemon peel and basil mixture here gives a savory lift to undersalted foods.

4 to 6 servings

1 tablespoon vegetable oil
2 medium garlic cloves, chopped
1 pound escarole, rinsed, torn into 1-inch pieces
6 cups rich unsalted chicken stock, degreased
1 carrot, peeled, sliced into thin rounds
Salt
½ cup small macaroni, freshly cooked
2 tablespoons chopped fresh basil or Italian parsley
2 teaspoons chopped lemon peel
1 tablespoon thinly sliced green onions
⅛ teaspoon coarsely ground pepper

Heat oil in heavy large saucepan over medium-low heat. Mix in garlic. Add escarole. Cover and cook until tender, stirring occasionally, 12 minutes.

Add stock and carrot to escarole. Season with salt. Simmer until carrot is just tender, about 6 minutes. Stir in macaroni. Finely mince basil and lemon peel together and stir into soup. Simmer 3 minutes. Sprinkle with green onions and pepper and serve.

Italian Tortellini Soup

Serve this hearty soup with crusty garlic bread. The recipe halves easily.

Makes 5 quarts

4 14½-ounce cans beef broth
7 cups water
1 pound sweet Italian sausage, cut into ½-inch pieces
1 9-ounce box tortellini
1 9-ounce box spinach tortellini
½ pound cabbage, shredded
1 small green bell pepper, cored and diced

1 medium zucchini, sliced
1 small red onion, chopped
1 medium tomato, diced
1 tablespoon chopped fresh basil
Salt and freshly ground pepper
Freshly grated Parmesan cheese (optional)

Combine first 11 ingredients in large pot. Season with salt and pepper. Bring to slow boil over medium-high heat. Reduce heat and simmer until vegetables are tender, about 15 minutes. Ladle soup into bowls. Pass grated Parmesan separately if desired. (*Soup can be prepared 1 day ahead, covered and refrigerated.*)

Double Chicken Consommé with Shrimp, Corn and Cilantro

4 servings

3 tablespoons vegetable oil
3 pounds chicken necks and backs
2 medium onions (about 1 pound), chopped
1 large carrot, peeled and chopped
6 garlic cloves, peeled and crushed
2 bay leaves
8 whole black peppercorns
8 uncooked medium shrimp, peeled and deveined, shells reserved
7 cups unsalted chicken stock (preferably homemade)

10 fresh parsley sprigs
1 fresh thyme sprig
1 fresh oregano sprig

2 egg whites

Salt
2 plum tomatoes, seeded and diced
3 green onions, sliced
½ cup fresh or frozen corn kernels, drained
¼ cup minced fresh cilantro
4 thin lime slices

Heat oil in heavy large saucepan over high heat. Add chicken necks and backs and brown on all sides, about 12 minutes. Transfer chicken to bowl. Reduce heat to medium-low. Add onions, carrot, garlic, bay leaves, peppercorns and reserved shells to saucepan. Cover and cook for 20 minutes, stirring occasionally. Add chicken pieces, stock, parsley, thyme and oregano and bring to boil, skimming surface. Reduce heat, cover partially and simmer 2 hours, stirring occasionally.

Strain stock through sieve into large measuring cup. (Stock should measure 5 cups; if not, boil until reduced to 5 cups.) Cool completely. Cover stock and refrigerate overnight.

Remove fat from surface of stock. Bring stock to room temperature. Whisk egg whites with 1 cup stock in large bowl. Bring remaining stock to boil in large saucepan. Slowly whisk hot stock into egg white mixture. Return mixture to saucepan. Bring just to a simmer. Reduce heat so liquid is barely shaking and cook 20 minutes; do not stir and do not let boil.

Line fine sieve set over large bowl with double layer of cheesecloth. Gently ladle stock into sieve without disturbing egg whites. (*Can be prepared 1 day ahead, covered and refrigerated.*) Transfer consommé to saucepan.

Bring consommé to simmer; do not boil. Taste and adjust seasoning with salt. Add shrimp and cook until almost opaque, about 3 minutes. Divide tomatoes, green onions, corn and cilantro among 4 bowls. Ladle consommé over. Float lime slice in each. Serve immediately.

Yellow Pepper Soup

6 servings

1/4 cup olive oil
1 small onion, coarsely chopped
4 large garlic cloves, crushed
2 tablespoons capers, rinsed
1/8 teaspoon dried red pepper flakes
4 large yellow bell peppers (about 1 3/4 pounds), cored, seeded and cut into large pieces

Salt
2 cups beef stock (preferably homemade)

Heat oil in heavy large saucepan over medium-low heat. Add onion and garlic and cook until golden, stirring frequently, about 15 minutes. Add 1 tablespoon capers and red pepper flakes and cook 3 minutes, stirring frequently. Add bell peppers and salt. Cover and cook 10 minutes, stirring frequently. Add stock. Reduce heat, cover saucepan and simmer until peppers are soft, stirring occasionally, about 30 minutes.

Puree mixture in blender or processor in batches. Strain back into saucepan, pressing with spoon. (*Can be prepared 2 days ahead. Cover and refrigerate.*) Stir remaining 1 tablespoon capers into soup. Rewarm over low heat. Ladle into bowls and serve.

Tomato-Mushroom Soup with Vermouth

6 servings

2 tablespoons vegetable oil
3 celery stalks, chopped
1 leek (white part only), chopped
1 garlic clove, chopped
1/2 pound mushrooms, chopped
5 cups peeled, seeded and chopped tomatoes
3 cups chicken stock
1 cup whipping cream
3/4 cup dry vermouth
2 teaspoons tomato paste

1/4 teaspoon sugar
Bouquet garni (2 parsley sprigs, 1 thyme sprig, 1 oregano sprig, 1 basil sprig and 1 bay leaf)
Salt and freshly ground pepper

1 tablespoon butter
1/4 pound mushrooms, sliced
1/2 cup chopped watercress
Snipped fresh chives

Heat oil in heavy large saucepan over medium-low heat. Add celery, leek and garlic and sauté until softened, about 7 minutes. Increase heat to high. Add chopped mushrooms and sauté until lightly browned, about 5 minutes. Add tomatoes, stock, cream, vermouth, tomato paste, sugar and bouquet garni. Season with salt and pepper. Bring to boil. Reduce heat, cover and simmer until vegetables are tender, about 30 minutes. Discard bouquet garni. Puree soup in blender. Return to saucepan; keep warm.

Melt butter in small skillet over medium heat. Add sliced mushrooms and sauté until tender, about 5 minutes. Stir into soup. Mix in watercress. Adjust seasoning. Ladle into bowls. Garnish with snipped chives.

Creamy Greens Soup

8 servings

1 tablespoon vegetable oil
¹/₂ medium onion, chopped
2 celery stalks, diced
6 to 7 cups vegetable stock
³/₄ cup split peas, rinsed
1 bay leaf

6 cups diced zucchini
¹/₂ teaspoon dried basil, crumbled
   Salt and freshly ground pepper
1 pound spinach, chopped
¹/₂ cup chopped fresh parsley

Heat oil in heavy large saucepan over medium heat. Add onion and celery and stir until softened, about 5 minutes. Add 4 cups vegetable stock, split peas and bay leaf. Bring soup to boil. Reduce heat, cover partially and simmer 40 minutes.

Stir zucchini, 2 cups stock and basil into soup. Season with salt and pepper. Simmer 10 minutes. Discard bay leaf. Puree soup in blender or processor in batches. Return to saucepan. Stir in spinach and parsley. Thin soup with remaining stock, if desired. Stir soup over medium heat until warmed through, about 5 minutes. Serve immediately.

Cream of Spinach Soup with Prosciutto and Peppered Croutons

4 servings

1¹/₂ tablespoons safflower oil
1 medium onion, thinly sliced
1 pound fresh spinach, stemmed
   Salt and freshly ground pepper
3¹/₂ cups unsalted chicken broth

1 cup whipping cream
1 tablespoon (or more) fresh lemon juice
¹/₄ pound prosciutto, cut julienne
   Peppered Croutons*

Heat oil in heavy deep skillet over medium-low heat. Add onion and cook until tender, stirring frequently, about 10 minutes. Add spinach and stir 1 minute. Season with salt and pepper. Add broth. Increase heat and bring to boil. Reduce heat and simmer 7 minutes to blend flavors.

Puree soup in batches in processor or blender. Transfer to large bowl. Stir in cream and 1 tablespoon lemon juice. Refrigerate until well chilled. (*Can be prepared 1 day ahead.*)

Adjust seasoning of soup, adding more lemon juice, salt and pepper, if desired. Ladle soup into bowls. Garnish with prosciutto and croutons.

*Peppered Croutons

Makes 8

8 3-inch-wide ¹/₃-inch-thick slices
   French bread
6 tablespoons (about) safflower oil

2 teaspoons (about) coarsely ground
   pepper

Lightly brush both sides of bread with some of oil. Sprinkle generously on both sides with pepper. Heat 2 tablespoons oil in heavy large skillet over medium heat. Add bread and cook until golden brown on first side, about 1¹/₂ minutes. Add 2 more tablespoons oil to skillet. Turn bread over and cook until second side is golden brown, about 1¹/₂ minutes. Drain croutons well on paper towels.

Zucchini and Yellow Squash Soup

6 to 8 servings

¼ cup olive oil
1 medium onion, thinly sliced
2 tablespoons minced shallots
1½ teaspoons minced garlic
¼ cup all purpose flour
2 medium zucchini, sliced into ¼-inch-thick rounds (about 1½ cups)

2 large crookneck squash, sliced into ¼-inch-thick rounds (about 1½ cups)
3 cups rich chicken stock
3 cups whipping cream
2 teaspoons minced fresh basil
2 teaspoons minced fresh oregano
Salt and freshly ground pepper

Heat oil in heavy large saucepan over medium-low heat. Add onion, shallots and garlic and cook until onion is translucent, stirring occasionally, about 10 minutes. Add flour and stir 3 minutes. Add zucchini and crookneck squash and cook until softened, stirring frequently, about 5 minutes. Stir in stock, cream, basil and oregano. Reduce heat and simmer 20 minutes. Season with salt and pepper to taste. Serve immediately.

Butternut Squash Bisque

Makes about 20 cups

½ pound salt pork, diced

2 cups chopped onions
1 cup chopped celery with leaves
2 garlic cloves, minced
2 teaspoons curry powder
4 quarts water
4 pounds butternut squash, peeled, seeded and cubed
6 carrots, peeled and sliced
2 large potatoes, peeled and cubed

2 bay leaves
1 tablespoon dried thyme, crumbled

⅓ cup dark rum
¼ cup fresh lime juice
2 tablespoons sugar
Salt and freshly ground pepper
Minced fresh parsley
Curried Whipped Cream*

Cover salt pork with water in large saucepan. Bring to boil. Reduce heat and simmer 5 minutes. Drain and rinse under cold water. Pat dry.

Transfer salt pork to heavy large pot. Sauté over medium heat until just beginning to color, about 7 minutes. Reduce heat to low. Add onions, celery, garlic and curry and cook until vegetables are tender, about 5 minutes. Add 4 quarts water, squash, carrots, potatoes, bay leaves and thyme. Bring to boil. Reduce heat, cover and simmer 1 hour. Cool soup slightly.

Remove salt pork and bay leaves. Degrease soup. Puree in batches in blender or processor. Return to pot and stir in rum, lime juice and sugar. Season with salt and pepper. Simmer 5 minutes. Garnish with parsley. Serve hot with Curried Whipped Cream.

*Curried Whipped Cream

Makes 2 cups

2 teaspoons curry powder

1 cup whipping cream, whipped
Salt

Place curry powder in heavy small skillet and stir over low heat until slightly darkened, about 3 minutes. Cool. Fold into whipped cream. Season with salt.

South of the Border Soup

Makes about 20 cups

1 1/2 cups dried pinto beans

4 tablespoons vegetable oil
6 pounds boneless pork shoulder, cut into 1-inch cubes, patted dry
1 1/2 cups chopped onions
4 garlic cloves, minced
1 1/2 tablespoons chili powder
1 1/2 teaspoons dried oregano, crumbled
1 1/2 teaspoons cumin seeds
12 cups beef stock

6 cups peeled and thinly sliced carrots
1 10-ounce package frozen corn
Salt and freshly ground pepper
Sour cream
Tortilla chips
Chopped avocado
Chopped tomatoes
Chopped green onions
Chopped fresh cilantro
Minced jalapeño chilies

Cover beans with cold water; soak overnight. Drain; rinse under cold water.

Heat 2 tablespoons oil in heavy large pot over high heat. Add pork in batches and brown well. Remove using slotted spoon. Heat remaining 2 tablespoons oil in same pot over medium heat. Add onions and garlic and cook until softened, about 3 minutes. Add chili powder, oregano and cumin and stir 1 minute. Add beans and stock. Return pork to pot. Bring to boil. Reduce heat, cover and simmer until pork and beans are tender, 1 1/2 hours.

Degrease soup. Return to boil. Add carrots. Reduce heat, cover and simmer until carrots are tender, about 20 minutes. Stir in corn and simmer until tender. Season with salt and pepper. Serve accompanied with sour cream, tortilla chips, avocado, tomatoes, green onions, cilantro and chilies.

Five-Bean Soup

This meatless soup has a rich, hearty flavor. Accompany with a thick slice of Three-Grain Wild Rice Bread (see page 75).

6 servings

1/2 cup dried navy beans
1/2 cup dried white lima beans
1/2 cup dried chick-peas (garbanzo beans)
1/2 cup dried red kidney beans
1/2 cup dried black beans

3 1/2 cups water or beef stock
Salt

2 tablespoons vegetable oil
1 large onion, chopped
2 tablespoons dry Sherry
3 garlic cloves, minced

1 large green bell pepper, cored, seeded and diced
1 large carrot, diced
1 celery stalk, diced
1 1/2 teaspoons ground cumin
1 teaspoon coarsely ground coriander seeds
1 teaspoon grated orange peel
1/4 teaspoon freshly ground pepper
1/4 teaspoon (or more) dried red pepper flakes
Freshly cooked rice (optional)
Yogurt or sour cream
Chopped fresh cilantro

Rinse and sort beans. Place beans in large pot; add enough cold water to cover by 3 inches. Let stand overnight.

Drain beans and return to pot. Add 3 1/2 cups water. Bring to boil. Adjust heat so liquid barely simmers. Cover and cook until beans are tender, stirring occasionally, about 1 1/2 hours. Season to taste with salt.

Heat oil in heavy skillet over low heat. Add onion, Sherry and garlic. Cover and cook until onion is soft, stirring occasionally, about 15 minutes. Add bell pepper, carrot, celery, cumin and coriander. Cover and continue cooking until vegetables are tender, stirring occasionally, about 15 minutes. Add vegetable mixture to beans. Stir in orange peel, pepper and ¼ teaspoon red pepper flakes. Taste, adding more red pepper flakes if desired. Place rice in bowls. Spoon soup over. Top each with dollop of yogurt. Garnish with chopped cilantro and serve.

Fish and Fresh Vegetable Soup

4 servings

3 tablespoons olive oil
½ medium onion, chopped
½ medium green bell pepper, seeded and chopped
1 green onion, chopped
1 garlic clove, minced
¼ cup dry white wine
2 medium tomatoes, cut into ¼-inch dice
1 medium baking potato, peeled and cut into ¼-inch dice
1 medium carrot, peeled and cut into ¼-inch dice
1 medium celery stalk, cut into ¼-inch dice

1 tablespoon tomato paste
2 bay leaves
½ teaspoon dried thyme, crumbled
3 cups water
1 6- to 8-ounce red snapper fillet, cut into 1-inch chunks
1 6- to 8-ounce sea bass fillet, cut into 1-inch chunks
8 uncooked medium shrimp, peeled and deveined
¼ cup chopped fresh parsley
⅛ teaspoon cayenne pepper
Salt
Fresh lemon juice

Heat olive oil in heavy large saucepan over medium-low heat. Add onion, bell pepper, green onion and garlic and cook until softened, stirring occasionally, about 10 minutes. Add wine and boil 1 minute. Stir in tomatoes, potato, carrot, celery, tomato paste, bay leaves and thyme. Add water and bring to boil. Reduce heat and simmer until vegetables are almost tender, about 15 minutes. Add fish and shrimp and simmer gently until just opaque, about 2 minutes; do not overcook. Add parsley and cayenne. Adjust seasoning with salt and lemon juice to taste. Serve immediately.

❦ *Salads*

Radicchio, Endive and Fennel Salad

4 servings

1 medium head radicchio, quartered and cut crosswise into ¾-inch-wide pieces
2 large Belgian endives, cut crosswise into ¾-inch-wide pieces
1 medium fennel bulb, trimmed, tough outer leaves removed, cored and cut lengthwise into thin strips

¼ cup minced fresh Italian parsley
16 small fresh basil leaves, halved
¼ cup extra-virgin olive oil
Salt and freshly ground pepper
4 teaspoons balsamic vinegar
8 slices imported Parmesan cheese (preferably Reggiano)

Combine first 5 ingredients in large bowl. (*Can be prepared 4 hours ahead. Cover with barely damp towel and refrigerate.*) Just before serving, toss salad with oil until well coated. Season with salt and pepper and toss. Add vinegar and toss well. Top with cheese.

Spicy Greens with Toasted Breadcrumbs and Basil Vinaigrette

8 servings

1/2 teaspoon minced garlic
1/2 teaspoon Dijon mustard
3 tablespoons red wine vinegar
1 tablespoon balsamic vinegar
1/2 cup olive oil
4 teaspoons minced fresh basil
  Salt and freshly ground pepper

1 medium head escarole
1 small head radicchio
1/2 pound arugula
1/4 cup (1/2 stick) unsalted butter
1 cup coarse breadcrumbs made
  from stale Italian bread

In mortar with pestle, mash garlic with mustard to paste. Whisk in both vinegars. Gradually whisk in oil. Mix in basil and season with salt and pepper.

Tear escarole, radicchio and arugula into bite-size pieces. Place in large bowl. Melt butter in heavy large skillet over medium-high heat. Add breadcrumbs and stir until golden brown, about 5 minutes. Add vinaigrette to salad and toss well. Arrange on plates. Sprinkle with breadcrumbs.

Summer Greens with Bacon, Olives, Eggs and Zucchini

4 servings

3 tablespoons white wine vinegar
1 teaspoon Dijon mustard
1/3 cup olive oil
  Salt and freshly ground pepper

1/2 pound slab bacon, cut into
  3/8-inch-thick slices

5 cups packed assorted greens, such
  as red and green leaf lettuce,
  mâche, dandelion greens,
  watercress and sorrel

4 hard-cooked eggs, peeled, each cut
  into 8 wedges
1/2 cup black Niçoise olives
1/2 cup green Niçoise olives
1 1/2 cups zucchini julienne
1/3 cup freshly grated Parmesan
  cheese (about 1 1/2 ounces)

Blend vinegar and mustard in small bowl. Gradually whisk in oil in thin steady stream. Add salt and pepper.

Cut bacon into 2 1/2-inch pieces and cook in heavy medium skillet over medium-high heat until crisp. Drain thoroughly on paper towels.

Mound greens in center of large platter. Arrange egg wedges around border. Sprinkle olives inside egg border. Arrange zucchini strips down center of greens. Sprinkle with bacon. Mix Parmesan cheese into dressing. Spoon dressing over salad and serve.

Cucumber Salad

For a more assertive flavor, marinate the salad in the refrigerator for up to two weeks before serving.

Makes about 7 cups.

4 cucumbers (about 3/4 pound each)
1 tablespoon plus 1 teaspoon salt

5 tablespoons sugar
1/4 cup plus 2 tablespoons cider
  vinegar

3 medium white onions (about
  1 pound), thinly sliced
  Freshly ground pepper

Peel cucumbers with vegetable peeler, leaving thin evenly spaced lengthwise strips of rind. Slice cucumbers into $1/16$-inch-thick rounds. Place in colander. Toss with salt. Cover with towel. Weight with heavy object. Let stand 1 hour.

Pat cucumbers dry. Dissolve sugar in vinegar in large bowl. Add cucumbers and onions. Season with pepper; toss well. Cover and refrigerate.

Jicama-Sunchoke Salad with Mustard Dressing

10 to 12 servings

1 $1^1/2$-pound jicama, peeled and cut julienne
2 cups peeled sunchokes, cut julienne
$1^1/2$ cups drained canned red kidney beans, rinsed
1 large bunch watercress, coarsely chopped
1 bunch mustard greens, torn into bite-size pieces
1 medium green bell pepper, cored and cut julienne

1 medium yellow or red bell pepper, cored and cut julienne
4 green onions, finely chopped
$1/2$ cup cider vinegar
$1/2$ cup Dijon mustard
2 garlic cloves, minced
1 cup sunflower seed oil or vegetable oil
3 tablespoons minced fresh parsley
1 teaspoon minced fresh dill
1 teaspoon minced fresh cilantro
Salt and freshly ground pepper

Combine first 8 ingredients in large bowl. Combine vinegar, Dijon mustard and garlic in medium bowl. Gradually whisk in oil. Add parsley, dill and cilantro. Season with salt and pepper. Add to salad and toss well. Let marinate at least 1 hour at room temperature. Toss again before serving.

Mexican Salad

2 servings; can be doubled or tripled

1 orange, peeled and diced
1 medium tomato, seeded and diced
$1/2$ avocado, peeled, pitted and diced
$1/3$ cup frozen corn kernels, thawed
2 tablespoons minced red onion

3 tablespoons olive oil
1 tablespoon fresh lime juice
Salt and freshly ground pepper
1 tablespoon minced fresh cilantro
Red leaf lettuce

Combine first 5 ingredients in medium bowl. Using fork, gradually mix oil into lime juice in small bowl. Season with salt and pepper. Add to salad with cilantro and mix. Line plates with lettuce. Mound salad on lettuce.

Molded Cranberry Salad with Honey Mayonnaise

Pink grapefruit juice adds a refreshing note to this festive salad.

8 servings

3 packages unflavored gelatin
$1/2$ cup cold water
6 cups cranberries (about 23 ounces)
$1^1/2$ cups sugar

2 cups fresh grapefruit juice (preferably pink)

Lettuce leaves
Honey Mayonnaise*

Sprinkle gelatin over water in small bowl. Coarsely chop cranberries with sugar in processor in batches. Transfer to heavy medium saucepan. Stir in grapefruit juice. Cover and cook over low heat until sugar dissolves, stirring occasionally, about 12 minutes. Uncover, increase heat and bring to boil, stirring occasionally.

Remove pan from heat. Add gelatin and stir until dissolved. Cool slightly.

Rinse 5-cup mold with water and drain. Pour cranberry mixture into mold. Refrigerate until completely set, at least 8 hours. (*Can be prepared 2 days ahead.*)

Line large platter with lettuce leaves. Invert mold onto platter. Wrap in hot damp towel; shake gently. Let stand until cranberry salad loosens from mold. (*Can be prepared 4 hours ahead and refrigerated.*) Serve, passing Honey Mayonnaise separately.

*Honey Mayonnaise

Makes about 2¼ cups

2 egg yolks	¼ teaspoon salt
3 tablespoons cider vinegar	Freshly ground pepper
3 tablespoons honey	1½ cups vegetable oil
3 tablespoons Dijon mustard	

Whisk first 6 ingredients in medium bowl. Gradually whisk in oil in slow steady stream. Taste; adjust seasoning. (*Can be prepared 3 days ahead. Cover and refrigerate until ready to serve.*)

Bread Salad Layered with Mushrooms, Tomatoes and Panfried Onions with Pesto Vinaigrette

A superb light supper offering. For a more substantial dinner, serve it with some grilled Italian sausages.

8 to 10 main-dish servings

1 1-pound loaf crusty French bread, halved lengthwise and cut into ½-inch-thick slices	¼ pound fresh shiitake mushrooms, stemmed and cut into ¼-inch-wide strips
1 ounce dried porcini mushrooms	Salt and freshly ground pepper
1 whole head garlic, halved crosswise	1¾ pounds tomatoes, sliced into ¼-inch-thick rounds
¼ cup plus 2 tablespoons olive oil	½ cup minced fresh Italian parsley
2 large onions, halved and thinly sliced	Freshly ground pepper
½ teaspoon sugar	Pesto Vinaigrette*
½ pound button mushrooms, cut into ⅛-inch-thick slices	1 cup Kalamata olives

Arrange bread slices on large baking sheets. Let stand 2 hours at room temperature. Meanwhile, soak porcini mushrooms in hot water to cover until softened, about 1 hour. Rinse and drain. Pat dry. Cut mushrooms into ¼-inch pieces, discarding any hard stems.

Preheat oven to 325°F. Bake bread until slightly dry, about 10 minutes. Rub garlic over bread slices.

Heat 2 tablespoons oil in heavy large skillet over medium-high heat. Add onions; sprinkle with sugar and cook until onions just begin to color, stirring frequently, about 5 minutes. Transfer to medium bowl. Heat remaining ¼ cup oil in same skillet over medium-high heat. Add button and shiitake mushrooms and cook until tender, stirring frequently, about 3 minutes. Add porcini and stir until all liquid has evaporated, about 1 minute. Season with salt and pepper.

Place ¼ of toasted bread in bottom of large deep bowl. Layer with ¼ of onion mixture, ¼ of mushroom mixture, ¼ of sliced tomatoes, ¼ of parsley, pepper and ¼ of Pesto Vinaigrette. Repeat layering 3 times, ending with vinaigrette. Cover with plastic wrap. (*Can be prepared 12 hours ahead and refrigerated.*) Let stand 3 hours at room temperature. Garnish with olives.

*Pesto Vinaigrette

Makes about 2¹/₂ cups

1¹/₂ cups packed fresh basil leaves
¹/₃ cup freshly grated Romano cheese
¹/₄ cup packed fresh Italian parsley leaves
2 large garlic cloves

1 teaspoon salt
¹/₂ teaspoon grated lemon peel
1¹/₃ cups olive oil
¹/₄ cup white wine vinegar
¹/₄ cup fresh lemon juice

Blend basil, cheese, parsley, garlic, salt and lemon peel in processor to paste, stopping occasionally to scrape down sides of work bowl. With machine running, add oil in slow steady stream until completely incorporated. Add vinegar and lemon juice and blend. (*Can be prepared 1 day ahead and refrigerated. Bring to room temperature before using.*)

Hot Beef Satay on Kale and Romaine

Arrange this on a large platter, with Peanut Dressing passed on the side. Make the beverage ice-cold lager or iced tea with fresh lime. Steamed soft flour tortillas make a nice complement.

6 main-dish servings

1 large onion, coarsely chopped
¹/₂ lemon, seeded and coarsely chopped
3 tablespoons soy sauce
2 tablespoons tomato paste
2 tablespoons firmly packed light brown sugar
2 tablespoons oriental sesame oil
3 garlic cloves, chopped
1 teaspoon ground cumin
1 teaspoon salt
1 teaspoon ground coriander
¹/₂ teaspoon cinnamon
¹/₄ teaspoon ground cloves
1³/₄ pounds flank steak, cut across grain into ¹/₂-inch-thick strips

1 cup roasted, salted peanuts

8 large carrots, peeled and cut into 2 × ¹/₄-inch julienne

1 pound haricots verts or slender green beans
³/₄ pound daikon (Japanese white radish), peeled, cut crosswise into paper-thin slices

¹/₄ cup rice vinegar
Salt
6 tablespoons oriental sesame oil
¹/₄ cup peanut oil

Bamboo skewers

2 large heads romaine lettuce, cut into ¹/₄-inch-wide strips (about 11 cups)
¹/₄ pound kale, rinsed and cut into ¹/₄-inch-wide strips (about 2 cups)
Peanut Dressing*

Blend onion, lemon, soy, tomato paste, brown sugar, 2 tablespoons sesame oil, garlic, cumin, salt, coriander, cinnamon and cloves in processor until smooth, stopping occasionally to scrape down sides of work bowl. Transfer to large bowl. Add steak and toss to coat with mixture. Cover tightly and let steak marinate 3 hours at room temperature.

Preheat oven to 325°F. Toast peanuts on baking sheet until golden brown, 8 to 10 minutes. Cool completely.

Bring large pot of salted water to boil. Add carrots and cook until just crisptender. Transfer to large bowl of ice water using slotted spoon. Add haricots verts to boiling water and cook until just crisp-tender. Drain well; add to carrots. Add daikon to carrot, with more ice water if necessary to cover.

Mix vinegar with salt in small bowl. Whisk in 6 tablespoons sesame oil and peanut oil in thin steady stream.

Preheat broiler. Drain steak, reserving marinade. Thread 1 steak strip on each skewer, ruffling slightly. Broil 3 inches from heat source until slightly charred but still tender, turning once and brushing with marinade, 8 minutes.

Meanwhile, combine romaine and kale in large bowl. Rewhisk vinaigrette and add enough to greens to season to taste. Toss to blend. Line large platter with greens. Drain carrots, haricots verts and daikon. Toss with vinaigrette to taste. Arrange atop greens. Top with hot satay skewers. Sprinkle with chopped nuts. Serve immediately, passing Peanut Dressing separately.

*Peanut Dressing

Makes about 2 cups

1 cup chunky peanut butter
1/4 cup light soy sauce
2 tablespoons fresh lemon juice
1 tablespoon grated lemon peel
1 large garlic clove

1/2 teaspoon ground star anise or
   five-spice powder
1 teaspoon hot chili oil**
6 tablespoons (about) ice water

Blend first 7 ingredients in processor until smooth, stopping occasionally to scrape down sides of work bowl. With machine running, add just enough water in thin steady stream to thin dressing to consistency of mayonnaise. Taste and adjust seasoning. Transfer to container. Refrigerate overnight to let flavors blend. Serve at room temperature.

**Hot chili oil is available at oriental markets and some supermarkets.

Farmer's Market Turkey and Lentil Salad

6 main-dish servings

1 cup lentils
4 cups water

2 large garlic cloves
1 medium shallot
4 sun-dried tomatoes packed in oil,
   patted dry
1/4 cup olive oil (preferably extra-
   virgin)
2 1/2 tablespoons Sherry wine vinegar
2 1/2 tablespoons fresh orange juice
1 tablespoon water
1 tablespoon fresh thyme
1/2 teaspoon salt

2 large tomatoes, seeded and cut
   into 6 pieces each

1 medium red bell pepper

6 ounces cooked turkey breast, cut
   into chunks
4 cups broccoli florets, steamed
1 cup fresh basil leaves, cut julienne
1/2 cup cooked fresh corn kernels
1 head romaine lettuce, cut into
   1/3-inch-wide strips
   Fresh basil leaves

Bring lentils and 4 cups water to boil in medium saucepan. Reduce heat, cover and simmer until just tender, about 30 minutes. Drain well. Transfer lentils to medium bowl.

With processor machine running, drop garlic and shallot through feed tube and mince. Add sun-dried tomatoes, oil, vinegar, orange juice, 1 tablespoon water, thyme and salt and mix until smooth, about 2 minutes. Add half of dressing to lentils; toss gently. Add fresh tomatoes to remaining dressing in work bowl and chop coarsely using about 6 on/off turns. Leave dressing in work bowl.

Cut bell pepper lengthwise into 4 pieces; discard core and seeds. Cut each piece in half lengthwise.

Using medium slicer in processor, stand pepper pieces in feed tube, packing tightly. Slice bell pepper using light pressure.

Transfer contents of work bowl to large bowl. Mix in turkey, broccoli, basil julienne and corn. Arrange lettuce on plates. Spoon ½ cup lentils in center of each. Top each with turkey salad. Garnish with basil leaves.

Smoked Salmon, Beet and Cucumber Pasta Salad

2 main-dish servings; can be doubled or tripled

2½ cups dried fusilli

⅓ cup sour cream
⅓ cup mayonnaise
4 teaspoons minced fresh dill
2½ teaspoons fresh lemon juice
1½ teaspoons Dijon mustard
   Salt and freshly ground pepper

⅓ pound thinly sliced smoked salmon, cut into ½-inch pieces
½ hothouse cucumber, quartered lengthwise and sliced
2 celery stalks, diced
½ cup diced drained pickled beet slices

Add pasta to large pot of rapidly boiling salted water, stirring to prevent sticking. Cook until just tender but still firm to bite. Drain. Rinse under cold water until cool. Drain well. Shake off any water. Transfer to bowl.

Combine sour cream, mayonnaise, dill, lemon juice, mustard, salt and pepper. Stir into pasta with all remaining ingredients except beets. Just before serving, top with beets.

Scallop Salad with Peppers and Tomatoes

The yogurt dressing, accented with jalapeño and some minced ginger, is a wonderful complement to the scallops.

4 appetizer servings

1 pound red bell peppers, roasted (see page 13)
½ pound tomatoes, peeled, seeded and diced
½ cup diced green bell peppers
½ cup fresh corn kernels (from about 1 medium ear)
¼ cup diced red onions
1 teaspoon minced seeded jalapeño chili
4 cups torn assorted greens, such as curly endive, red leaf lettuce, arugula and/or watercress

¼ cup peanut oil
1 teaspoon minced peeled fresh ginger
2 tablespoons thinly sliced green onions
½ teaspoon minced garlic
½ pound bay scallops

Creamy Yogurt Dressing*
Fresh cilantro sprigs
Sliced Italian plum tomatoes

Dice enough red bell pepper to measure ¼ cup. Mix with tomatoes, green bell peppers, corn, red onions and chili in small bowl. Cut remaining red bell peppers into ¾-inch-wide strips. Combine with greens in large bowl.

Heat wok or heavy medium skillet over high heat until drops of water sizzle vigorously. Add oil and heat until very hot. Add ginger and stir-fry 20 seconds. Add green onions and garlic and stir-fry 20 seconds. Add scallops and stir-fry until just opaque, about 2 minutes. Drain mixture in sieve.

Add half of dressing to greens and toss. Divide among plates. Add warm scallops to tomato mixture; stir in 2 tablespoons dressing. Spoon atop greens. Drizzle remaining dressing over. Garnish each plate with cilantro sprigs and sliced plum tomatoes and serve.

*Creamy Yogurt Dressing

Makes about 1/2 cup

1/4 cup peanut oil
1 1/2 tablespoons fresh lemon juice
1 1/2 tablespoons plain nonfat yogurt
1 teaspoon oriental sesame oil
1/2 teaspoon (or more) minced seeded jalapeño chili

1/2 teaspoon (or more) minced peeled fresh ginger
1/4 teaspoon salt

Whisk peanut oil, lemon juice, yogurt, sesame oil, 1/2 teaspoon chili, 1/2 teaspoon ginger and salt in medium bowl until smooth. Taste and add more chili and/or ginger if desired.

3 ❦ Pasta and Pizza

These two categories of food have become so popular in the American diet that they deserve a chapter of their own. You will note, though, that our recipes go beyond the ordinary fare of the average pizza parlor. They emphasize lightness, freshness, new techniques and innovative combinations of ingredients.

Pasta, long a trendy favorite, has become something of an art form—but one that keeps in mind classic techniques and quality ingredients. Try our colorful presentation of pasta half-moons filled with a puree of artichokes and cheese and topped with green tomato sauce (page 31) or tiny bean-filled pasta packets served with a fresh tomato sauce and a cream sauce accented with greens (page 33). On the more traditional side, we offer easy Fettuccine with Parsley-Walnut Pesto (page 29) and delicious do-ahead Oriental Noodles with Spiced Pork and Carrots (page 28).

Who would have thought that those wonderfully cheesy, gooey pizzas—the staple diet of college days—could have evolved into such sophisticated and nutritious fare? Our recipes are perfect for quick light snacks, dinner party openers, or even the focus of a terrific, do-it-yourself party. Our innovative grilled pizzas come from a professional pair who are credited with introducing these golden, cracker-crisp appetizers. Brushed with olive oil and dappled with colorful toppings like grilled bell peppers and goat cheese (page 38), Gorgonzola and herbs (page 37) or bitter greens and tomato (page 37), these appetizers are easy and deliciously trendy. Spa Pizzas (page 35) are a super-quick, extra-light version, made from tortillas instead of dough and topped with easy homemade tomato sauce, fresh vegetable toppings and cheese.

🍒 Pasta

Noodles with Spiced Pork and Carrots

8 servings

1/3 cup soy sauce
1 tablespoon Chinese rice wine or dry Sherry
2 teaspoons minced fresh ginger
1 teaspoon sugar
1 1/2 pounds pork loin, cut into 1/4 × 1 1/2-inch julienne

4 quarts water
1 tablespoon oriental sesame oil
1 pound fresh fettuccine

6 tablespoons peanut oil
3 small dried red chilies
4 carrots, peeled, cut into fine julienne
2 celery stalks, cut into fine julienne
4 green onions, cut into fine julienne
1 teaspoon oriental sesame oil

Combine soy sauce, rice wine, ginger and sugar in bowl. Add pork, stirring to coat. Let stand 30 minutes.

Bring 4 quarts water and 1 tablespoon sesame oil to boil in large pot. Add pasta and cook until just tender but still firm to bite, stirring to prevent sticking, about 5 minutes. Drain. Transfer to large deep serving bowl.

Heat 3 tablespoons peanut oil in wok or heavy large skillet over high heat. Add chilies and stir-fry 30 seconds. Add carrots and stir-fry 30 seconds. Add celery and green onions and stir-fry 1 minute. Remove vegetables using slotted spoon. Add remaining 3 tablespoons peanut oil to wok and heat over high heat. Add pork mixture and stir-fry until pork is browned, about 8 minutes. Return vegetables to wok. Blend in 1 teaspoon sesame oil.

Add pork to noodles and toss. Serve warm or at room temperature.

Penne with Rapini, Red Pepper and Spicy Olive Oil

6 first-course or 4 main-course servings

3 tablespoons olive oil
3 large garlic cloves, peeled and halved

1 large red bell pepper, cored, seeded and cut into 1- to 2-inch-long strips

1/2 teaspoon dried red pepper flakes

1 pound penne, ziti, rigatoni or other tubular pasta
1 1/4 pounds rapini* or mustard or turnip greens, stemmed
Salt

Heat oil in heavy medium skillet over medium-low heat. Add garlic and cook until light golden and soft, stirring occasionally, about 6 minutes. Remove from heat. Transfer garlic to small bowl using slotted spoon. Mash to paste with fork.

Return skillet with oil to medium heat. Add bell pepper and pepper flakes and sauté until edges of bell pepper brown slightly, stirring occasionally, about 3 minutes. Remove from heat.

Add penne to large pot of boiling salted water. Boil until slightly undercooked. Stir in rapini and boil until penne and greens are tender, stirring frequently, 2 to 3 more minutes. Drain penne and greens, reserving 1/4 cup cooking liquid. Mix reserved liquid with penne, rapini, garlic and oil-pepper mixture in large pot. Season with salt. Toss well. Serve immediately.

*Also known as broccoli rabe.

Pasta with Tomatoes, Basil and Romano

This is a typical dish from the Abruzzi region of Italy, where the noodles are made on a special device known as a "guitar" (chitarra), consisting of a rectangular frame strung with steel wires.

6 appetizer servings

¹/₂ cup olive oil
¹/₂ cup chopped onions
1¹/₂ pounds tomatoes, peeled, seeded and diced
  8 fresh basil leaves, cut julienne

1 pound fresh angel hair pasta
¹/₂ cup freshly grated pecorino Romano cheese

Heat oil in heavy large skillet over medium heat. Add onions and cook until golden brown, stirring frequently, about 10 minutes. Reduce heat to low. Add tomatoes and cook until almost all liquid evaporates, stirring occasionally, 15 minutes. Mix in basil.

Meanwhile, add pasta to large amount of rapidly boiling salted water, stirring to prevent sticking. Cook until pasta is just tender but still firm to bite. Drain thoroughly.

Add pasta to tomato mixture and toss well. Divide among 6 plates. Serve hot, passing cheese separately.

Fettuccine with Parsley-Walnut Pesto

8 servings

Pesto
  1 cup packed fresh parsley leaves
  ²/₃ cup coarsely chopped walnuts (about 3 ounces)
  1 garlic clove, coarsely chopped
    Salt and freshly ground pepper
  ³/₄ cup olive oil

Pasta
  4 eggs

¹/₂ teaspoon salt
2¹/₂ to 3 cups durum wheat flour*

  2 ounces freshly grated Parmesan cheese (about ¹/₂ cup)
  2 tablespoons (¹/₄ stick) unsalted butter, melted
    Additional freshly grated Parmesan cheese

For pesto: Coarsely chop parsley in food processor. Add walnuts and process until finely chopped. Blend in garlic, salt and pepper. With machine running, add oil through feed tube in thin steady stream. (*Can be prepared 5 days ahead. Cover and refrigerate. Bring to room temperature before using.*)

For pasta: Blend eggs with salt in processor. Add 1 cup flour and blend until mixture resembles thick pancake batter. With machine running, gradually add enough flour through feed tube to form smooth ball. Wrap dough in plastic and let stand 30 minutes.

Cut dough into 4 pieces. Flatten 1 piece of dough (keep remainder covered), then fold in thirds. Turn pasta machine to widest setting and run dough through several times until smooth and velvety, folding before each run and dusting with flour if sticky. Adjust machine to next narrower setting. Run dough through machine without folding. Repeat narrowing rollers after each run until pasta is ¹/₈ inch thick, dusting with flour as necessary. Hang dough sheet on drying rack or place on kitchen towels. Repeat with remaining dough pieces. Set aside until sheets look leathery and edges begin to curl, 10 to 30 minutes. *Pasta sheets must be cut at this point or dough will become too brittle.*

Run sheets through fettuccine blade of pasta machine (or cut by hand into ¹/₄-inch-wide strips). Arrange pasta on towel-lined baking sheets, overlapping as little as possible, until ready to cook. (*Can be prepared 2 days ahead. Cover with flour-dusted towels.*)

Add pasta to large pot of boiling salted water. Cook until just tender but still firm to bite, stirring occasionally to prevent sticking, about 4 minutes. Drain. Transfer to large serving bowl. Toss with pesto. Add 2 ounces Parmesan and butter and toss again. Divide pasta among plates and serve, passing additional Parmesan separately.

*Available at natural foods stores and some specialty foods stores.

Fettuccine with Shrimp and Tasso

Substitute smoked ham if tasso, spicy Creole ham, is unavailable.

4 servings

¼ cup clarified butter
16 uncooked medium shrimp, peeled and deveined
¼ cup 1 × ½-inch strips tasso* or smoked ham
   Creole Seasoning**
2 green bell peppers, seeded and cut into 1 × ¼-inch julienne
2 red bell peppers, seeded and cut into 1 × ¼-inch julienne
2 teaspoons minced garlic
2 large tomatoes, peeled, seeded and cut into ¾-inch dice
1⅓ cups rich brown chicken stock***

4 teaspoons Creole mustard
¾ cup (1½ sticks) well-chilled unsalted butter, cut into tablespoons
   Salt and freshly ground pepper

3 tablespoons butter
½ pound spinach leaves
2 Creole or beefsteak tomatoes, cut into ½-inch-thick slices

4 ounces dried fettuccine, freshly cooked

Heat clarified butter in heavy large skillet over high heat. Add shrimp and tasso. Sprinkle shrimp with Creole Seasoning. Stir 30 seconds. Add bell peppers and garlic and stir 1½ minutes. Add diced tomatoes and stock. Boil until reduced by half, stirring frequently, about 5 minutes. Mix in Creole mustard. Reduce heat to low. Whisk in ¾ cup butter 1 piece at a time. Season with salt and pepper.

Meanwhile, melt 2 tablespoons butter in heavy large skillet over high heat. Add spinach; season with salt and pepper. Stir until just wilted, about 1 minute. Place mound of spinach on each side of each plate. Melt remaining tablespoon butter in same skillet. Sprinkle sliced tomatoes with Creole seasoning. Add to skillet and cook until heated through, about 1 minute per side. Arrange 2 slices on each plate between mounds of spinach.

Add fettuccine to sauce and stir to coat. Roll pasta with fork and place in center of plates. Pour shrimp and tasso sauce over and serve immediately.

*A spiced smoked Creole ham, available at specialty foods stores and some supermarkets.

**Creole Seasoning

Use this spice mix on roasted or grilled seafood, meat and poultry.

Makes about ¾ cup

¼ cup salt
1 tablespoon granulated or powdered garlic
1 tablespoon freshly ground pepper
1 tablespoon paprika

¾ teaspoon granulated or powdered onion
¼ teaspoon cayenne pepper
¼ teaspoon dried thyme, crumbled
¼ teaspoon dried oregano, crumbled

Mix all ingredients. Store in glass jar.

***To make brown chicken stock, roast chicken parts and vegetables for standard stock in 350°F oven until brown, about 40 minutes, before proceeding with recipe.

Artichoke-filled Half-Moon Pasta with Green Tomato Sauce

If you can find the miniature artichokes, use them for this delicate dish. When trimming, keep some of the stem and the soft leaves on.

6 to 8 servings

2 pounds artichokes
  Lemon halves

3 tablespoons olive oil
1 small onion, minced
1 large garlic clove, minced
6 tablespoons dry white wine
½ pound whole milk ricotta cheese
½ pound Gorgonzola cheese

1 egg yolk
1 teaspoon minced fresh parsley
  Salt and freshly ground white pepper

Basic Egg Dough,* rolled to sheets

Green Tomato Sauce**

Cut off stem of each artichoke and rub exposed area with lemon. Starting from base, bend each leaf back and snap off at natural break. Cut off tight cone of leaves above heart. Trim and shape heart carefully with knife until no dark green areas remain. Rub with lemon. Cut hearts into fine julienne.

Heat oil in heavy large skillet over medium-low heat. Add onion and garlic and cook until onion is translucent, stirring occasionally, about 10 minutes. Add artichoke julienne and cook until tender, stirring occasionally, about 30 minutes. Add wine and cook until evaporated. Transfer mixture to processor and chop finely (do not puree), using on/off turns, about 30 seconds. Blend in cheeses, yolk and parsley; do not overmix. Season with salt and pepper. (*Can be prepared 1 day ahead. Cover and refrigerate.*)

Flour baking sheets. Lay dough sheets on work surface. Cut out 3-inch rounds using tortellini cutter or glass. Place ½ tablespoon filling in center of each round. Moisten edges with water. Fold dough over filling, pressing edges to seal. Bend edges to form half-moon shapes. Arrange pasta on sheets.

Cook pasta in large amount of boiling salted water until just tender but still firm to bite, about 5 minutes. Drain well. Divide among bowls. Spoon sauce over. Serve immediately.

*Basic Egg Dough

Makes about ¾ pound

1⅔ cups all purpose flour
2 eggs
1 teaspoon olive oil

Pinch of salt and freshly ground white pepper

Mound flour on work surface or in large bowl. Make well in center. Add eggs, oil and salt and pepper to well and blend with fork. Gradually draw flour from inner edge of well into center until all flour is incorporated. Turn dough out onto lightly floured surface and knead until dough comes together. Wrap in plastic or waxed paper and let stand 30 minutes.

Cut dough in half. Flatten 1 piece of dough (keep remainder covered to prevent drying). Fold in thirds. Turn pasta machine to widest setting and run dough through several times until smooth and velvety, folding before each run and dusting with flour if sticky. Adjust machine to next narrower setting. Run dough through machine without folding. Repeat narrowing rollers after each run until pasta is 1/16 inch thick (about thickness of dime), dusting with flour as necessary. Repeat with remaining dough. For flat pasta, set aside until sheets look leathery and edges begin to curl, 10 to 30 minutes depending on dampness of dough. *Pasta must be cut at this point or dough will be too brittle.* Cook according to directions in individual recipe. For filled pasta, do not dry. Proceed to cut, fill and cook pasta according to directions in recipe.

**Green Tomato Sauce

Makes about 3 cups

1/4 cup olive oil
2 carrots, finely chopped
4 garlic cloves, minced
4 pounds unripened green tomatoes (not tomatillos), peeled, seeded and coarsely chopped

2 cups chicken broth
2 bay leaves
12 basil leaves, chopped
Salt and freshly ground pepper

Heat olive oil in heavy large skillet over medium-low heat. Add carrots and garlic and stir 1 minute. Add tomatoes, broth, bay leaves and basil and simmer until thick, stirring occasionally, about 30 minutes. Remove bay leaves. Season sauce generously with salt and pepper. (*Can be prepared 1 day ahead. Cool, cover and refrigerate. Reheat sauce gently before serving.*)

Pasta Daisies with Radicchio in Saffron Sauce

6 servings

1¹/4 pounds radicchio

1 tablespoon olive oil
2¹/2 ounces pancetta* or unsmoked bacon, minced
1 small onion, minced
2 jumbo egg yolks
5 tablespoons freshly grated Parmesan cheese
Salt and freshly ground pepper

1 recipe Basic Egg Dough (see page 31), rolled to sheets

Saffron Sauce**
Poppy seeds

Separate radicchio into leaves. Blanch in boiling salted water until wilted. Drain well. Twist radicchio in towel to eliminate excess water, then mince.

Heat oil in heavy medium skillet over medium-low heat. Add pancetta and onion and cook until onion is translucent, stirring occasionally, about 10 minutes. Add radicchio and stir to coat. Remove from heat and cool slightly. Stir in yolks and Parmesan. Season with salt and pepper.

Flour baking sheets. Arrange dough sheets on work surface. Cut out rounds of dough using daisy ravioli cutter or any 2¹/2-inch fluted cutter. Place about 3/4 tablespoon filling in center of half of rounds, leaving small border. Moisten edges with water. Top with remaining rounds, pressing down around filling to force out air and seal dough. Arrange pasta on sheets.

Cook pasta in large amount of boiling salted water until just tender but still firm to bite, about 3 to 3¹/2 minutes. Drain well. Divide among bowls. Spoon sauce over. Sprinkle with poppy seeds. Serve immediately.

*Pancetta, unsmoked bacon cured in salt, is available at Italian markets.

**Saffron Sauce

Makes about 1¹/4 cups

2 tablespoons (1/4 stick) butter
1/3 cup minced onion
1/2 cup dry white wine

1¹/2 teaspoons saffron threads, crushed
2 cups whipping cream
Salt and freshly ground pepper

Melt butter in heavy small saucepan over medium-low heat. Add onion and cook until translucent, stirring occasionally, about 10 minutes. Add wine and saffron and boil until reduced to glaze. Add cream and boil until reduced. Add salt and pepper to taste. (*Can be prepared 4 hours ahead.*)

Bean-filled Pasta with Two Sauces

A tomato sauce and a cream one accented with bitter greens and pancetta complement these whimsically shaped packets, which originated in Tuscany.

6 to 8 servings

1/4 **pound dried cannellini beans**
1/4 **pound lentils**
1/4 **pound fresh or frozen shelled fava beans**

2 **tablespoons olive oil**
1 **small onion, finely chopped**
2 **ounces thinly sliced prosciutto, chopped**
2 **large garlic cloves, minced**
2 1/2 **cups chicken broth**
1/2 **cup dry white wine**
2 **bay leaves**

4 **ounces pecorino cheese, grated**
1 **egg**
2 **tablespoons minced fresh parsley**
Salt and freshly ground white pepper

1 **recipe Basic Egg Dough (see page 31), rolled to sheets**

Fresh Tomato Sauce*
Sauce of Pancetta and Bitter Greens**

Combine beans in large bowl. Add enough water to cover and let stand overnight. Drain beans; rinse well.

Heat oil in heavy large skillet over medium heat. Add onion, prosciutto and garlic and stir until lightly browned, about 5 minutes. Add beans, broth, wine and bay leaves and simmer gently until beans are tender, about 1 hour. Remove bay leaves.

Transfer mixture to blender and puree. Work puree through fine sieve into bowl. Stir in cheese, egg and parsley. Season filling generously with salt and pepper. (*Can be prepared 1 day ahead. Let cool. Cover and refrigerate.*)

Flour baking sheets. Lay dough sheets on work surface. Cut out 2 × 2-inch squares. Place about 1 teaspoon filling in center of each square. Bring two adjacent corners together. Bring in third, then fourth corner. Pinch center to seal, then pinch seams together. Or, bring 2 diagonal corners into center. Bring other 2 diagonal corners into center. Pinch center to seal, then pinch seams together. Arrange pasta on prepared sheets. (*Can be prepared 1 day ahead and refrigerated.*)

Cook pasta in large amount of boiling salted water until just tender but still firm to bite, about 5 minutes. Drain.

Spoon Fresh Tomato Sauce onto plates. Top with pasta. Spoon Sauce of Pancetta and Bitter Greens over pasta.

*Fresh Tomato Sauce

Makes about 2 cups

1/4 **cup olive oil**
1 **medium onion, minced**
2 **large garlic cloves, minced**

3 **pounds ripe tomatoes, peeled, seeded and coarsely chopped**
1/4 **cup minced fresh basil**
Salt and freshly ground pepper

Heat oil in heavy large skillet over medium-low heat. Add onion and garlic and cook until translucent, stirring occasionally, about 10 minutes. Add tomatoes and stir until warmed through. Mix in basil. Season with salt and pepper. Serve immediately. (*Can be prepared 2 days ahead. Cool, cover and chill.*)

** Sauce of Pancetta and Bitter Greens

Makes about 1³/₄ cups

2 tablespoons olive oil
1 medium onion, minced
3 ounces pancetta*** or unsmoked bacon, minced
1 large garlic clove, minced

¹/₂ pound bitter greens (such as mustard greens or dandelion leaves), trimmed and chopped
2 cups chicken broth
1¹/₂ cups whipping cream

Heat oil in heavy large skillet over medium-low heat. Add onion, pancetta and garlic and cook until onion is translucent, stirring occasionally, about 10 minutes. Add greens and stir until wilted. Add broth and boil until reduced to about ¹/₂ cup. Add cream and boil until reduced to 1³/₄ cups, about 20 minutes. Serve immediately. (*Can be prepared 6 hours ahead.*)

***Pancetta, unsmoked bacon cured in salt, is available at Italian markets.

Salmon Ravioli with Tomato-Vodka Sauce

8 servings

1 tablespoon olive oil
1 tablespoon minced green onion (white part only)
³/₄ pound skinned and boned salmon, cut into 1-inch cubes
3 tablespoons dry white wine
1 tablespoon minced fresh parsley
¹/₂ teaspoon minced fresh thyme
2 tablespoons freshly grated Parmesan cheese

1 egg yolk
Salt and freshly ground white pepper
Cayenne pepper

1 recipe Basic Egg Dough (see page 31), rolled to sheets

Tomato-Vodka Sauce*

Heat oil in heavy medium skillet over medium heat. Add green onion and stir until translucent, about 1 minute. Add salmon, wine, parsley and thyme and cook until fish is opaque outside but still very pink inside, about 5 minutes, turning once. Transfer mixture to processor. Add Parmesan and yolk and puree using on/off turns. Season with salt, pepper and cayenne. Transfer to bowl. Cool completely. Cover and refrigerate. (*Can be prepared 1 day ahead.*)

Flour baking sheets. Set sheet of dough on work surface. Place 1 teaspoon filling at 2-inch intervals. Top with another sheet. Press around filling to force out air and seal dough. Cut into 2-inch squares. Arrange on prepared sheets.

Cook pasta in large amount of boiling salted water until tender but still firm to bite, about 4 minutes. Transfer to bowls. Spoon sauce over and serve.

*Tomato-Vodka Sauce

Makes about 2 cups

2 tablespoons (¹/₄ stick) butter
2 green onions (white part only), chopped
¹/₃ cup vodka
³/₄ pound ripe tomatoes, peeled, seeded and chopped

2 cups whipping cream
2 teaspoons pink peppercorns, crushed
Salt and freshly ground white pepper

Melt butter in heavy medium skillet over medium heat. Add green onions and stir until translucent, about 1 minute. Add vodka and boil until evaporated. Add tomatoes, cream and peppercorns and simmer until reduced and thickened. Season with salt and freshly ground white pepper.

🍅 *Pizza*

Spa Pizzas

Use any combination of the toppings here. Sautéed eggplant and squash, artichoke hearts, tomatoes and onions are some other delicious possibilities.

Makes 4 individual pizzas

3 tablespoons olive oil
1/2 cup minced onions
1 cup tomato sauce
2 garlic cloves, minced
1/2 teaspoon dried oregano, crumbled
1/4 teaspoon Italian herb seasoning

3/4 cup sliced mushrooms
1/2 medium zucchini, thinly sliced

4 8-inch flour or 6-inch corn tortillas
1 cup grated mozzarella cheese
1/2 cup diced green bell pepper
1/2 cup diced red bell pepper
1/2 cup sliced black olives

Heat 2 tablespoons oil in heavy medium saucepan over medium heat. Add onions and cook until golden, stirring occasionally, about 5 minutes. Stir in tomato sauce, garlic, oregano and Italian seasoning. Simmer until thickened, about 5 minutes. Set sauce aside.

Heat remaining 1 tablespoon oil in heavy medium skillet over medium heat. Add mushrooms and zucchini and cook until tender, stirring occasionally, about 5 minutes. Set aside.

Preheat oven to 350°F. Place tortillas on baking sheet and bake until crisp, about 4 minutes. Spread about 1/4 cup sauce over each. Sprinkle each with 1/4 cup cheese. Top pizzas with mushrooms, zucchini, bell peppers and olives. Bake until cheese melts, about 5 minutes.

Personal Pizzas

Three pizzas per person may sound like a lot, but as dinner progresses and the guests become more adventurous with toppings, you will want to have enough to go around. Any extras can be kept in the freezer for fast future dinners or snacks. For ease in handling, make the dough in two batches.

Makes 36

6 tablespoons (6 envelopes) dry yeast
9 cups warm water (105°F to 115°F)
1 cup olive oil

20 cups (or more) unbleached all purpose flour

4 1/2 cups whole wheat flour
3 tablespoons salt

Coarsely ground yellow cornmeal
Quick Tomato Sauce*
Toppings**

Sprinkle 3 tablespoons yeast over 4 1/2 cups warm water in small bowl; add 1/2 cup oil and stir to blend. Let yeast mixture stand 5 minutes.

Combine 10 cups all purpose flour, 2 1/4 cups whole wheat flour and 1 1/2 tablespoons salt in large bowl. Make well in center. Add yeast mixture and stir until stiff dough forms, adding more all purpose flour if necessary. Knead dough on lightly floured surface until smooth and elastic, about 5 minutes, adding more all purpose flour if necessary to prevent sticking. Transfer to oiled bowl, turning to coat entire surface. Cover with cloth and let rise in warm draft-free area until doubled in volume, about 1 hour.

Repeat, making second batch of dough with remaining yeast, water, oil, all purpose flour, whole wheat flour and salt. Repeat kneading and rising.

Punch down 1 batch of dough. Knead on lightly floured surface several minutes until smooth. Divide into 18 pieces; form into balls. Shape each into 6-inch round on lightly floured surface. Stack 6 rounds between sheets of waxed paper; wrap with plastic and freeze. Repeat with remaining rounds. Repeat with second batch of dough.

Preheat oven to 500°F. Oil 2 large baking sheets and sprinkle with cornmeal. Spread 12 frozen rounds with tomato sauce and add toppings as desired. Place on prepared sheets. Using spray bottle, spray oven with water to create steam. Bake pizzas until crusts are brown and toppings are bubbly, 15 to 20 minutes, rotating sheets halfway through. Serve immediately. Repeat with remaining frozen pizza rounds, tomato sauce and toppings.

*Quick Tomato Sauce

Makes about 8 cups

3 28-ounce cans Italian plum tomatoes (undrained)
1/3 cup tomato paste
3 garlic cloves, minced
4 fresh basil leaves, minced or 2 teaspoons dried, crumbled

2 teaspoons dried marjoram, crumbled
2 teaspoons dried oregano, crumbled
Salt and freshly ground pepper

Place tomatoes and juice in heavy large nonaluminum saucepan and crush with potato masher or fork. Add tomato paste, garlic and herbs. Season with salt and pepper. Bring to boil. Reduce heat and simmer 30 minutes. (*Can be prepared 1 week ahead and kept refrigerated.*)

**Toppings

Include any or all of the following. After baking the pizzas you could top them with sour cream and/or caviar.

Cheeses

Smoked or regular mozzarella
Goat cheese
Fontina
Parmesan
Romano
Provolone
Gorgonzola

Meats

Cooked sausages
Prosciutto
Pancetta

Vegetables

Slowly sautéed onions
Fresh mushrooms or reconstituted
dried wild mushrooms

Sun-dried tomatoes
Minced hot chilies
Roasted red and yellow bell peppers
Eggplant cubes sautéed in olive oil
Prepared caponata***

Miscellaneous

Anchovies
Prepared pesto
Oil-cured black olives
Fresh and dried herbs
Extra-virgin olive oil

***A cooked mixture of vegetables, olive oil and vinegar, available at supermarkets.

Grilled Pizza with Gorgonzola

Makes one 12-inch pizza

2 Italian plum tomatoes (fresh or canned), peeled, seeded and coarsely chopped
1 tablespoon unsalted butter
2 tablespoons whipping cream
Salt

¼ Pizza Dough*

Extra-virgin olive oil
2 tablespoons crumbled Gorgonzola cheese (preferably imported)
2 tablespoons coarsely chopped fresh Italian parsley
1 fresh sage leaf, coarsely chopped

Drain tomatoes in strainer. Melt butter in heavy small skillet over medium-high heat. Add tomatoes and stir 2 minutes. Add cream and bring to boil. Remove from heat. Season with salt.

Prepare barbecue grill (medium-high heat). Flatten dough on oiled surface to 12-inch free-form round. Place in center of grill rack. Cook until dough begins to puff slightly, underside is firm and grill marks appear, about 2 minutes. Turn dough over and move to edge of rack, using tongs. Brush cooked surface with oil. Top with tomatoes. Distribute Gorgonzola and herbs over surface. Drizzle with oil. Slide pizza into center of grill rack. Cook until underside is slightly charred, rotating frequently with tongs, 3 to 5 minutes. Serve pizza immediately.

*Pizza Dough

Makes about 1½ pounds

1 envelope dry yeast
Pinch of sugar
1 cup warm water (105°F to 115°F)
¼ cup white cornmeal
3 tablespoons whole wheat flour
1 tablespoon extra-virgin olive oil

2¼ teaspoons salt
2½ cups (about) unbleached all purpose flour

Extra-virgin olive oil

Sprinkle yeast and sugar over warm water in large bowl; stir to dissolve. Let stand 5 minutes. Mix in cornmeal, whole wheat flour, 1 tablespoon oil and salt. Mix in enough all purpose flour ½ cup at a time to form stiff dough. Knead dough on lightly floured surface until smooth and elastic, adding more all purpose flour to dough if sticky, about 10 minutes.

Grease large bowl with olive oil. Add dough, turning to coat entire surface. Cover and let rise in warm draft-free area until doubled, about 1 hour.

Punch dough down and knead in bowl until smooth. Cover and let rise until doubled in volume, about 30 minutes.

Punch dough down and knead until smooth. (*Can be prepared 2 hours ahead and refrigerated. Punch dough down and knead until smooth before using.*)

Grilled Pizza with Bitter Greens

Makes one 12-inch pizza

1 6-ounce tomato, peeled, seeded and coarsely chopped
¼ Pizza Dough (see above)
Extra-virgin olive oil
¼ cup (about 1 ounce) coarsely grated imported Parmesan cheese

1 medium garlic clove, minced
12 small arugula or curly endive leaves

Prepare barbecue grill (medium-high heat). Drain tomato. Flatten dough on oiled surface to 12-inch free-form round. Place in center of grill rack. Cook until dough begins to puff slightly, underside is firm and grill marks appear, about 2 minutes. Turn dough over and move to edge of rack, using tongs. Brush cooked surface with oil. Top with tomatoes. Sprinkle with Parmesan and garlic. Top with arugula. Drizzle with oil. Slide pizza into center of grill rack, using tongs. Cook until underside is slightly charred, rotating frequently, 3 to 5 minutes. Serve immediately.

Grilled Pizza with Grilled Peppers "Agrodolce"

Goat cheese, olives and the special marinated peppers combine to make a fabulous pizza topping.

Makes one 12-inch pizza

2/3 cup Grilled Peppers "Agrodolce"*
1 Italian plum tomato, peeled, seeded and coarsely chopped
1/4 Pizza Dough (see page 37)

Extra-virgin olive oil
3 tablespoons goat cheese
6 Kalamata olives, pitted and quartered
10 fresh Italian parsley leaves

Prepare barbecue grill (medium-high heat). Drain peppers 5 minutes. Drain tomato in strainer. Flatten dough on oiled surface to 12-inch free-form round. Place on grill rack. Cook until dough begins to puff slightly, underside is firm and grill marks appear, about 2 minutes. Turn dough over and move to edge of rack, using tongs. Brush cooked surface with oil. Scatter peppers and tomato over dough. Add cheese in 1-teaspoon mounds. Scatter olives and parsley over pizza. Drizzle with oil. Slide pizza into center of grill rack. Cook until underside is slightly charred, rotating frequently with tongs, 3 to 5 minutes.

*Grilled Peppers "Agrodolce"

Agrodolce—sweet and sour—peppers are terrific on the pizza, in a mozzarella salad or as part of an antipasto.

Makes about 2 cups

2 tablespoons golden raisins
1 yellow bell pepper, halved and seeded
1 red bell pepper, halved and seeded

1/2 cup extra-virgin olive oil
1/3 cup balsamic vinegar
1 garlic clove, minced
Salt

Soak raisins in hot water to cover while preparing peppers.

Prepare barbecue grill (high heat). Arrange peppers on grill rack cut side down and cook until beginning to char, about 8 minutes. Cut into thin strips. Place in medium bowl. Drain raisins; add to peppers. Mix in oil, vinegar and garlic. Season with salt. Let marinate at least 30 minutes. (*Can be prepared 3 days ahead and refrigerated. Bring to room temperature before using.*)

4 ❦ Main Courses

Among the meat and poultry main dishes, familiar cooking techniques predominate. There are plenty of country stews and casseroles, hearty roasts and always-popular grilled foods. Strong ethnic and regional American influences add interest and taste along the way.

Traditionalists will enjoy the hearty Cheese-crusted Flank Steak (page 40) and sweet and tangy Mustard-glazed Corned Beef Brisket (page 40). The adventurous will love the Cajun Meat Loaf (page 42), a spicy twist on an old favorite, or Red Beef Stew (page 41), not the meat-and-potatoes kind but a spicy Chinese Szechwan version. Veal Ragout with Red Pepper (page 45) is a rustic Italian dish; Lamb and Orzo Stew (page 47), with a cinnamon-scented tomato sauce, comes from Greece; and Juniper-glazed Ham (page 51) is an easy Scandinavian-flavored entrée.

Poultry and seafood also come in an array of international recipes, including home-style baked chicken, simple and satisfying, surrounded by tender onions, carrots, parsnips and rutabagas (page 51); Texcoco-style Green Mole Chicken (page 52) and Creole Roast Turkey (page 54) basted with zingy Creole butter and filled with Jambalaya Stuffing (page 54), a spicy melange of rice, bell peppers, crabmeat and andouille sausage. Fish and Shellfish selections range from Southwestern Grilled Salmon with Corn Ragout and Ancho Chili Sauce (page 56) to Chinese Steamed Trout (page 59) and Provençal Shellfish Stew with Rouille (page 60).

With the growing interest in light and healthy eating, non-meat entrées are gaining in popularity as a nutritious menu change of pace. Some terrific examples are French Tian of Roasted Bell Peppers, Tomatoes, Eggplant and Cheese (page 66), innovative Mexican Tamale Spinach Roll with Corn, Chili and Tomato Sauce (page 64) and Poached Eggs with Creole Sauce and Fried Eggplant (page 62). All are ideal main courses for brunch, luncheon or light suppers.

❦ Beef

Grilled Steak with Provençal Herbs

4 servings

4 1¹/₂-inch-thick 12-ounce New York (top loin) or Delmonico steaks
1 tablespoon olive oil
2 garlic cloves, minced
2 teaspoons minced fresh rosemary or 1 teaspoon dried, crumbled

2 teaspoons minced fresh thyme or 1 teaspoon dried, crumbled
2 teaspoons minced fresh basil or 1 teaspoon dried, crumbled
Freshly ground pepper

Place steaks in shallow dish. Rub both sides with oil, garlic and herbs. Season with pepper. Let stand 1 hour.

Prepare barbecue (high heat) or preheat broiler. Cook steaks 2 inches from heat source to desired doneness, about 4 minutes per side for rare.

Cheese-crusted Flank Steak

The secret to tender flank steak is all in the cutting: Slice it thinly across grain on the diagonal and serve.

6 servings.

1 cup dry red wine
2 tablespoons olive oil
2 tablespoons red wine vinegar
2 garlic cloves, minced
1 tablespoon minced fresh oregano or 1 teaspoon dried, crumbled

2 1¹/₂-pound flank steaks, trimmed

1 cup grated cheddar cheese
2 teaspoons Dijon mustard
1 teaspoon Worcestershire sauce

Combine wine, oil, vinegar, garlic and oregano in shallow nonaluminum baking pan. Add steaks, turning to coat. Cover and refrigerate 24 to 48 hours, turning occasionally.

Prepare barbecue (high heat). Combine cheese, mustard and Worcestershire in small bowl. Drain steaks. Grill 5 minutes. Turn over and spread with cheese mixture. Grill about 5 more minutes for medium rare.

Mustard-glazed Corned Beef Brisket

6 servings

1 4- to 5-pound corned beef brisket

8 whole black peppercorns
2 bay leaves

¹/₂ cup Dijon mustard
1 teaspoon dry mustard

¹/₂ cup honey
¹/₃ cup Sherry wine vinegar
¹/₃ cup firmly packed light brown sugar
1 tablespoon oriental sesame oil

Place brisket in large pot. Add enough water to cover. Cover pot. Refrigerate brisket at least 6 hours or overnight.

Drain brisket. Add water to cover, peppercorns and bay leaves. Bring to boil. Reduce heat, cover and simmer until tender, about 3¹/₂ hours. Drain brisket. Cool. Cover and chill overnight.

Transfer brisket to roasting pan, fat side up. Bring to room temperature.

Preheat oven to 350°F. Whisk mustards in heavy small saucepan. Stir in remaining ingredients. Simmer 5 minutes, stirring constantly. Spread glaze evenly over top of brisket. Bake until heated through, about 45 minutes.

Roast Tenderloin of Beef with Pancetta, Marjoram and Red Wine

4 servings

2 tablespoons (¼ stick) butter, room temperature
1 2-pound beef tenderloin, trimmed of outside fat and sinew
Coarsely ground pepper
¼ pound ⅛-inch-thick slices pancetta* or bacon

1 tablespoon butter
3 ounces pancetta* or bacon, chopped
⅓ cup minced shallots

¼ cup Cognac
1½ cups dry red wine
3 marjoram sprigs
3 cups unsalted beef stock (preferably homemade), boiled until reduced to 1½ cups
1 teaspoon tomato paste
¼ cup (½ stick) butter, cut into 4 pieces
Freshly ground pepper
Minced fresh marjoram

Preheat oven to 450°F. Spread 2 tablespoons butter over beef. Sprinkle liberally with pepper. Wrap with ¼-pound pancetta, securing with toothpicks. Place on rack in roasting pan just large enough to accommodate beef. Bake until thermometer inserted in thickest part of meat registers 120°F for rare, about 30 minutes. Transfer beef to heated platter and tent with foil to keep warm.

Set roasting pan over medium heat. Add 1 tablespoon butter and chopped pancetta and stir 1 minute. Add shallots and stir until tender, about 3 minutes. Pour off all but thin film of fat. Add Cognac and boil until reduced to glaze, scraping up any browned bits, about 1½ minutes. Add ¾ cup wine and marjoram and boil until reduced to glaze, about 5 minutes. Add remaining wine and boil until reduced to glaze, about 5 minutes. Add stock and tomato paste and boil until reduced to ¾ cup mixture, adding juices on beef platter, about 8 minutes. Strain into heavy small saucepan, pressing to extract as much liquid as possible. Bring sauce to simmer and whisk in ¼ cup butter 1 piece at a time. Season generously with pepper. Cut meat into ½-inch-thick slices, discarding toothpicks. Arrange on heated plates. Spoon sauce over. Sprinkle with marjoram and serve.

*Pancetta, unsmoked bacon cured in salt, is available at Italian markets.

Red Beef Stew

Carrots, onions and a generous amount of ginger highlight this fiery Szechwan dish, traditionally spooned over thin egg noodles in clear broth.

4 servings

2 pounds boneless beef shanks, cut into 1½ × 2-inch pieces

1 medium onion, thinly sliced
10 large ⅛-inch-thick slices ginger
5 garlic cloves, thinly sliced
4 small dried red chilies
1 star anise*
2 tablespoons soy sauce
4 teaspoons dark soy sauce
1 tablespoon brown bean sauce*

1 teaspoon sugar
½ teaspoon salt

7 teaspoons hot chili oil*
3 cups water

3 large carrots, cut on diagonal into ¾ × ½-inch pieces
1 teaspoon cornstarch
5 tablespoons minced green onions

Bring large pot of water to boil. Add beef and boil 10 seconds. Drain; rinse under running water 1 minute.

Combine onion, ginger, garlic, chilies and star anise in bowl. Blend soy sauces, brown bean sauce, sugar and salt in another bowl.

Heat hot chili oil in wok over high heat 1 minute (be careful; fumes may be intense). Add onion mixture to wok and stir-fry 2 minutes. Add beef and stir-fry 3 minutes. Transfer to saucepan. Add 2¾ cups water and bring to boil. Reduce heat, cover and simmer until beef is tender but not falling apart, stirring occasionally, about 1 hour and 40 minutes, adding more water if necessary.

Add carrots to beef. Cover and simmer until tender, stirring occasionally, about 20 minutes. Remove chilies, ginger and star anise. Increase heat to high. Dissolve cornstarch in remaining ¼ cup water. Add to stew and stir 75 seconds. Transfer to platter. Garnish with green onions. Serve immediately.

*Available at oriental markets.

Cajun Meat Loaf

Leftovers of this meat loaf make a great sandwich.

2 to 4 servings

2 tablespoons (¼ stick) butter
½ large onion, chopped
½ cup chopped green bell pepper
1 teaspoon salt
¾ teaspoon cayenne pepper
½ teaspoon dried thyme, crumbled
½ teaspoon freshly ground pepper

¼ teaspoon ground cumin

1 pound lean ground beef
1 egg, beaten to blend
½ cup fine dry breadcrumbs
½ cup catsup
1 teaspoon Worcestershire sauce

Preheat oven to 375°F. Melt butter in heavy medium skillet over medium-low heat. Add next 7 ingredients and cook until vegetables are tender, stirring frequently, about 10 minutes.

Combine meat, egg, breadcrumbs, ¼ cup catsup and Worcestershire sauce in medium bowl. Blend in sautéed vegetables. Form mixture into loaf 1¾ inches high and 5 inches wide in baking dish. Bake 20 minutes. Spread top with remaining ¼ cup catsup and bake for 40 more minutes.

Sautéed Liver with Garlic and Sage

2 servings; can be doubled or tripled

3 tablespoons butter
5 large garlic cloves, thinly sliced
8 large sage leaves, torn into pieces

All purpose flour
Salt and freshly ground pepper

12 to 14 ounces ¼- to ½-inch-thick beef or calf's liver slices

¾ cup unsalted chicken broth
1 tablespoon dry white wine

Melt 1½ tablespoons butter in heavy large skillet over low heat. Add garlic and sage and cook until garlic begins to brown, stirring frequently, about 6 minutes. Transfer garlic and sage to small bowl using slotted spoon.

Season flour generously with salt and pepper. Pat liver dry. Dredge in flour, shaking off excess. Add remaining 1½ tablespoons butter to same skillet and melt over medium-high heat. Add liver and cook until beginning to brown on outside but still pink inside, about 1 minute per side. Transfer sautéed liver to heated plates; keep warm.

Return garlic and sage to skillet. Add broth and wine and bring to boil, scraping up any browned bits. Boil until thickened to sauce consistency. Spoon sauce over liver and serve.

🍎 *Veal*

Veal Pisarek

8 servings

3 pounds veal scaloppine
3 cups all purpose flour
4 teaspoons salt
4 teaspoons freshly ground white pepper
1 cup clarified butter

24 asparagus spears (peeled), blanched
4 cups fresh mushrooms, sliced
6 large shallots, finely chopped
½ cup dry Marsala

2 pounds Havarti or Jarlsberg cheese, grated

Place veal between sheets of waxed paper and pound with mallet until thin. Mix flour, salt and pepper in shallow pan. Heat butter in heavy large skillet over medium-high heat. Dredge veal in flour, shaking off excess. Add to skillet in batches (do not crowd). Cook until light brown, 1 to 2 minutes per side. Transfer to heated plate.

Pour off all but 2 tablespoons butter from skillet. Add asparagus, mushrooms and shallots and cook until asparagus is almost tender, stirring frequently, about 4 minutes. Transfer vegetables to shallow dish using slotted spoon. Add Marsala to corner of skillet and heat slightly. Ignite with match. Bring mixture to boil, scraping up any browned bits. Return veal to skillet and return to boil.

Preheat oven to 425°F. Grease large baking pan. Arrange veal in single layer in pan. Spoon asparagus mixture over, dividing evenly. Pour sauce over. Top with cheese. Bake until cheese melts, 5 to 7 minutes. Serve hot.

Veal Loin Hungarian Style

Serve this colorful entrée with glazed carrot ovals and potato rounds.

6 servings

3 bunches fresh spinach, stemmed
2 cups dry Riesling wine
⅓ cup chopped shallots
4 cups Veal Stock*
1½ tablespoons Hungarian sweet paprika, soaked in ¼ cup dry Riesling wine

Salt
5 tablespoons unsalted butter

Clarified butter
6 4- to 5-ounce veal loin medallions, flattened slightly
Freshly ground pepper
All purpose flour

Blanch spinach in a large pot of boiling salted water until just wilted. Drain; refresh under cold water. Squeeze dry. (*Can be prepared 1 day ahead, wrapped in plastic and refrigerated.*)

Boil wine and shallots in heavy medium saucepan until liquid is reduced to 1 tablespoon. Add stock and dissolved paprika and boil until reduced to consistency of light cream or about 1½ cups. Adjust seasoning with salt. Strain through fine sieve. Whisk in 2 tablespoons butter. Keep sauce warm in double boiler or vacuum bottle.

Melt remaining 3 tablespoons butter in heavy medium-large skillet over medium heat. Add spinach and cook until slightly browned, fluffing with fork. Season to taste with salt.

Heat thin layer of clarified butter in heavy large skillet over medium heat.

Pat veal dry. Season with salt and pepper. Dredge in flour, shaking off excess. Add to skillet and cook until firm to touch, about 3 minutes per side.

Cut veal diagonally into ⅛-inch-thick slices. Mound spinach in center of plate. Top with veal. Surround with sauce. Serve immediately.

*Veal Stock

Makes about 4 cups

4 **pounds veal bones, cut into 2-inch pieces**
3 **tablespoons peanut oil**
2 **carrots, coarsely chopped**
1 **celery stalk, coarsely chopped**
1 **medium onion, coarsely chopped**
¼ **cup tomato paste**

2 **garlic cloves, chopped**
3 **fresh parsley sprigs**
2 **fresh thyme sprigs**
1 **small bay leaf**
1 **teaspoon whole black peppercorns**

Preheat oven to 375°F. Arrange bones in roasting pan and roast until golden brown, stirring occasionally, about 1 hour. Transfer to stockpot. Add water to cover and bring to boil.

Meanwhile, heat oil in heavy large skillet over medium heat. Add carrots, celery and onion and cook until lightly browned, stirring frequently, about 15 minutes. Add to stockpot. Add remaining ingredients and bring to boil, skimming foam from surface. Reduce heat and simmer very gently 12 hours. Strain into clean saucepan, pressing on solids to extract as much liquid as possible. If necessary, boil until reduced to 4 cups. Cool.

Braised Veal with Vegetable and Porcini Sauce

This dish can also be made with a three-pound boneless turkey breast half. Allow approximately 15 more minutes cooking time or until a meat thermometer registers 160°F.

6 to 8 servings

1 **ounce dried porcini mushrooms or other dried European mushrooms**

1 **fresh rosemary sprig or 1 teaspoon dried, crumbled**
1 **3-pound boned and rolled veal roast (cut from leg), about 5 inches thick, with thin layer of fat tied around meat**
1 **tablespoon unsalted butter**
3 **tablespoons light olive oil**
  Salt and freshly ground pepper

1 **medium onion, halved lengthwise**
2 **medium carrots, peeled and cut into feed-tube lengths**
2 **small celery stalks, cut into feed-tube lengths**

½ **cup dry, fruity white wine, such as Italian Chardonnay**
1 **bay leaf**

½ **cup whipping cream**

Soak porcini in hot water to cover 20 minutes. Rinse well; squeeze dry. Discard any hard stems.

Position rack in center of oven and preheat to 350°F. Tuck fresh rosemary under fat around roast or rub surface with dried rosemary. Melt butter with oil in heavy stove-to-oven casserole over medium-high heat. Add veal and brown well on all sides, about 10 minutes. Season with salt and pepper.

Using thin or medium slicer in processor, arrange onion in feed tube and slice. Stand carrots in feed tube and slice. Stand celery in feed tube and slice. Add vegetables to veal. Carefully remove slicing disc; insert steel knife.

Add ¼ cup wine and bay leaf to veal. Bring to boil, basting veal and vegetables with liquid. Remove from heat. Add remaining ¼ cup wine to casserole. Cover, transfer to oven and bake until thermometer inserted in thickest part of meat registers 140°F, about 75 minutes, basting 4 times with juices.

Transfer veal to platter and tent with foil to keep warm. Discard bay leaf. Transfer vegetables to processor using slotted spoon. Pour pan juices into measuring cup and degrease.

Puree vegetables in processor until smooth, stopping occasionally to scrape down sides of work bowl. Add porcini and mince, about 3 seconds.

Return vegetable puree and pan juices to casserole and stir over medium-high heat 3 minutes. Add cream and cook until thickened to consistency of whipping cream, about 4 minutes. Cut veal into thin slices, discarding string. Spoon some sauce over. Serve, passing remaining sauce separately.

Veal Ragout with Red Pepper

A do-ahead stew with the flavors of osso bucco, the classic Italian dish made with veal shanks and vegetables.

8 servings

5 tablespoons (about) olive oil
3 pounds veal stew meat, cut into 1½-inch pieces, trimmed
½ cup chopped carrots
½ cup chopped onion
¼ cup all purpose flour
4 cups chicken stock
1 28-ounce can Italian plum tomatoes, drained
1 cup dry white wine
3 parsley sprigs
2 medium garlic cloves, crushed
1 bay leaf, crumbled

1 teaspoon dried thyme, crumbled
½ teaspoon dried basil, crumbled
Salt and freshly ground pepper

1 large red bell pepper, seeded and cut into 1-inch squares

½ cup chopped fresh parsley
¼ cup minced green onions
2 teaspoons minced garlic
2 teaspoons grated lemon peel
1¾ pounds fresh fettuccine
3 tablespoons butter

Heat 5 tablespoons oil in heavy Dutch oven over medium-high heat. Pat veal dry. Add to pan in batches (do not crowd) and cook until brown on all sides, adding more oil if necessary, about 10 minutes. Drain on paper towels. Add carrots and onion to pan and cook 5 minutes, stirring frequently. Return veal to pan; sprinkle with flour. Stir 3 minutes. Add stock and bring to boil, scraping up any browned bits. Mix in tomatoes, wine, parsley sprigs, crushed garlic, bay leaf, thyme, basil, salt and pepper. Bring to simmer, stirring constantly and breaking up tomatoes. Reduce heat, cover and simmer 1 hour. Uncover and simmer until veal is tender, about 20 minutes.

Add bell pepper and cook until just tender, about 10 minutes. Transfer meat and bell pepper to bowl, using slotted spoon. Discard parsley. Skim surface of cooking liquid. Boil until reduced to 2 cups, stirring occasionally, about 20 minutes. Return meat and pepper to pan. (*Can be prepared 2 days ahead. Cover and refrigerate. Rewarm over medium heat before continuing.*)

Combine chopped parsley, green onions, minced garlic and lemon peel. Cook fettuccine in large pot of boiling salted water until just tender but still firm to bite. Drain well. Return to pot and mix with butter. Arrange around outer edge of large deep platter. Spoon ragout into center of platter. Sprinkle with parsley mixture and serve.

🍎 Lamb

Marinated Smoked Leg of Lamb

The smoking time will vary considerably depending on the size of the barbecue or smoke oven, among other things. Be sure to start with enough charcoal to burn the entire time.

8 servings

1 5- to 6-pound leg of lamb
9 garlic cloves, chopped
18 juniper berries
3 tablespoons fresh lemon juice
1 tablespoon grated lemon peel
1½ teaspoons freshly ground pepper

¾ teaspoon dried red pepper flakes
½ cup olive oil

3 cups hickory chips (or other smoke flavoring), soaked in water to cover 30 minutes and drained

Trim excess fat from lamb. Make ½-inch cuts over surface. Place in non-aluminum pan. Combine next 6 ingredients in mortar and mash with pestle until paste forms. Slowly mix in olive oil. Rub mixture into lamb. Cover and refrigerate overnight.

Prepare covered barbecue or smoker (low heat). Spread 1 cup hickory chips over coals. Set water pan over coals and fill with water. Oil grill rack. Set lamb on rack, cover and smoke until thermometer inserted in thickest part registers 145°F for medium-rare, turning lamb and adding more water and chips occasionally, 3 to 5 hours. Slice lamb and serve hot or at room temperature.

Mediterranean Lamb Skewers

6 servings

⅓ cup olive oil
⅓ cup red wine vinegar
2 large garlic cloves, minced
1 teaspoon dried basil, crumbled
   Salt and freshly ground pepper

5 pounds boneless leg of lamb, trimmed and cut into 1½-inch cubes

Spicy Pepper Sauce*

Combine first 4 ingredients in large bowl. Season with salt and pepper. Pierce meat with fork. Add to marinade. Cover and chill 2 days, stirring occasionally.

Prepare barbecue (medium-high heat) or preheat broiler. Drain meat and thread on skewers. Grill to desired doneness, turning once, about 10 minutes for medium. Serve immediately, passing Spicy Pepper Sauce separately.

*Spicy Pepper Sauce

Makes about 4 cups

1 12¼-ounce jar brine-packed red and yellow bell pepper strips, drained (brine reserved) and chopped
3 2¼-ounce cans sliced black olives, drained

1 4-ounce can mushroom stems and pieces, drained
3 garlic cloves, minced
1 teaspoon dried basil, crumbled
⅛ teaspoon dried red pepper flakes
1 cup olive oil
   Salt and freshly ground pepper

Combine bell peppers, olives, mushrooms, garlic, basil and red pepper flakes in medium bowl. Add 1 cup reserved brine and olive oil. Season with salt and pepper. Refrigerate in airtight container until ready to use. Serve at room temperature. (*Can be made 5 days ahead.*)

Greek Lamb and Orzo Stew

6 servings

½ cup olive oil
1 5- to 7-pound leg of lamb, boned,
  cut into 1½-inch chunks and
  patted dry
2 pounds ripe tomatoes, chopped
1 medium onion, studded with
  5 whole cloves
2 large garlic cloves, minced
2 tablespoons tomato paste

¼ teaspoon cinnamon
  Pinch of sugar
  Salt and freshly ground pepper

½ cup (1 stick) butter
1 pound orzo (rice-shaped pasta)*
3 cups water
½ cup freshly grated kefalotyri** or
  Parmesan cheese

Heat olive oil in Dutch oven over medium-high heat. Add lamb and brown well on all sides. Add tomatoes, onion, garlic, tomato paste, cinnamon, sugar and salt and pepper. Reduce heat to low. Cover and simmer 45 minutes.

Preheat oven to 350°F. Melt butter in heavy large skillet over medium heat. Add orzo and sauté until completely coated. Stir into lamb mixture. Add water. Cover and bake 1 hour. Remove onion. Sprinkle mixture with cheese. Bake 5 minutes. Transfer to platter and serve immediately.

*Available at Italian markets, specialty foods stores and many supermarkets.

**A nutty-flavored hard cheese similar to Parmesan. Available at Greek markets.

Lamb Shanks with White Beans and Savory

Partner this hearty dish with a red wine from the Rhone Valley or a California Zinfandel.

4 servings

2 cups dried white beans such as
  Great Northern

Lamb
4 lamb shanks (from fore shank),
  trimmed
  Salt
2 tablespoons olive oil
1 10-ounce can Italian plum
  tomatoes
1 small bunch fresh parsley,
  chopped
1 teaspoon minced fresh savory or
  ½ teaspoon dried
1 teaspoon minced fresh thyme or
  ½ teaspoon dried
½ teaspoon minced fresh rosemary
  or ¼ teaspoon dried
¼ teaspoon minced fresh lavender
  (optional) or pinch dried

2 bay leaves
  Freshly ground pepper
1 cup dry white wine

Beans
6 cups water
1 lamb bone (optional)
½ onion, cut into 2 pieces
2 garlic cloves, crushed
1 small dried red chili
1 bay leaf
½ teaspoon minced fresh thyme or
  ¼ teaspoon dried
½ teaspoon minced fresh savory or
  ¼ teaspoon dried

16 garlic cloves, peeled and halved
½ cup extra-virgin olive oil
  Fresh savory sprigs

Soak beans overnight in water to cover by 3 inches.

For lamb: Preheat oven to 325°F. Pat lamb dry. Sprinkle with salt. Heat oil in heavy large skillet over medium-high heat. Add lamb and brown on all sides.

Transfer to oven casserole just large enough to accommodate in single layer. Pour off drippings from skillet. Add all remaining ingredients except wine and bring to boil, scraping up any browned bits and breaking up tomatoes with spoon. Reduce heat and simmer 12 minutes. Add wine and return liquid to simmer. Pour sauce over lamb. Cover tightly. Place casserole in oven and roast until lamb is very tender, about 2¼ hours.

Meanwhile, prepare beans: Drain beans. Place in heavy medium saucepan. Add 6 cups water, lamb bone, onion, crushed garlic, dried chili, bay leaf, thyme and ½ teaspoon minced savory. Simmer until beans are just tender, about 1½ hours. Drain.

Transfer lamb to platter, using slotted spoon. Tent with foil to keep warm. Degrease cooking juices in casserole. Add beans and halved garlic and simmer 15 minutes, stirring occasionally. Discard bay leaves and dried chili. Mix extra-virgin olive oil into beans. Adjust seasoning. Spoon around lamb shanks. Garnish with savory sprigs and serve.

Moroccan Couscous of Lamb, Fruit and Vegetables

6 servings

²/₃ **cup quick-cooking couscous**
²/₃ **cup dried currants**
½ **cup boiling chicken stock**

3 **large garlic cloves**
1 **6-ounce unpeeled Jonathan apple, cored and cut into 6 pieces**
1 **4-ounce red bell pepper, seeded and cut into 1-inch pieces**

6 **medium green onions, cut into thirds**

6 **1-ounce slender carrots, peeled, cut into feed-tube lengths**

10 **ounces lean boneless lamb (preferably from leg), cut into 1-inch cubes, well chilled**

¼ **cup olive oil**
  Salt
¼ **cup pine nuts**
2 **teaspoons fresh lemon juice, or to taste**
1 **teaspoon cinnamon**
¼ **teaspoon cayenne pepper, or to taste**

Place couscous and currants in small bowl. Pour boiling stock over. Stir with fork. Cover bowl and set aside.

With processor machine running, drop garlic through feed tube and mince. Remove from work bowl and set aside. Add apple and bell pepper to processor and chop coarsely using about 8 on/off turns. Transfer apple mixture to small bowl. Set aside.

Insert thick slicer. Stand green onions in feed tube and slice using light pressure. Add onions to apple mixture.

Insert thin slicer. Stand carrots in feed tube and slice using firm pressure. Remove from work bowl and set aside.

Coarsely chop lamb in processor with steel knife using 6 on/off turns.

Heat oil in heavy large skillet over high heat. Mix in lamb, garlic and salt and stir 15 seconds. Reduce heat to medium. Add carrots, cover and cook until lamb is no longer pink, stirring occasionally, about 4 minutes. Add couscous mixture, apple mixture, pine nuts, lemon juice, cinnamon and cayenne, tossing gently to blend. Cover and cook just until heated through, stirring occasionally, about 3 minutes. Adjust seasoning. Serve immediately.

❧ *Pork*

Ginger and Garlic Pork Loin

Slivers of whole nutmeg enhance this dish.

10 servings

1 5- to 6-pound boneless pork loin
4 large garlic cloves, slivered
1½ whole nutmegs, slivered
1 walnut-size piece fresh ginger, peeled and slivered
2 teaspoons salt
1 teaspoon freshly ground pepper

6 tablespoons dark rum
3 tablespoons dark brown sugar

1 teaspoon ground ginger
1 teaspoon freshly grated nutmeg
2½ cups chicken stock

1½ tablespoons fresh lime juice
1 teaspoon grated lime peel
1 tablespoon cornstarch mixed with ¼ cup cold water
Raisin and Almond Rice (see page 73)

Preheat oven to 450°F. Score cross-hatch pattern ½ inch deep on fat side of pork. Pierce 1-inch holes at intervals in pork. Insert garlic, nutmeg and ginger slivers into holes. Rub pork with salt and pepper. Set on rack in roasting pan and roast 15 minutes. Reduce heat to 325°F and continue roasting pork 25 minutes.

Blend 2 tablespoons rum with brown sugar, ginger and grated nutmeg. Rub mixture over pork. Stir chicken stock into roasting pan. Continue roasting until juices run clear when pork is pierced, about 50 more minutes.

Strain juices from roasting pan into saucepan. Warm remaining rum in another saucepan. Remove from heat; ignite rum. When flames subside, add to juices. Blend in lime juice and peel. Bring to boil. Stir in cornstarch mixture and cook over medium heat until thickened, stirring constantly. Adjust sauce seasoning with salt and pepper.

Cut pork into thin slices. Mound rice in center of platter. Surround with pork. Pass sauce separately.

Grilled Skewered Pork Rolls

8 servings

5 garlic cloves, minced
2 tablespoons minced fresh sage or 2 teaspoons dried, crumbled
1 tablespoon (generous) grated peeled fresh ginger
½ teaspoon cinnamon
Pinch of ground cloves
8 3-ounce pork loin scallops, trimmed

Salt and freshly ground pepper
8 thin slices prosciutto

16 1½-inch-square Italian bread cubes
Olive oil
16 paper-thin slices pancetta*

Combine first 5 ingredients in small bowl. Pound pork between sheets of waxed paper to thickness of ¼ inch. Season with salt and pepper. Spread garlic mixture evenly over one side of each scallop. Cover with prosciutto slice. Cut scallop crosswise in half. Starting at short ends, roll up loosely jelly roll fashion.

Brush bread cubes generously on all sides with olive oil. Wrap each with one pancetta slice. Alternate 2 bread cubes and 2 pork rolls on each skewer, using skewer to secure ends of pancetta and pork rolls, and leaving ⅛-inch space between each. (*Can be prepared 4 hours ahead. Cover and refrigerate. Bring to room temperature before cooking.*)

Prepare barbecue (medium heat) or preheat broiler. Arrange skewers on rack and cook until pork is tender, basting bread with more oil, about 5 minutes per side. Serve immediately.

*Pancetta, unsmoked bacon cured in salt, is available at Italian markets.

Mustard-glazed Spareribs

Any leftovers are delicious cold or can be wrapped in foil and reheated.

2 servings; can be doubled or tripled

2 teaspoons minced fresh rosemary
2 medium garlic cloves, minced
1 rack (about 3 pounds) pork spareribs
Salt and freshly ground pepper

Mustard Glaze
⅓ cup firmly packed dark brown sugar

¼ cup coarse-grained Dijon mustard
2 tablespoons plus 1½ teaspoons cider vinegar
1 tablespoon molasses
1½ teaspoons dry mustard

Preheat oven to 350°F. Rub rosemary and garlic into both sides of ribs. Sprinkle with salt and pepper. Arrange meaty side down on baking sheet. Bake 1 hour, turning once. (*Can be prepared 1 day ahead. Cool completely, cover with plastic wrap and refrigerate.*)

Meanwhile, prepare glaze: Combine all ingredients in heavy small saucepan. Bring to simmer, stirring. Cool.

Prepare barbecue grill (medium heat). Place ribs on grill rack, meaty side up. Spread top with ⅓ of glaze. Cook until bottom side is crisp, about 5 minutes. Turn, spread second side with glaze and cook until bottom side is crisp, about 5 minutes. Turn, spread top with glaze and cook until bottom side is glazed, about 5 minutes. Transfer to platter. Cut into individual ribs.

White Bean and Pork Chili

Like any chili, this is even better the second day. Warm corn tortillas are the perfect accompaniment.

2 to 4 servings

3 tablespoons olive oil
1 medium onion, chopped
2 medium carrots, chopped
2 medium celery stalks, chopped
2 large garlic cloves, minced

1 pound pork sirloin cutlets, cut into ½-inch dice
Salt and freshly ground pepper

1 teaspoon chili powder (or to taste)
½ teaspoon cumin

½ teaspoon dried oregano, crumbled
⅛ teaspoon ground sage
1 cup beef broth
1 14½-ounce can peeled tomatoes (undrained)

2 15-ounce cans cannellini or Great Northern beans, rinsed and drained
Grated cheddar and/or Monterey Jack cheese
Minced fresh cilantro

Heat 2 tablespoons oil in heavy large saucepan over medium-low heat. Add onion, carrots, celery and garlic and cook until tender, about 10 minutes.

Meanwhile, heat remaining 1 tablespoon oil in heavy large skillet over high heat. Pat pork dry. Add to skillet, season with salt and pepper and cook until browned, stirring frequently, approximately 6 minutes.

Add pork to vegetables. Blend in chili, cumin, oregano and sage and stir 3 minutes. Add broth to skillet and bring to boil, scraping up any browned bits. Stir into pork mixture. Add tomatoes with liquid and bring to boil. Reduce heat, cover and simmer until pork is tender, stirring occasionally, about 1 hour.

Add beans to mixture and stir until heated through. Spoon into bowls. Top with cheese and cilantro.

Juniper-glazed Ham

The quality of the ham is of prime importance. Ask your butcher for a bone-in, ready-to-eat whole leg ham. Do not use a shoulder cut.

12 servings

2 cups gin
²/₃ cup dried juniper berries
¹/₂ cup firmly packed dark brown sugar

¹/₄ cup dark beer
2 teaspoons dry mustard

1 12- to 14-pound bone-in ready-to-eat ham

Preheat oven to 325°F. Boil gin and juniper berries in heavy small saucepan until liquid is reduced to ¹/₄ cup. Strain into heavy medium saucepan; reserve ¹/₄ cup berries. Add sugar, beer and mustard to gin. Stir mixture over medium heat until reduced to syrupy glaze, about 3 minutes.

Place ham in large roasting pan. Trim any skin remaining on ham. Cut ¹/₂-inch-deep, ¹/₂-inch-long pockets in ham, spacing ¹/₃ inch apart. Fill cut pockets with reserved berries. Brush half of glaze over ham. Bake 40 minutes. Brush ham with remaining glaze and bake 40 minutes more. (*Can be prepared 1 week ahead. Cool completely. Cover and refrigerate.*) Transfer ham to large platter. Cut into thin slices. Serve warm, at room temperature or cold.

❦ Poultry

Baked Chicken Pieces and Root Vegetables

2 servings; can be doubled or tripled

2 large carrots, peeled and cut diagonally into 1¹/₂-inch pieces
2 parsnips, peeled and cut diagonally into 1¹/₂-inch pieces
1 rutabaga, peeled and cut into 1¹/₂-inch pieces
1 medium onion, quartered
2 tablespoons plus 2 teaspoons olive oil

1¹/₄ teaspoons rubbed sage
³/₄ teaspoon dried rosemary, crumbled
Salt and freshly ground pepper

2 leg-thigh chicken pieces
2 large garlic cloves, crushed

Preheat oven to 375°F. Combine first 4 ingredients in baking pan. Add 2 tablespoons oil, ³/₄ teaspoon sage and ¹/₂ teaspoon rosemary. Sprinkle with salt and generous amount of pepper. Mix to coat vegetables. Bake 15 minutes.

Meanwhile, rub chicken with garlic, then with remaining ¹/₂ teaspoon sage and ¹/₄ teaspoon rosemary, salt and pepper and finally with 2 teaspoons oil. Add to pan with vegetables. Cook until juices run clear when thigh is pierced in thickest part, about 1 hour, stirring vegetables occasionally.

Chicken Stuffed with Mushrooms, Pine Nuts and Feta

Roasted potatoes are a nice accompaniment to this easy-to-make Greek dish.

4 servings

2 tablespoons olive oil
1/4 pound mushrooms, thinly sliced
3 tablespoons pine nuts
1 garlic clove, minced
1/2 pound feta cheese, crumbled
1 tablespoon minced fresh parsley
Freshly ground pepper

1 3-pound chicken
Salt and freshly ground pepper
1/4 cup (1/2 stick) butter, melted
3 tablespoons fresh lemon juice
1 teaspoon Dijon mustard

Heat olive oil in heavy medium skillet over medium-high heat. Add mushrooms, pine nuts and garlic and stir until golden brown, about 5 minutes. Stir in feta and parsley. Season with pepper. Cool stuffing completely.

Position rack in center of oven and preheat to 425°F. Pat chicken dry. Sprinkle inside and out with salt and pepper. Spoon stuffing into chicken; truss chicken. Set chicken breast side up in roasting pan. Blend butter, lemon juice and mustard. Brush chicken lightly with mixture. Roast 5 minutes. Turn on left side and roast 5 minutes. Turn on right side and roast 5 minutes. Return to upright position. Reduce oven temperature to 350°F. Roast chicken until juices run clear when thigh is pierced, 30 to 40 minutes, basting frequently with butter mixture and pan juices.

Texcoco-style Green Mole Chicken

Mole recipes vary considerably within the different regions of Mexico. This one has a combination of spices typical of the Texcoco style.

4 servings

3 tablespoons raw, unsalted hulled pumpkin seeds
Salt
1/2 cup sesame seeds
3 tablespoons slivered almonds
3 tablespoons raw Spanish peanuts
1 1/2-inch piece thin cinnamon stick, coarsely chopped
Scant 1/2 teaspoon whole black peppercorns, crushed

3 tablespoons vegetable oil
1/2 small onion, diced (about 1/2 cup)
2 large ripe plantains, peeled and cut diagonally into 1/4-inch-thick slices
1 corn tortilla, cut into thirds
1 teaspoon minced garlic clove

1/2 of 1/4-inch-thick slice French bread, toasted

1 pound tomatillos, husked and quartered
1 romaine lettuce leaf
2 teaspoons fresh cilantro leaves
1 fresh serrano chili

1/4 cup vegetable oil
1 3 1/2-pound chicken, cut into 8 pieces or 4 large leg-thigh pieces
1/3 cup rich reduced chicken stock (preferably homemade)

Vegetable oil

Red, yellow and green bell pepper rings
Cilantro sprigs

Sprinkle pumpkin seeds lightly with salt in heavy small skillet (preferably cast iron). Stir over medium-high heat until toasted, about 5 minutes. Grind coarsely in processor using on/off turns. Transfer to plate. Stir sesame seeds in same skillet until toasted, about 2 minutes. Transfer to processor. Repeat with almonds, then peanuts. Stir cinnamon and peppercorns in skillet until aromatic, about 2 minutes. Add to nuts and process to fine powder, using on/off turns, stopping occasionally to scrape down sides of bowl, about 30 seconds.

Heat 3 tablespoons oil in same skillet over low heat. Add onion, cover and cook until translucent, stirring occasionally, about 10 minutes. Add two ¼-inch slices plantain and 1 piece of tortilla to skillet (remainder is not used). Cook over medium heat until plantain is golden brown, stirring occasionally, about 2 minutes. Add garlic and cook 1 minute. Add to mixture in processor and cool.

Add bread to processor and finely grind mixture, stopping occasionally to scrape down sides of work bowl, about 4 minutes. Add tomatillos, lettuce, cilantro and chili. Puree, stopping occasionally to scrape down sides of work bowl, about 3 minutes.

Preheat oven to 425°F. Heat ¼ cup oil in heavy large ovenproof skillet over medium-high heat. Pat chicken dry. Add dark meat to skillet and brown on all sides, about 10 minutes. Transfer to plate. Add breast to skillet skin side down and brown, about 5 minutes. Add to other chicken pieces. Add stock to skillet, scraping up any browned bits. Stir in puree. Season with salt. Return chicken to skillet and bring sauce to simmer. Cover and cook chicken for 10 minutes. Turn and continue cooking until juices run clear when chicken is pierced with fork, 10 to 15 more minutes.

Meanwhile, heat ¼ inch oil in heavy small skillet over medium-high heat. Fry remaining plantains until golden brown, about 2 minutes per side. Drain on paper towels.

Stir ground pumpkin seeds into chicken mixture. Taste and adjust seasoning. Arrange chicken on plates. Spoon sauce over. Arrange plantain slices on side of each plate. Garnish with bell pepper. Sprinkle with cilantro and serve.

Curried Game Hens

For additional flavor, start marinating the birds the night before.

8 servings

6 medium onions, quartered	1 tablespoon salt
¾ cup grated unsweetened coconut	3 garlic cloves
9 tablespoons poppy seeds	3 cups plain yogurt
6 tablespoons cumin seeds	
2 tablespoons chopped seeded small dried red chilies	8 small Cornish game hens
1 tablespoon cardamom seeds	Butter
	Solid vegetable shortening

Puree first 8 ingredients in blender or processor. Add yogurt and blend well.

Arrange hens in nonaluminum baking dish. Pour marinade over. Turn hens to coat completely. Cover with plastic and refrigerate overnight.

Preheat oven to 300°F. Remove hens from marinade, scraping off and reserving excess. Melt enough mixed butter and shortening to come 1½ to 2 inches up sides of heavy large skillet. Add hens (in batches; do not crowd) and brown well on all sides. Transfer to large ovenproof casserole. Stir marinade into skillet set over medium heat and stir 2 minutes. Pour over hens. Cover and bake 2 hours. Pour or spoon off excess fat. (*Can be prepared 1 day ahead. Cool completely; cover and chill.*) Serve hot or at room temperature.

Creole Roast Turkey with Jambalaya Stuffing

The sensational Creole Butter helps keep the breast moist and adds flavor and color to the turkey. Half of the stuffing is cooked in the turkey; bake the remainder separately.

8 servings

1 16-pound turkey, room temperature
Creole Butter*

7 cups Jambalaya Stuffing**

2 cups rich chicken stock (preferably homemade)

Position rack in lower third of oven and preheat to 325°F. Pat turkey dry. Gently slide fingers between turkey breast skin and meat to loosen skin. Rub Creole Butter under skin over breast meat. Spoon stuffing into cavity, packing firmly. Truss turkey. Arrange breast side up in shallow roasting pan. Roast turkey until juices run clear when thigh is pierced or meat thermometer inserted in thickest part of thigh registers 170°F, basting about every 20 minutes with pan juices, 3¼ hours to 3½ hours.

Transfer turkey to heated platter. Tent with foil; let stand 30 minutes.

Degrease pan juices. Set roasting pan with pan juices over medium-high heat. Add stock and bring to boil, scraping up any browned bits. Boil 5 minutes. Strain into heated sauceboat. Serve turkey, passing pan juices separately.

*Creole Butter

Makes about ⅔ cup

½ cup (1 stick) unsalted butter, room temperature
3 medium garlic cloves, mashed
2 teaspoons Worcestershire sauce
1 teaspoon hot pepper sauce
1 teaspoon dried thyme, crumbled

½ teaspoon rubbed sage
½ teaspoon freshly ground pepper
½ teaspoon freshly ground white pepper
½ teaspoon cayenne pepper
¼ teaspoon ground allspice

Blend all ingredients in processor until smooth. Transfer to bowl. (*Can be prepared 4 days ahead, covered and refrigerated or 1 month ahead and frozen. Bring to room temperature before using.*)

**Jambalaya Stuffing

8 servings

¼ cup olive oil
1 pound andouille*** or other spicy smoked sausage, thinly sliced
2 red bell peppers, cored and diced
1 large onion, coarsely chopped
3 celery stalks, diced
3 garlic cloves, minced
2 teaspoons dried thyme, crumbled
2 bay leaves
1 teaspoon freshly ground pepper
1 teaspoon freshly ground white pepper

1 teaspoon filé powder****
¼ teaspoon cayenne pepper

5 cups chicken stock (preferably homemade)
1 28-ounce can Italian plum tomatoes, crushed and drained
2 teaspoons salt
2½ cups long-grain rice
1 cup sliced green onions

1 pound lump crabmeat

Heat oil in heavy 5-quart saucepan over medium heat. Add andouille and stir until crisp and brown, about 10 minutes. Transfer to bowl using slotted spoon. Add bell peppers, onion, celery, garlic, thyme, bay leaves, pepper, white pepper, filé and cayenne to saucepan. Cover and cook over low heat until vegetables are tender, stirring occasionally, about 15 minutes.

Mix in stock, tomatoes and salt. Increase heat and bring to boil. Stir in rice. Reduce heat to low. Cover and cook until rice has absorbed all liquid, about 22 minutes. Transfer rice to bowl. Mix in andouille and green onions. Cool completely. (*Can be prepared 1 day ahead. Cover and refrigerate. Bring to room temperature before continuing.*)

Preheat oven to 375°F. Stir crab into stuffing. Reserve 7 cups stuffing for turkey. Spoon remaining stuffing into 2-quart baking dish. Cover tightly. (*Can be prepared 4½ hours ahead and refrigerated.*) Bake until hot, about 40 minutes.

***A smoked pork and beef sausage, available at specialty foods stores. Smoked bratwurst, kielbasa or smoked Hungarian sausage can be substituted.

****A powder made from ground sassafras leaves. Available at specialty foods stores.

❦ *Fish and Shellfish*

Catfish with Coarse-grained Mustard Sauce

The perfect accompaniments for this are spoon bread and mustard greens cooked with bacon.

4 servings

½ cup dry white wine
¼ cup white wine vinegar
2 shallots, minced
1 bay leaf
Pinch of dried tarragon, crumbled
1 tablespoon whipping cream
1 cup (2 sticks) chilled unsalted butter, room temperature
2 tablespoons coarse-grained mustard
1 tablespoon chopped fresh parsley
Fresh lemon juice

8 4-ounce ½-inch-thick catfish fillets
1 cup all purpose flour
2 eggs, beaten to blend
1 cup fresh breadcrumbs
Salt and freshly ground pepper
3 tablespoons clarified butter

Fresh parsley sprigs

Boil first 5 ingredients in heavy small saucepan until reduced to syrupy glaze, about 8 minutes. Remove from heat and add cream. Set over low heat and whisk in butter 1 tablespoon at a time, removing pan from heat briefly if drops of melted butter appear. (If sauce breaks down at any time, remove from heat and whisk in 2 tablespoons cold butter.) Strain sauce into medium bowl. Whisk in mustard and parsley. Season with lemon juice.

Dip fish in flour, then egg; roll in breadcrumbs, coating thoroughly. Season with salt and pepper. Heat butter in heavy large skillet over medium-high heat. Add fish (in batches if necessary; do not crowd) and cook until crisp and golden, about 4 minutes per side.

Ladle sauce onto plates. Top with 2 fillets each. Garnish with parsley.

Grilled Salmon with Corn Ragout and Ancho Chili Sauce

6 servings

Sauce
6 ancho (dried) chilies

3 Italian plum tomatoes
1 small red onion, quartered
2 garlic cloves
2 cups chicken stock
1 tablespoon honey
2 tablespoons (¼ stick) unsalted butter
2 tablespoons fresh lime juice
Salt and freshly ground pepper

Ragout
4 ears fresh corn, husked

¼ cup (½ stick) butter
1 medium red bell pepper, finely chopped
1 medium green bell pepper, finely chopped
2 green onions, minced
1 jalapeño chili, minced
¼ cup whipping cream

6 7- to 8-ounce salmon fillets
Peanut or olive oil

Sour cream
Fresh cilantro sprigs

For sauce: Toast chilies in heavy small skillet over medium heat until aromatic, turning frequently, about 5 minutes. Stem, seed and cut into small pieces. Transfer chilies to blender.

Prepare barbecue (high heat) or preheat broiler. Grill tomatoes, onion and garlic on rack until tomatoes blister, about 5 minutes. Transfer to blender. Add stock and honey and mix to rough puree, about 30 seconds. Pour into heavy small saucepan. Whisk in butter and lime juice. Season to taste with salt and pepper. Keep sauce warm over very low heat.

For ragout: Prepare barbecue (medium heat) or preheat broiler. Grill corn until cooked through, turning frequently, about 10 minutes depending on freshness. Cut kernels from cobs.

Melt butter in heavy medium skillet over medium heat. Add bell peppers, green onions and chili and cook until softened, stirring frequently, about 5 minutes. Add corn and heat through. Add cream and cook until thickened.

Rub fish with oil. Grill until translucent, 2 to 3 minutes per side.

Spoon sauce onto plates. Top with salmon. Surround with ragout. Garnish with sour cream and cilantro sprigs. Serve immediately.

Peppercorn Shrimp with Jalapeño and Garlic

2 to 4 servings

25 medium uncooked, unshelled shrimp
¼ cup tapioca starch* or cornstarch
¼ cup all purpose flour
1½ teaspoons salt
¼ teaspoon freshly ground white pepper

1 cup vegetable oil

2 teaspoons minced seeded jalapeño chili
2 teaspoons minced ginger
2 teaspoons minced garlic

½ teaspoon Szechwan peppercorn powder**
1½ cups parsley leaves
2 radishes, very thinly sliced

Using scissors, cut through shell and meat along back of each shrimp; devein (do not remove shell). Rinse shrimp and drain; dry well. Combine starch, flour, 1¼ teaspoons salt and pepper. Dredge shrimp in flour mixture.

Heat oil in wok to 350°F. Slide 5 shrimp down side of wok into oil and fry

Seafood and Sausage Gumbo

Brian Leatart

Grilled Skewered Pork Rolls; Summer Vegetable Stew; Fettuccine with Parsley-Walnut Pesto; Orange-Raisin Cake

*Clockwise from far left: Poached Eggs
with Creole Sauce and Fried Eggplant;
fried oysters (recipe not included);
Creamed Fish, Ham and Egg Pilaf; Apple,
Honey and Cottage Cheese Griddle Cakes*

Irwin Horowitz

Clockwise from bottom left: Black Walnut Wagon Wheels; Bourbon Butter Pecan Cheesecake; Apricot Chocolate Soufflé Cake; Chocolate Mocha Sauce

Clockwise from top right: Pineapple Ginger Upside-down Cake; Bread Pudding with Maple Pecan Sauce; Plum Hazelnut Crisp with vanilla ice cream; Lemon Honey Fritters with Apricots Poached in Vanilla Syrup, served with sour cream

Irwin Horowitz

30 seconds per side. Remove using slotted spoon and drain on paper towels. Repeat with remaining shrimp. Clean wok, reserving 1 tablespoon oil.

Heat 1 tablespoon oil in wok over high heat 1 minute. Combine jalapeño, ginger and garlic. Add to wok and stir-fry until brown and crunchy, 1 minute. Transfer to bowl. Clean wok.

Heat wok over high heat 1 minute. Add shrimp and stir-fry 15 seconds. Combine peppercorn powder and remaining 1/4 teaspoon salt. Sprinkle over shrimp. Add jalapeño mixture and toss 1 minute. Mound parsley on platter. Top with shrimp. Garnish with radishes. Serve immediately.

*Available at natural foods stores.

**Available at oriental markets.

Stir-fried Shrimp with Noodles

2 servings; can be doubled or tripled

8 dried shiitake mushrooms
1/2 pound uncooked medium shrimp, peeled and deveined
1 teaspoon dry Sherry
1 teaspoon cornstarch

6 ounces spaghettini
2 teaspoons oriental sesame oil
1/2 cup chicken broth
3 tablespoons soy sauce
1 tablespoon dry Sherry

3 tablespoons vegetable oil
1 bunch green onions, trimmed and thinly sliced
2 tablespoons slivered fresh ginger

4 ribs bok choy, trimmed and cut into 3/4-inch-thick slices
6 ounces snow peas, trimmed
1/2 teaspoon crushed Szechwan peppercorns (optional)

Soak shiitake in hot water to cover until softened, about 20 minutes. Drain; squeeze out excess liquid. Cut mushrooms into slices, discarding stems. Combine shrimp, 1 teaspoon Sherry and cornstarch in small bowl; mix until well blended.

Cook spaghettini in large pot of boiling salted water until just tender but still firm to bite. Drain. Rinse under cold water until cool. Drain well. Mix with sesame oil in medium bowl. Combine broth, soy sauce and 1 tablespoon Sherry in another small bowl.

Heat 2 tablespoons vegetable oil in wok or heavy large skillet over high heat. Add half of green onions and half of ginger and stir until aromatic, about 30 seconds. Add shiitake and stir-fry 30 seconds. Add shrimp and stir-fry until starting to turn pink, about 2 minutes. Remove from wok.

Add remaining 1 tablespoon oil and heat. Add half of remaining green onions and all of remaining ginger and stir until aromatic, about 30 seconds. Add bok choy and stir-fry until bok choy begins to soften, about 2 minutes. Add snow peas and stir-fry until snow peas begin to turn dark green, about 1 minute. Add peppercorns, then noodles and stir-fry until heated through, about 30 seconds. Return shrimp mixture to wok and stir 30 seconds. Add broth mixture and stir until absorbed by noodles and shrimp are cooked through, about 1 minute. Transfer to heated platter. Sprinkle with remaining green onions.

Red Snapper with Pinot Noir Sauce and Winter Vegetables

Offer this fish dish with a bottle of chilled Pinot Noir to complement the lovely sauce.

4 servings

1 10-ounce sweet potato, peeled
2 small turnips, peeled
2 small carrots, peeled

12 shallots
   Olive oil

Pinot Noir Sauce
1 cup California Pinot Noir wine
1/4 cup Sherry wine vinegar
2 shallots, minced
2 bay leaves
2 thyme sprigs
1 rosemary sprig
   Pinch of dried red pepper flakes

2 tablespoons whipping cream
1 cup (2 sticks) unsalted butter, cut into 16 pieces
   Salt and freshly ground pepper

Sautéed Fish
4 8-ounce Gulf red snapper, grouper, black bass or striped bass fillets
   Salt and freshly ground pepper
   All purpose flour
3 tablespoons vegetable oil

   Fresh thyme and rosemary sprigs
   Minced fresh parsley

Cut potato, turnips and carrots into 3/4-inch cubes. Blanch in large pot of boiling salted water until just tender, about 10 minutes. Drain. Pat dry.

Preheat oven to 375°F. Rub shallots with oil. Place in heavy small pan and roast until soft and golden brown, about 30 minutes.

Meanwhile, prepare sauce: Boil wine, vinegar, shallots, herbs and dried pepper flakes in heavy medium saucepan until reduced to glaze, about 10 minutes. Add cream and boil until thickened, about 1 minute. Reduce heat and whisk in butter 1 piece at a time, removing pan from heat briefly if beads of melted butter appear. (If sauce breaks down at any point, remove from heat and whisk in 2 tablespoons cold butter.) Strain sauce into heated bowl. Season to taste with salt and pepper.

For fish: Sprinkle fish with salt and pepper; dust with flour. Heat oil in heavy large skillet over high heat until almost smoking. Add fish skin side up. Cook until light golden brown and just opaque, turning once, about 8 minutes per inch of thickness. Transfer to heated platter.

Meanwhile, rewarm potato, turnips and carrots in boiling water. Drain well. Ladle sauce onto heated plates, tipping to coat completely. Place 1 fillet in center of each plate. Spoon blanched vegetables around fish. Add 3 shallots to each plate. Garnish with thyme and rosemary sprigs. Sprinkle with parsley.

Broiled Swordfish with Marmalade-Ginger Glaze

2 servings; can be doubled or tripled

2 8-ounce 1 1/2-inch-thick swordfish steaks
   Soy sauce
   Oriental sesame oil
   Freshly ground pepper

6 tablespoons strained fresh orange juice

6 tablespoons strained fresh lemon juice
2 tablespoons orange marmalade
2 teaspoons minced peeled fresh ginger
1/4 cup vegetable oil

2 orange slices, twisted

Brush swordfish with soy sauce and sesame oil on both sides. Top with pepper. Let stand while preparing glaze.

Boil orange juice, lemon juice, marmalade and ginger in small saucepan until reduced to 4 tablespoons, stirring occasionally, about 6 minutes. Cool slightly. Mix in vegetable oil.

Preheat broiler. Arrange fish on foil-lined broiler pan. Brush with half of glaze and cook 3 minutes. Turn, brush with remaining glaze and continue cooking until just opaque, about 4 minutes. Transfer to plates. Garnish with orange slices and serve.

Chinese-style Steamed Trout

2 servings

2 whole 8-ounce trout
1 teaspoon salt
   Freshly ground pepper
12 thin quarter-size slices peeled fresh ginger, slivered

6 green onions, thinly sliced
2 tablespoons soy sauce
2 teaspoons oriental sesame oil

Pat trout dry. Make several slashes on each side, spacing ³/₄ inch apart and cutting almost to bone. Rub salt and pepper into trout inside and out. Press some of ginger and green onions into slashes and inside fish. Place trout on heatproof plate. Sprinkle with soy sauce and top with remaining ginger and green onions.

Bring water to boil in steamer. Place plate with fish on steamer rack. Cover and cook until fish is just opaque, about 9 minutes per inch of thickness. Remove fish from steamer. Sprinkle with oil and serve.

Fresh Tuna with Piquant Sauce

Serve with lots of crusty Italian bread to soak up the zesty sauce.

6 servings

Sauce
¹/₂ cup olive oil (preferably extra-virgin)
¹/₂ cup minced fresh Italian parsley
¹/₂ cup pickled red bell pepper strips, drained and diced
¹/₃ cup thinly sliced green onions
2 to 3 tablespoons fresh lemon juice
2 tablespoons minced fresh oregano or 2 teaspoons dried, crumbled

1 to 2 tablespoons capers, drained and rinsed
   Salt

6 ³/₄-inch-thick 8-ounce tuna steaks
¹/₄ cup olive oil
2 tablespoons fresh lemon juice
   Freshly ground pepper
4 fresh oregano sprigs

For sauce: Combine oil, parsley, bell pepper strips, onions, 2 tablespoons lemon juice, oregano, 1 tablespoon capers and salt in heavy medium saucepan over low heat. Cook 5 minutes to blend flavors, stirring occasionally. Taste, adding more lemon juice and capers if desired. (*Can be prepared 2 weeks ahead, covered and refrigerated. Bring to room temperature before serving.*)

Place fish in nonaluminum dish just large enough to accommodate in single layer. Drizzle with ¹/₄ cup oil and 2 tablespoons lemon juice. Sprinkle with pepper. Turn to coat both sides. Place oregano sprigs under and over fish. Cover and let stand 30 minutes.

Prepare barbecue grill (high heat) or preheat broiler. Set fish on rack and cook to desired doneness, about 4 minutes per side for medium. Transfer fish to plates. Top with sauce and serve.

Provencal Shellfish Stew with Rouille

Yellow bell peppers add color to the rouille, a spicy mayonnaise that traditionally complements the fish soups served in the south of France.

4 servings

4 tablespoons olive oil
1 pound uncooked large shrimp, peeled and deveined (shells reserved and patted dry)
1 cup dry white wine
1 cup water

1 small onion, chopped
1 garlic clove, crushed
3 pounds red and/or yellow tomatoes, peeled, seeded and coarsely chopped (juices reserved) Yellow bell pepper juices reserved from Rouille**

¼ cup minced fresh basil
¼ cup minced fresh Italian parsley
1 teaspoon minced fresh oregano or ½ teaspoon dried, crumbled

1 teaspoon salt
½ teaspoon fresh thyme leaves or ¼ teaspoon dried, crumbled Freshly ground pepper
12 littleneck clams, scrubbed and soaked in cold water 1 hour
12 mussels, scrubbed, debearded and soaked in cold water 1 hour
2 6-ounce lobster tails (unshelled), cut crosswise into ¾-inch pieces

Garlic Croutons*
Fresh basil leaves
Fresh parsley leaves
Rouille**

Heat 2 tablespoons oil in heavy Dutch oven or large skillet over medium heat. Add shrimp shells and cook until translucent, stirring frequently, about 5 minutes. Increase heat to medium-high. Add wine and boil until liquid is reduced by half, stirring occasionally, about 5 minutes. Add water and boil until liquid is reduced by half, stirring occasionally, about 5 minutes. Finely chop shells with liquid in processor. Let stand 15 minutes. Strain through sieve into medium bowl, pressing with back of spoon to extract liquid; reserve liquid.

Dry Dutch oven and set over low heat. Add remaining 2 tablespoons oil and heat. Add onion and cook until golden, stirring frequently, about 15 minutes. Add garlic and stir 1 minute. Add tomatoes with their juices and pepper juices. Cover and simmer until mixture resembles chunky sauce, stirring occasionally, about 20 minutes.

Add reserved shrimp-shell liquid, minced basil, minced parsley, oregano, salt, thyme and pepper to tomato mixture. Simmer 5 minutes. Add clams and cook 3 minutes. Add mussels and cook 3 minutes. Add shrimp and lobster. Cover and cook just until clams and mussels open and shrimp and lobster are opaque, 3 minutes. Discard any clams or mussels that do not open.

Place 3 croutons in bottom of each of 4 large shallow soup bowls. Divide shellfish among bowls. Ladle liquid over. Garnish with basil and parsley leaves. Serve, passing Rouille separately.

*Garlic Croutons

Makes 12

12 ½-inch-thick slices French bread
1 garlic clove, halved

2 tablespoons olive oil

Preheat oven to 400°F. Rub 1 side of each bread slice with cut side of garlic. Arrange bread on large baking sheet, garlic side up. Brush with oil. Bake until golden brown, about 15 minutes. Cool completely.

**Rouille

Makes about 2⅓ cups

1 pound yellow bell peppers,
  roasted (see page 13) and cut into
  1-inch pieces (reserve juices for
  shellfish stew)
1 tablespoon chopped garlic

1 teaspoon salt
½ teaspoon cayenne pepper
1 egg
1 cup olive oil

Puree bell peppers, garlic, salt and cayenne in processor. Add egg and blend 10 seconds. With machine running, add oil in slow steady stream. Transfer to bowl. (*Can be prepared 1 day ahead. Cover and refrigerate. Bring to room temperature before serving.*)

Seafood and Sausage Gumbo

20 servings

1 cup vegetable oil
1 cup all purpose flour

3 large onions, chopped
8 celery stalks, chopped
1 large green bell pepper, chopped
½ cup minced fresh parsley
6 garlic cloves, minced

2 tablespoons solid vegetable
  shortening
1 pound okra, cut crosswise into ½-
  inch rounds
1 teaspoon distilled white vinegar

4 pounds uncooked unshelled
  medium shrimp

4 quarts chicken stock
1 pound spicy sausage (such as
  andouille), cut into ½-inch
  rounds and sautéed quickly on
  both sides

½ cup Worcestershire sauce
½ cup catsup
1 large tomato, chopped
2 tablespoons Pickapeppa Sauce*
1 tablespoon salt
1 teaspoon cayenne pepper
1 teaspoon minced fresh thyme or
  ¼ teaspoon dried, crumbled
1 teaspoon minced fresh rosemary
  or ¼ teaspoon dried, crumbled
1 teaspoon dried red pepper flakes
2 bay leaves

1 pound lump crabmeat
1 quart shucked oysters, drained
2 cups chopped cooked chicken
½ cup light brown sugar
2 tablespoons fresh lemon juice
1 tablespoon filé powder
  Freshly cooked white rice

Heat oil in heavy large pot over very low heat. Gradually add flour and stir with wooden spoon until roux is nicely browned, about 30 minutes.

Increase heat to medium. Add onions, celery, bell pepper, parsley and garlic to roux and cook until vegetables are soft, stirring often, about 45 minutes.

Melt shortening in heavy large skillet over medium-low heat. Add okra and vinegar and cook until okra is no longer stringy, stirring occasionally, 25 to 30 minutes. Add to onion mixture.

Meanwhile, poach shrimp in boiling water to cover until pink. Drain, reserving liquid. Shell shrimp.

Add reserved shrimp liquid, stock, sausage, Worcestershire sauce, catsup, tomato, Pickapeppa Sauce, salt, cayenne, thyme, rosemary, pepper flakes and bay leaves to okra mixture and simmer until very thick, stirring occasionally, about 3 hours. (*Can be prepared 2 days ahead. Cool completely, cover and refrigerate. Bring to simmer before continuing with recipe.*)

Add shrimp, crabmeat, oysters and chicken to gumbo and cook until edges of oysters begin to curl, about 5 minutes. Stir in brown sugar and lemon juice. Adjust seasoning. Remove gumbo from heat. Stir in filé powder. To serve, spoon rice into soup bowls. Ladle gumbo over.

*Available at specialty foods stores.

❦ Eggs, Cheese and Vegetables

Poached Eggs with Creole Sauce and Fried Eggplant

Although this recipe involves several components, they can be prepared ahead of time. The dish is also delicious served with only one of the sauces.

4 servings

Creole Sauce
- 1 tablespoon unsalted butter
- 1/2 medium onion, chopped
- 1 small green bell pepper, seeded and chopped
- 1 7-ounce ripe tomato, peeled, seeded and chopped or 2/3 cup chopped drained canned tomatoes
- 1/2 cup chicken stock (preferably homemade)
- 1/2 cup tomato juice
- 1 teaspoon fresh thyme or 1/4 teaspoon dried, crumbled
- 1/2 teaspoon paprika
- 1 small bay leaf
- 1 teaspoon cornstarch dissolved in 1 tablespoon cold water
  Salt
  Cayenne pepper

Eggplant
- 1 14-ounce eggplant, cut into 1/2-inch-thick rounds

- 1/2 cup fresh breadcrumbs
- 1/4 cup freshly grated Parmesan cheese (preferably imported)
- 1/4 teaspoon dried thyme, crumbled
- 1/4 teaspoon dried basil, crumbled
  Salt and freshly ground pepper
  All purpose flour
- 1 egg beaten with 1/2 cup milk

Chive Hollandaise Sauce
- 3/4 cup (1 1/2 sticks) unsalted butter
- 2 egg yolks
- 1/2 teaspoon white wine vinegar
- 1/2 teaspoon cold water
- 2 tablespoons fresh lemon juice
  Salt and freshly ground white pepper
- 1 tablespoon chopped fresh chives

- 1 tablespoon white wine vinegar
- 4 to 8 eggs

  Vegetable oil

  Fresh watercress sprigs

For Creole sauce: Melt butter in heavy medium saucepan over medium-high heat. Add onion and bell pepper and cook until onion is translucent, stirring frequently, about 8 minutes. Mix in tomato, stock, tomato juice, thyme, paprika and bay leaf. Bring to boil. Reduce heat, cover and simmer 30 minutes, stirring occasionally. Add cornstarch mixture and boil until slightly thickened, stirring constantly, about 2 minutes. Season with salt and cayenne pepper. Cover partially and simmer 10 minutes. Puree sauce in blender or processor. Return to saucepan. Taste and adjust seasoning. (*Can be prepared 1 day ahead, covered and refrigerated.*)

For eggplant: Line baking sheet with waxed paper. Cut eggplant into eight 2 1/2-inch rounds, using biscuit cutter. Combine breadcrumbs, Parmesan, thyme, basil, salt and pepper in shallow dish. Dip eggplant rounds into flour; shake off excess. Dip into egg mixture, then breadcrumbs, coating thoroughly. Transfer to prepared sheet. Refrigerate at least 30 minutes. (*Can be prepared 1 day ahead. Cover and refrigerate.*)

For hollandaise: Melt butter in heavy small saucepan over low heat. Remove from heat and spoon white foam off surface. Pour clarified butter into cup, discarding milky residue. Combine 2 yolks, ¹/₂ teaspoon vinegar and water in top of double boiler. Whisk over barely simmering water until eggs thicken, double in volume and are pale yellow, about 4 minutes. Remove from heat. Gradually whisk in clarified butter. Add lemon, salt and pepper. Stir in chives. (*Can be prepared up to 3 hours ahead. Keep sauce warm in vacuum bottle.*)

Add 2 inches salted water to large skillet. Add 1 tablespoon vinegar and bring to simmer. One at a time, break eggs into cup and slide into water. Poach until whites are set but yolks are still runny, about 4 minutes. Transfer to bowl of cold water using slotted spoon. (*Can be prepared 3 hours ahead.*)

Pour ¹/₂ inch oil into another heavy large skillet. Heat to 350°F. Add eggplant rounds in batches (do not crowd) and cook until tender and golden brown, about 2 minutes per side. Drain on paper towels.

Meanwhile, reheat Creole sauce over medium heat. Coat heated plates with Creole sauce. Place 2 eggplant rounds in center of each plate. Add eggs to large skillet of simmering water and reheat, about 30 seconds. Remove with slotted spoon and drain briefly. Place 1 or 2 eggs atop eggplant on each plate. Nap each egg with hollandaise and garnish with watercress. Serve, passing remaining hollandaise sauce separately.

Eggs with Tortillas, Salsa and Cheese

This piquant dish can be prepared with either fried or poached eggs.

4 servings

Salsa
- 3 medium tomatoes, cored, seeded and cut into ¹/₄-inch dice
- 4 pickled or canned jalapeño chilies, drained, seeded and finely diced
- 3 green onions, trimmed and chopped

Tortillas and Eggs
- Vegetable oil
- 8 blue or yellow corn tortillas

- 3 tablespoons unsalted butter
- 8 eggs
- 1¹/₄ cups grated Monterey Jack cheese (about 5 ounces)

For salsa: Combine tomatoes, jalapeños and green onions in small bowl.

For tortillas and eggs: Line baking sheets with paper towels. Add ¹/₂ inch oil to heavy large skillet and heat over medium heat until very hot but not smoking. Add 1 tortilla and cook until lightly toasted around edges and beginning to blister, pressing down with tongs, about 30 seconds. Drain on prepared sheet. Repeat with remaining tortillas. Keep warm.

Pour off oil from skillet, add butter and melt over medium heat. Break eggs into skillet and cook until whites are set and yolks are still runny. Place 2 tortillas on each heated plate. Top each with egg. Sprinkle with cheese. Top each with spoonful of salsa. Serve, passing remaining salsa separately.

Creamed Fish, Ham and Egg Pilaf

Also known as kedgeree, this favorite English breakfast dish is usually made with smoked haddock.

8 servings

1 cup long-grain rice
1 13³/₄-ounce can chicken broth
4 tablespoons (¹/₂ stick) unsalted butter
2 medium boiling potatoes, peeled, cut into ¹/₄-inch dice, boiled until almost tender
2 green bell peppers, seeded, cut into ¹/₄-inch dice
¹/₂ cup fresh peas (about ³/₄ pound unshelled) or frozen, thawed
   Coarse salt
   Freshly ground pepper

1 cup half and half
1 teaspoon cornstarch dissolved in 1 tablespoon cold water
³/₄ pound sole fillets (preferably gray sole), cut into 1¹/₂-inch pieces
³/₄ cup slivered smoked ham (about 3¹/₂ ounces)
³/₄ cup chopped green onions
4 hard-cooked eggs, sliced
   Toasted bread triangles (crusts trimmed)
   Fresh cilantro or parsley sprigs

Combine rice and broth in heavy small saucepan. Bring to boil. Reduce heat to low, cover and cook until liquid is absorbed, about 20 minutes. Melt 3 tablespoons butter in heavy large saucepan over medium heat. Mix in potatoes, green pepper and fresh peas if using. Cover and cook 4 minutes, stirring occasionally. Uncover and continue cooking until vegetables are just tender, stirring occasionally, about 6 minutes; do not brown vegetables. Mix in frozen peas if using. Season with salt and pepper.

Fold rice, half and half and cornstarch into vegetables. Stir gently until cream coats rice, about 5 minutes. Gently fold in fish, ham, green onions and remaining 1 tablespoon butter. Reduce heat to low, cover and cook until heated through, stirring occasionally, about 5 minutes. Adjust seasoning. Mound on heated platter. Alternate eggs and toast around edge of platter. Sprinkle generously with pepper. Garnish with cilantro and serve immediately.

Tamale Spinach Roll with Corn, Chili and Tomato Sauce

This light and colorful variation on the traditional tamale involves wrapping and steaming the dough in one long roll lined with spinach leaves.

6 to 8 servings

6 tablespoons vegetable oil
3 medium onions, finely chopped
2 medium garlic cloves, minced
4 pounds tomatoes, quartered

4 fresh large poblano chilies, seeded, deveined and diced
   Kernels from 2 small ears of corn
   Salt

2¹/₂ pounds spinach, rinsed and dried

2 cups instant masa mix*
1 teaspoon salt
1 cup sour cream or Crema Fresca**

¹/₂ cup milk
¹/₂ cup butter (1 stick) or lard, room temperature

3 tablespoons butter
   Salt and freshly ground pepper

¹/₃ cup crumbled queso fresco* (optional)
   Minced fresh parsley
   Fresh cilantro sprigs
   Radish roses

Heat 3 tablespoons oil in heavy deep skillet over medium-low heat. Add 2 finely chopped onions and garlic. Cover and cook until onions are translucent, stirring occasionally, about 10 minutes. Transfer to processor with tomatoes. Puree, in batches if necessary. Strain back into skillet through fine sieve to eliminate seeds. Simmer until reduced to thick sauce, stirring occasionally, about 40 minutes.

(*Tomato sauce can be prepared 2 days ahead, covered and refrigerated.*)

Heat remaining 3 tablespoons oil in heavy large skillet over low heat. Add remaining onion. Cover and cook until translucent, stirring occasionally, about 10 minutes. Add chilies and cook 2 minutes. Add corn and continue cooking until vegetables are almost tender, stirring occasionally, about 3 minutes. Season with salt. Cool to room temperature.

Spread large white kitchen towel on work surface. Break off spinach leaves at stem. Arrange leaves vein side up in slightly overlapping rows, forming 12½ × 16-inch rectangle.

Cut two 17-inch strips waxed paper. Combine masa and 1 teaspoon salt in large bowl. Add sour cream, milk and butter and blend until soft, sticky dough forms. Using metal spatula, spread dough into rectangle in center of 1 piece of waxed paper. Cover with second piece of paper. Roll dough into 10½ × 14-inch rectangle. Peel off top sheet of paper. Invert dough atop spinach. Peel off top sheet of waxed paper, using spatula as aid. Spread onion-corn mixture over dough, leaving ½-inch border. Starting with short side, roll tamale up very tightly jelly roll fashion, using towel as aid. Tuck spinach in at ends. Roll towel up around tamale. Tie ends tightly with string to make firm sausage shape.

Fit fish poacher, wok or roasting pan with rack long enough to hold tamale roll. Add enough water to come 1 inch below rack. Bring to boil. Place tamale roll on rack. Cover and steam over medium-high heat 1 hour, replacing boiling water as necessary.

Remove tamale roll from steamer. Let rest for 15 minutes.

Meanwhile, rewarm tomato sauce over low heat. Whisk in butter 1 tablespoon at a time. Season with salt and pepper.

Carefully unwrap tamale and roll onto serving platter seam side down. Spoon some tomato sauce over. Sprinkle with cheese, if desired, and parsley. Garnish platter with cilantro sprigs and radishes. Slice roll with serrated knife, using spatula as aid. Pass remaining tomato sauce separately.

*Available at Latin American markets and many supermarkets.

**Crema Fresca

This is the Mexican version of crème fraîche.

Makes about 1½ cups

1½ **cups whipping cream**   3 **tablespoons sour cream**

Mix cream and sour cream in medium bowl. Cover and let stand at room temperature until thickened, 8 hours or overnight. Chill until ready to use.

Eggplant Pie

2 to 4 servings

1 **medium eggplant, peeled and cut lengthwise into ¼-inch-thick slices**
2 **tablespoons olive oil**

½ **cup chopped tomatoes**
½ **cup chopped green bell peppers**
½ **cup chopped onions**

½ **cup sliced mushrooms**
1 **teaspoon dried oregano, crumbled**
½ **teaspoon garlic powder**
½ **cup grated mozzarella cheese**
½ **cup grated sharp cheddar cheese**
2 **teaspoons freshly grated Parmesan cheese**

Preheat broiler. Brush eggplant slices on both sides with oil. Place on baking sheet or broiler pan. Broil until browned, 3 to 5 minutes per side.

Preheat oven to 350°F. Arrange eggplant slices in 9-inch pie plate, overlapping slices in spoke pattern. Press edges together to form a crust. Combine tomatoes, bell peppers, onions and mushrooms in medium bowl. Spoon vegetable mixture over eggplant. Sprinkle with oregano and garlic powder. Combine grated mozzarella and cheddar cheeses and sprinkle over vegetables. Top with Parmesan. Bake until cheese is melted and golden, 20 to 25 minutes.

Tian of Roasted Bell Peppers, Tomatoes, Eggplant and Cheese

For the tian—*a round or oval earthenware baking dish used in southern France—substitute any two-quart baking dish two inches deep.*

6 to 8 servings

1 1-pound eggplant, peeled and cut into ¹/₂-inch-thick rounds
Salt
¹/₂ pound small zucchini, cut into ¹/₄-inch-thick rounds

3 tablespoons olive oil
1 medium white onion, chopped
1 garlic clove, minced
1¹/₂ pounds red and/or yellow tomatoes, peeled, seeded and coarsely chopped (juices reserved)
¹/₄ cup minced fresh basil with stems
1 teaspoon minced fresh thyme
1 teaspoon minced fresh oregano

¹/₂ teaspoon minced orange peel
¹/₂ teaspoon salt
¹/₄ teaspoon freshly ground pepper

Olive oil

1¹/₂ cups shredded mozzarella cheese (about 5 ounces)
3 tablespoons freshly grated Parmesan cheese
2 pounds red, green and/or yellow bell peppers, roasted (see page 13), cut into 1-inch-wide strips
¹/₄ cup fresh Italian breadcrumbs

Line large baking sheet with double layer of paper towels. Cover with eggplant in single layer. Sprinkle lightly with salt. Place another double layer of paper towels atop eggplant. Cover with zucchini. Sprinkle lightly with salt. Place another layer of paper towels atop zucchini. Cover with large baking sheet. Weight with heavy object. Let stand 1 hour. Rinse and pat dry.

Heat 2 tablespoons oil in heavy large saucepan over low heat. Add onion and cook until just golden, stirring frequently, about 15 minutes. Add garlic and cook 5 minutes, stirring occasionally. Add tomatoes and reserved juices and bring to simmer. Cook until thickened, stirring frequently, about 20 minutes. Remove pan from heat. Stir in basil, thyme, oregano, orange peel, salt and pepper.

Preheat broiler. Brush eggplant very lightly with oil. Arrange in single layer on heavy large baking sheet. Broil 6 inches from heat source until lightly browned, about 5 minutes per side.

Preheat oven to 400°F. Lightly oil shallow 2-quart gratin dish. Cover bottom of dish with overlapping slices of eggplant. Spread half of tomato mixture over. Top with half of mozzarella and 1 tablespoon Parmesan. Cover with zucchini. Spread remaining tomato mixture over. Sprinkle with remaining mozzarella and 1 tablespoon Parmesan. Cover with bell pepper strips in decorative pattern. Sprinkle with breadcrumbs, then remaining 1 tablespoon Parmesan. Drizzle with remaining 1 tablespoon oil. (*Can be prepared 8 hours ahead and refrigerated. Bring to room temperature before baking.*)

Bake tian until top is golden brown and knife pierces vegetables easily, about 30 minutes. Let cool 5 minutes before cutting and serving.

5 ❦ Vegetables, Grains and Breads

To enhance the exciting array of entrées, we include here a number of ideas for great side dishes. They range from the more traditional, such as Baby Carrots and Brussels Sprouts Glazed with Brown Sugar and Black Pepper (page 68), a perfect go-with for a holiday turkey or ham, to the bit more exotic, such as Gingered Pea Pods with Soy-flavored Butter (page 69). Accompaniments can be simple and well flavored, such as easy Garlic Mashed Potatoes (page 70), Summer Vegetable Stew (page 72) or Southwestern Sonoran Rice (page 72). Side dishes can also provide nice textural contrast to a main course; Kasha with Mushrooms and Swiss Chard (page 74), Cannellini Beans with Pancetta and Sage (page 69) and Eggplant with Herbs and Toasted Pine Nuts (page 68) are good examples.

It has been said that bread-bakers are nurturers, creative and patient. In this chapter they have a full range of recipes on which to practice their skills, from wholesome Three-Grain Wild Rice Bread (page 75) to the lovely Bread Wreath and Breadsticks (page 74), an attractive addition to any buffet table. There are also a few easy quick breads, such as Soda Muffins with Cheddar and Chives (page 77), Parsley-Sage Corn Bread (page 78) and Sweet Potato Corn Sticks (page 77).

Also in the bread category, we present some wonderful breakfast items that would brighten any morning: tender, golden Apple, Honey and Cottage Cheese Griddle Cakes (page 79), light and flaky Blueberry Ricotta Pancakes with Blueberry Syrup (page 79), and nutty Macadamia Nut Waffles with Papaya and Strawberries (page 80), enhanced with orange blossom-flavored honey.

❦ *Vegetables*

Baby Carrots and Brussels Sprouts Glazed with Brown Sugar and Pepper

8 servings

2 pounds baby carrots, peeled
2 pounds brussels sprouts, trimmed, cross cut in root ends

1½ cups chicken stock
6 tablespoons (¾ stick) unsalted butter

⅓ cup firmly packed light brown sugar
1 tablespoon freshly ground pepper

Blanch carrots in large pot of boiling salted water until crisp-tender, about 4 minutes. Transfer carrots to bowl of ice water using slotted spoon. Return water to boil. Add brussels sprouts and blanch until crisp-tender, about 5 minutes. Transfer to another bowl of ice water using slotted spoon. (*Can be prepared 1 day ahead. Drain well. Cover and refrigerate.*)

Bring stock, butter and sugar to boil in heavy large skillet, stirring until sugar dissolves. Boil until reduced by half, about 7 minutes. (*Can be prepared 6 hours ahead. Return to boil before continuing.*) Add carrots and cook until almost tender and sauce begins to coat, shaking pan occasionally, about 6 minutes. Add brussels sprouts and pepper and cook until heated through, stirring occasionally, about 4 minutes. Serve immediately.

Eggplant with Herbs and Toasted Pine Nuts

8 servings

2 12-ounce eggplants, peeled and cut into ⅛-inch-thick rounds
Salt and freshly ground pepper
4 eggs, beaten to blend
2 cups dry breadcrumbs
Vegetable oil
5 tablespoons plus 2 teaspoons cider vinegar
4 teaspoons chopped garlic

8 cherry tomatoes
¼ cup imported black olives (preferably Niçoise)
Fresh basil sprigs
¼ cup julienne of fresh basil
2 tablespoons pine nuts, toasted
4 teaspoons finely snipped fresh chives

Sprinkle 24 largest eggplant rounds with salt and pepper on both sides. Dip each slice in eggs, then breadcrumbs, coating thoroughly. Generously cover bottom of heavy large skillet with oil. Heat over medium-high heat. Add eggplant in batches (do not crowd) and cook until golden brown, about 3 minutes per side. Drain on paper towels. Pour half of vinegar into nonaluminum pan large enough to accommodate eggplant in single layer. Top with eggplant. Sprinkle with remaining vinegar and garlic. Let stand at room temperature 2 to 4 hours.

Discard garlic from eggplant. Arrange tomatoes, olives and basil sprigs in center of platter. Arrange eggplant around tomatoes, overlapping slightly. Sprinkle eggplant with basil, pine nuts and chives. Serve at room temperature.

Gingered Pea Pods with Soy-flavored Butter

4 servings

3 teaspoons safflower oil
1 1½-inch piece fresh ginger, peeled and cut into thin julienne
1 pound snow peas, strings removed

1 tablespoon soy sauce
1 tablespoon well-chilled unsalted butter, cut into small pieces

Heat 1½ teaspoons oil in wok or heavy large skillet over medium-high heat. Add ginger and stir-fry until light golden brown, about 1 minute. Remove from wok. Add remaining oil to wok and heat until hot. Add snow peas and stir-fry until almost crisp-tender, about 3 minutes. Return ginger to wok and stir-fry until heated through, about 30 seconds. Transfer vegetables to platter. Add soy sauce to wok. Immediately add butter and whisk until smooth, about 30 seconds. Pour over vegetables and toss well.

Peppery Sautéed Cabbage and Noodles

6 servings

½ cup (1 stick) butter, melted
6 cups shredded cabbage
2 tablespoons sugar

Salt and freshly ground pepper
12 ounces thin egg noodles, freshly cooked

Melt butter in heavy large skillet over medium-high heat. Add cabbage and sauté until lightly browned, about 8 minutes. Mix in sugar, salt and pepper. Add noodles and toss to combine. Reduce heat to low and stir until warmed through. Serve immediately.

Cannellini with Pancetta and Sage

6 servings

½ pound small dried cannellini beans* (1¼ cups)

½ cup loosely packed fresh sage leaves
1 medium onion, quartered
2 ounces pancetta** or regular bacon, cut into 1-inch pieces

5 tablespoons plus 1 teaspoon extra-virgin olive oil

1 medium tomato, halved, seeded and cut into ⅓-inch dice
2 tablespoons (or more) balsamic vinegar
½ teaspoon salt
½ teaspoon freshly ground pepper
Fresh sage leaves

Place beans in bowl. Add cold water to cover by 3 inches and let soak overnight.
Drain beans. Place in heavy large saucepan. Add cold water to cover. Bring to boil. Reduce heat and simmer until beans are tender but not mushy, about 45 minutes. Drain beans; cool completely. Return to saucepan.
Mince ½ cup sage in processor. Remove from work bowl and set aside. Combine onion and pancetta in work bowl and process until minced.
Heat 2 tablespoons oil in heavy 8-inch skillet over medium-high heat. Add onion mixture and cook until onion is translucent, stirring occasionally, about

4 minutes. Add tomato and minced sage and cook 2 minutes. Add to beans. Mix in remaining 3 tablespoons plus 1 teaspoon oil, 2 tablespoons vinegar, salt and pepper. (*Can be prepared 2 days ahead. Cover and refrigerate.*) Taste and adjust seasoning, adding more vinegar if desired. Garnish with fresh sage leaves. Serve warm or at room temperature.

*White kidney beans, available at Italian markets. If unavailable, Great Northern or navy beans can be substituted.

**Pancetta, unsmoked bacon cured in salt, is available at Italian markets.

Garlic Mashed Potatoes

2 servings; can be doubled

1¹/₃ **pounds baking potatoes (about 2 large), peeled and quartered**
12 **garlic cloves, peeled**
3 **tablespoons half and half or whipping cream**

2 **tablespoons (¹/₄ stick) butter, room temperature**
Salt and freshly ground pepper
Minced fresh Italian parsley

Combine potatoes and garlic in medium saucepan. Cover with cold water. Cover and bring to boil. Cook until potatoes are tender, about 25 minutes. Drain through food mill. Puree through food mill into same pan. Stir in half and half and butter. Season generously with salt and pepper. Sprinkle with minced Italian parsley and serve.

Roasted Potatoes with Chilies, Bacon and Cheese

4 servings

2 **large baking potatoes**

4 **bacon slices**
¹/₂ **cup minced onion**
1 **jalapeño chili, seeded and minced**

Salt and freshly ground pepper
4 **ounces mozzarella cheese**
Sour cream

Preheat oven to 350°F. Roast potatoes until tender, about 1¹/₂ hours. Let stand until just cool enough to handle. Halve potatoes lengthwise. Using small, sharp knife, cut 4 lines lengthwise and 7 lines crosswise forming ¹/₂-inch cubes in potato pulp of each half; cut down to but not through skin.

Fry bacon in heavy small skillet over medium heat until crisp. Remove and drain on paper towels. Do not wash skillet. Finely chop bacon. Transfer to bowl. Stir in onion and chili. Press some of bacon mixture into each potato half. (*Can be prepared several hours ahead and stored at room temperature.*)

Heat rendered bacon fat in same skillet over medium heat. Sprinkle potatoes with salt and pepper. Add flat side down to skillet and cook until golden brown and heated through. Turn and cook until skin side is crisp.

Preheat broiler. Sprinkle potatoes with cheese. Arrange in broiler pan. Broil until cheese melts, watching carefully.

Carrot Potato Pancakes

6 servings

2 eggs, beaten to blend
3 tablespoons all purpose flour
2 tablespoons milk
1½ pounds baking potatoes, peeled and finely shredded
2 large carrots, peeled and finely shredded

3 tablespoons minced green onions (white and light green parts)
3 tablespoons minced fresh parsley
Salt and freshly ground pepper

Vegetable oil
Melted butter

Combine eggs, flour and milk in large bowl. Add potatoes, carrots, onions and parsley. Season with salt and pepper. Mix until thoroughly combined.

Add enough oil to heavy large skillet to coat thinly. Heat over medium-high heat. Using ⅓ cup batter for each pancake, drop into skillet in batches and flatten slightly. Cook until browned, about 12 minutes per side. Serve immediately with melted butter.

Herbed Turnips Dauphinois

4 servings

1 large garlic clove
Butter
1 pound young turnips, peeled and thinly sliced
2 tablespoons all purpose flour

¼ cup snipped fresh chives
1¼ cups whipping cream
½ teaspoon (or more) salt
½ teaspoon freshly ground pepper
¼ teaspoon freshly grated nutmeg

Preheat oven to 350°F. Rub 7 × 10-inch porcelain or glass baking dish with garlic. Butter generously. Add ⅓ of turnips. Sprinkle with 1 tablespoon flour, then ⅓ of chives. Add ⅓ of turnips, sprinkle with 1 tablespoon flour and ⅓ of chives. Top with remaining turnips and sprinkle with remaining chives. Scald cream with ½ teaspoon salt, pepper and nutmeg. Taste cream mixture, adding more salt if desired. Pour over turnips. Cover with foil and bake 30 minutes. Remove foil and continue baking until turnips are tender, top browns and cream thickens, about 20 minutes. Serve hot.

Summer Vegetable Skewers with Cumin Butter

2 servings; can be doubled or tripled

1 small red bell pepper, seeded and cut into 1½-inch squares
1 small yellow bell pepper, seeded and cut into 1½-inch squares
2 small ears fresh corn, husked and cut into 1-inch-thick rounds

¼ teaspoon dried red pepper flakes
Salt and freshly ground pepper
1½ tablespoons chopped fresh cilantro

Cumin Butter
6 tablespoons (¾ stick) butter
⅜ teaspoon ground cumin

Prepare barbecue grill (medium heat). Alternate vegetables on 4 skewers.

For butter: Melt butter with cumin, red pepper flakes, salt and pepper in heavy small saucepan. Remove from heat and stir in chopped cilantro.

Arrange skewers on barbecue rack. Brush with some of butter. Grill until vegetables are just crisp-tender and beginning to char, turning and basting occasionally, about 15 minutes. Remove from grill. Brush with butter.

Summer Vegetable Stew

This colorful dish is known by many dialect names throughout southern Italy. The variations are almost as numerous as the names themselves since the vegetables change according to season and region: Use whatever is abundant in the garden or market.

8 servings

¹/₃ cup olive oil
3 medium onions, cut into ¹/₄-inch-thick wedges
4 large garlic cloves, crushed
3 baking potatoes (about 1 pound), peeled and cut into ¹/₄-inch slices
1 large red bell pepper, cored, seeded and cut into 1-inch squares
1 large yellow bell pepper, cored, seeded and cut into 1-inch squares
1 large green bell pepper, cored, seeded and cut into 1-inch squares
Salt
4 medium tomatoes (about 1 pound), peeled, seeded and coarsely chopped
Freshly ground pepper
2 tablespoons water (optional)

Heat oil in heavy large skillet over medium-low heat. Add onions and garlic and cook until onions are translucent and garlic is golden brown, stirring frequently, 15 to 20 minutes. Reduce heat to low. Add potatoes and bell peppers. Season with salt. Cover and cook 20 minutes, stirring occasionally. Add tomatoes, salt and pepper. Cover and cook until potatoes are tender, stirring occasionally, adding water if necessary, 20 to 35 minutes. (*Can be prepared 1 day ahead. Cover and refrigerate.*) Serve hot or at room temperature.

❧ Grains

Sonoran Rice

6 to 8 servings

1 28-ounce can whole peeled tomatoes, drained and chopped
2 cups tomato juice
1¹/₂ cups finely chopped onions
1 cup water
1 cup canned diced mild green chilies, drained
2 tablespoons (¹/₄ stick) butter
1 small jalapeño chili, seeded and finely chopped
2 teaspoons chopped fresh basil or ³/₄ teaspoon dried, crumbled
2 teaspoons garlic powder
1¹/₂ teaspoons ground cumin
1 teaspoon freshly ground white pepper
³/₄ teaspoon ground coriander
Salt
1¹/₂ cups uncooked rice

Preheat oven to 375°F. Combine all ingredients except rice in 5-quart flameproof casserole. Stir over high heat until butter melts, about 4 minutes. Reduce heat to medium. Add rice. Cover, transfer to oven and bake until liquid is absorbed, about 35 minutes. Serve hot.

Raisin and Almond Rice

This makes a nice accompaniment to roast pork.

10 servings

3¹/₂ cups unsalted chicken stock
1¹/₂ cups long-grain rice
1¹/₂ teaspoons salt

1¹/₂ cups raisins
1 cup slivered almonds, toasted
¹/₄ cup (¹/₂ stick) butter
2 teaspoons dark brown sugar

Bring stock to boil in heavy medium saucepan. Stir in rice and salt. Reduce heat, cover and simmer until rice is tender and liquid is absorbed, about 15 minutes.

Stir remaining ingredients into rice. Cover and let stand 5 minutes to blend flavors. Serve immediately.

Vegetable Pullao

8 servings

1 cup (2 sticks) butter
³/₄ pound onions, thinly sliced

¹/₄ cup (generous) chopped onions
2 small garlic cloves, crushed
1¹/₂ tablespoons cayenne pepper
1 tablespoon salt
2¹/₄ teaspoons turmeric
³/₄ teaspoon ground ginger
1¹/₂ teaspoons ground coriander
3 medium baking potatoes, peeled and cut into ¹/₂-inch cubes

1¹/₂ large carrots, cut into ¹/₄-inch rounds
³/₄ pound green beans, blanched
1¹/₂ cups peas
1¹/₂ cups long-grain converted rice, cooked
3 medium tomatoes, thinly sliced
3 cooked beets, peeled and thinly sliced

Melt 10 tablespoons butter in heavy large skillet over medium-low heat. Add sliced onions and cook until golden brown, stirring occasionally, about 15 minutes. Remove; set aside.

Melt remaining 6 tablespoons butter in same skillet over medium heat. Add chopped onions, garlic, cayenne, salt, turmeric and ginger and cook until onions are softened, stirring frequently, about 10 minutes. Add coriander and stir 1 minute. Reduce heat to medium-low. Add potatoes and carrots. Cover and cook until almost tender, stirring occasionally, about 15 minutes. Add beans and peas. Cover and cook until almost tender, stirring occasionally, about 5 minutes.

Preheat oven to 300°F. Layer some of rice, sliced onions, tomatoes, mixed vegetables and beets in 2¹/₂-quart ovenproof glass casserole or deep baking dish. Continue layering with remaining ingredients, ending with beets. (Number of layers will depend on size of container used.) Cover and bake until heated through, about 45 minutes. Serve immediately.

Mixed Grains with Red Pepper and Green Onions

Three different types of rice compose a delicious side dish for roasted meats.

8 servings

1 large red bell pepper

²/₃ cup wild rice
²/₃ cup long-grain rice
²/₃ cup Italian Arborio rice
4 cups chicken broth

2 bunches green onions (white and light green parts only), cut into ¹/₂-inch pieces
2 tablespoons (¹/₄ stick) unsalted butter
Salt and freshly ground pepper

Char pepper in broiler until blackened on all sides. Wrap in paper bag and let stand 10 minutes to steam. Peel and seed. Rinse if necessary; pat dry. Cut into 1/8 × 1-inch strips.

Combine all rices in heavy medium saucepan. Add broth. Cover and bring to boil. Reduce heat and simmer 20 minutes without lifting lid. Turn off heat and let stand 5 minutes.

Meanwhile, cook green onions in heavy large skillet in 1 inch of simmering water until just tender, 3 to 4 minutes. Drain; set green onions aside. Melt butter in same skillet over medium heat. Add rice and stir until coated with butter. Mix in pepper strips and green onions and stir until heated through. Season to taste with salt and pepper.

Kasha with Mushrooms and Swiss Chard

2 servings; can be doubled or tripled

4 large Swiss chard stalks, trimmed
4 tablespoons (1/2 stick) butter
1/2 medium onion, chopped
1/2 pound mushrooms, sliced
Freshly ground pepper

1 cup chicken broth
Salt

1/2 cup whole kasha
1 egg, beaten to blend

Remove ribs from chard leaves. Halve ribs lengthwise and slice thinly crosswise. Shred leaves. Melt 2 tablespoons butter in heavy medium saucepan over medium-low heat. Add onion and chard ribs and cook until onion is tender, stirring occasionally, about 10 minutes. Add mushrooms and shredded chard leaves. Season generously with pepper. Stir until mushrooms soften, about 5 minutes. Add broth and salt and bring to boil.

Meanwhile, combine kasha and 1/2 of egg (reserve remainder for another use) in medium bowl. Heat heavy large skillet over high heat. Add kasha and stir until egg dries and kasha kernels separate, about 3 minutes. Reduce heat to low. Add stock and vegetables. Cover and cook until kasha is tender and liquid is absorbed, about 20 minutes. Add remaining 2 tablespoons butter and toss well.

❧ *Breads*

Bread Wreath and Breadsticks

Serve these breads the same day they are baked. For a festive presentation, garnish the wreath with herbs and flowers in the center.

Makes 1 loaf and 20 breadsticks

2 envelopes dry yeast
3 cups warm water (105°F to 115°F)

5 cups (about) unbleached all purpose flour
2 cups whole wheat flour
1/2 cup olive oil
1 tablespoon salt

Freshly ground pepper, sesame seeds, poppy seeds and/or chopped fresh rosemary

1 egg yolk beaten with 2 tablespoons milk (glaze)

Sprinkle yeast over warm water; stir to dissolve. Let stand 10 minutes.

Combine 4 cups unbleached flour and whole wheat flour in large bowl. Transfer 1 cup of mixture to another large bowl; add 1 cup yeast mixture, oil and salt and stir until smooth. Mix in remaining flour mixture alternately with remaining yeast mixture. Knead dough on floured surface until smooth and elastic, adding more all purpose flour if sticky, about 8 minutes.

Grease large bowl. Add dough, turning to coat entire surface. Cover bowl with plastic or towel. Let dough rise in warm draft-free area until doubled in volume, about 1 hour.

Grease 3 large baking sheets. Punch dough down. Divide into 2 pieces. Pat 1 piece into 14-inch-long rectangle. Cut into twenty 14-inch-long pieces. Cover and let stand while forming wreath. Cut second half of dough into 7 pieces. Form each into round. Arrange in ring on 1 prepared sheet, flattening slightly so sides just touch, forming wreath. Roll each 14-inch piece into rope. Roll in pepper, sesame seeds, poppy seeds and/or rosemary. Arrange on prepared sheets, spacing 1 inch apart. Place in warm draft-free area. Let breadsticks rise 20 minutes. Let wreath rise until almost doubled in volume, about 35 minutes.

Preheat oven to 350°F. Brush breadsticks with glaze. Bake until golden brown, about 20 minutes. Cool on racks. Bake wreath 20 minutes. Brush with glaze and continue baking until bread is golden brown and sounds hollow when tapped on bottom, about 10 minutes. Cool on rack.

Three-Grain Wild Rice Bread

Makes 1 large loaf

1 envelope dry yeast
⅓ cup warm water (105°F to 115°F)
2 cups buttermilk, room temperature
½ cup light molasses
2 tablespoons (¼ stick) butter, melted
2 teaspoons salt
2 cups whole wheat flour

1 cup cooked wild rice (about ¼ cup raw)
½ cup yellow cornmeal
½ cup rolled oats
4 to 4½ cups bread flour or unbleached all purpose flour

1 egg beaten with 1 tablespoon water (glaze)
½ cup hulled sunflower seeds

Sprinkle yeast over warm water in large bowl; stir to dissolve. Let stand 5 minutes. Mix in buttermilk, molasses, butter and salt. Stir in whole wheat flour, rice, cornmeal and oats. Add 2 cups bread flour and beat with wooden spoon until well blended. Cover and let rest 15 minutes.

Add enough of remaining bread flour ½ cup at a time to form stiff dough. Turn dough out onto lightly floured surface and knead until smooth and elastic, adding more flour if necessary to prevent sticking, about 10 minutes. Lightly grease large bowl. Add dough, turning to coat entire surface. Cover and let rise in warm draft-free area until doubled in volume, about 1 hour.

Grease heavy large baking sheet. Punch dough down. Knead on lightly oiled surface until smooth. Divide dough into 3 pieces. Roll each into 24-inch-long rope with tapering ends. Pinch ropes together at one end. Braid together tightly. Place loaf on prepared sheet, tucking ends under. Let rise in warm draft-free area until almost doubled, about 45 minutes.

Preheat oven to 375°F. Brush loaf with glaze. Sprinkle with sunflower seeds. Bake until bread sounds hollow when tapped on bottom, about 45 minutes. Cool completely on rack.

Cheese Bubble Loaf

20 servings

1½ cups milk
2 envelopes dry yeast
2 tablespoons sugar
3 tablespoons unsalted butter, melted
2½ teaspoons salt

4¾ to 5 cups all purpose flour

2 eggs
2 cups shredded sharp cheddar cheese

1 egg yolk beaten with 1 tablespoon water (glaze)
1 tablespoon sesame seeds

Scald milk in heavy small saucepan. Pour into large bowl and cool to 105°F to 115°F. Sprinkle yeast and sugar over milk; stir to dissolve. Let stand until foamy, about 15 minutes. Stir in melted butter and salt.

Using electric mixer, add 2 cups flour to yeast mixture and beat until smooth. Add 2 eggs and cheese and beat until thoroughly combined. Add 2 cups flour and beat until dough is soft. Using wooden spoon, mix in enough additional flour to make slightly firmer but manageable dough. Turn out onto floured surface and cover with towel. Let rest 10 minutes.

Knead dough until smooth and elastic, adding additional flour if sticky. Butter large bowl. Add dough, turning to coat entire surface. Cover bowl. Let dough rise in warm draft-free area until doubled, about 45 minutes.

Grease large baking sheet. Punch dough down. Turn out onto lightly floured surface. Knead until smooth. Roll into log and cut into 20 pieces. Shape each piece into smooth ball. Place 1 dough ball in center of prepared sheet. Surround with remaining dough balls in concentric circles, with sides touching, forming 1 large circle. Cover; let rise until doubled, 1 hour.

Preheat oven to 350°F. Brush top of loaf with glaze. Sprinkle with sesame seeds. Bake until loaf sounds hollow when tapped on bottom, about 30 minutes. Cool loaf completely on rack.

Parmesan Rolls

These savory yeast rolls can be prepared one day ahead and reheated.

Makes 8

1 cup warm water (105°F to 115°F)
1 tablespoon olive oil
1 teaspoon garlic salt
1 teaspoon sugar
1 teaspoon dry yeast
3 cups (about) unbleached all purpose flour

Olive oil
¼ cup freshly grated Parmesan cheese
1½ teaspoons dried rosemary, crumbled

Combine water, 1 tablespoon oil, garlic salt and sugar in large bowl. Sprinkle yeast over; stir to dissolve. Gradually mix in enough flour to form moderately firm dough that pulls away from sides of bowl (dough can also be mixed in heavy-duty electric mixer). Knead on lightly floured surface until smooth and elastic, adding more flour if sticky, 8 to 10 minutes.

Grease large bowl. Add dough, turning to coat entire surface. Cover with kitchen towel. Let dough rise in warm draft-free area until doubled in volume, about 1 hour.

Grease baking sheet. Punch dough down. Knead until smooth. Divide into

8 pieces. Shape each into slightly domed 3-inch round. Place on prepared sheet, spacing 2 inches apart. Brush top of each roll with oil; sprinkle with Parmesan and rosemary. Let rolls rise in warm draft-free area until almost doubled in volume, about 45 minutes.

Preheat oven to 400°F. Bake rolls until golden brown, about 15 minutes. Serve hot. (*Can be prepared 1 day ahead. Cool completely. Wrap tightly. Reheat in 200°F oven about 10 minutes.*)

Soda Muffins with Cheddar and Chives

This recipe makes a big basketful for dinner, plus enough for breakfast.

Makes 24

4 cups all purpose flour
2 teaspoons baking powder
1½ teaspoons salt
1 teaspoon baking soda
¼ cup (½ stick) well-chilled butter, cut into pieces

6 ounces coarsely grated sharp cheddar cheese
¼ cup snipped fresh chives
2 cups buttermilk
1 egg, beaten to blend

Preheat oven to 350°F. Generously grease two 12-cup muffin tins. Sift together flour, baking powder, salt and baking soda in large bowl. Cut in butter until mixture resembles coarse meal. Stir in cheese and chives. Mix buttermilk and egg and add to dry ingredients, stirring just until blended (batter will be thick). Spoon batter into prepared muffin tins. Bake until golden, about 30 minutes. Serve muffins warm.

Tomato Bruschetta

4 servings

8 ½-inch-thick slices French bread
Extra-virgin olive oil
2 garlic cloves, halved
Salt and freshly ground pepper

2 large tomatoes, cut into ⅓-inch-thick slices
8 fresh Italian parsley sprigs

Preheat broiler. Place bread slices on baking sheet and cook until brown on both sides. Brush one side with oil; rub with garlic. Sprinkle with salt and pepper. (*Can be prepared 4 hours ahead. Let stand at room temperature.*)

Place tomato slice atop each bread slice. Brush with oil; sprinkle with salt and pepper. Broil until heated through. Top with parsley and serve.

Sweet Potato Corn Sticks

Makes about 14

2 medium sweet potatoes (about 1¼ pounds)

Vegetable oil

½ cup buttermilk
6 tablespoons (¾ stick) unsalted butter, melted

2 eggs
1 cup yellow cornmeal
1 cup unbleached all purpose flour
½ cup sugar
2½ teaspoons baking powder
½ teaspoon salt

Position rack in center of oven and preheat to 400°F. Place sweet potatoes on pan on rack and bake until knife pierces potatoes easily, approximately 1 hour. Maintain oven temperature.

Peel potatoes. Puree. Transfer 1½ cups puree to large bowl (reserve any remainder for another use).

Generously brush cornstick pans (preferably cast iron) with vegetable oil. Heat pans in oven until oil smokes slightly, about 10 minutes.

Meanwhile, mix buttermilk, butter and eggs into potato puree. Combine cornmeal, flour, sugar, baking powder and salt. Add to puree and stir just until combined. Spoon batter into pans, filling each ¾ full. Bake until crisp and golden brown, 15 to 20 minutes. Unmold. (*Can be prepared 8 hours ahead. Cool completely. Wrap in foil. Rewarm in 350°F oven about 10 minutes before serving.*)

Parsley-Sage Corn Bread

8 to 10 servings

1 cup cornmeal
1 cup all purpose flour
1 tablespoon baking powder
1 tablespoon sugar
1 teaspoon salt
1 cup milk

3 tablespoons butter, melted
1 egg
1 tablespoon chopped fresh parsley
1 tablespoon thinly sliced fresh sage leaves

Preheat oven to 400°F. Grease 9-inch square baking pan. Combine first 5 ingredients in large bowl. Combine all remaining ingredients in another bowl. Add to dry ingredients and mix until just combined. Pour into prepared pan. Bake until tester inserted in center comes out clean, about 20 minutes. Serve bread warm or at room temperature.

Blue Cornmeal Sticks with Black Olive Butter

Substitute yellow cornmeal if blue cornmeal is unavailable.

Makes about 14

1 cup blue cornmeal*
1 cup unbleached all purpose flour
1½ tablespoons sugar
2 teaspoons baking powder
¼ teaspoon salt
⅔ cup half and half, room temperature

6 tablespoons (¾ stick) unsalted butter, melted
1 egg, room temperature

Vegetable oil
Black Olive Butter**

Position rack in middle of oven and preheat to 425°F. Mix first 5 ingredients in small bowl. Whisk half and half, butter and egg to blend in large bowl. Stir dry ingredients into liquid mixture until just combined.

Brush cornstick pans (preferably cast iron) with vegetable oil. Heat pans in oven until oil smokes slightly, about 10 minutes. Pour off excess oil. Spoon batter into molds, filling each ¾ full. Bake until puffed and golden brown, about 15 minutes. Serve hot, passing Black Olive Butter separately.

*Blue cornmeal is available at natural and some specialty foods stores.

**Black Olive Butter

Makes about 1¹/₂ cups

³/₄ cup (1¹/₂ sticks) unsalted butter, room temperature

12 Kalamata olives, pitted

Blend butter and olives in processor using on/off turns until almost smooth. (*Can be prepared 1 day ahead, covered and refrigerated. Bring olive butter to room temperature before using.*)

Apple, Honey and Cottage Cheese Griddle Cakes

Makes about 16

1 cup small curd cottage cheese
1 cup grated peeled cooking apple such as Granny Smith (1 large)
¹/₂ cup unbleached all purpose flour
¹/₄ cup whole wheat flour
1 tablespoon honey
1 teaspoon fresh lemon juice
¹/₂ teaspoon salt

¹/₂ teaspoon cinnamon
4 eggs, separated, room temperature
¹/₈ teaspoon cream of tartar

Melted unsalted butter
Vegetable oil
Powdered sugar

Combine first 8 ingredients in large bowl. Blend in yolks. Beat whites and cream of tartar in another bowl until stiff but not dry. Fold ¹/₄ of whites into batter; fold in remaining whites.

Heat griddle or heavy large skillet (preferably nonstick) over medium heat. Film lightly with butter and oil. Drop batter onto griddle by scant ¹/₄ cups, forming 4-inch pancakes. Adjust heat so butter sizzles gently. Cook pancakes until bubbles appear on tops and bottoms are golden brown, 3 to 4 minutes. Turn and cook until second sides are golden brown, about 3 minutes. Transfer to heated platter. Dust pancakes with powdered sugar and serve.

Blueberry Ricotta Pancakes with Blueberry Syrup

These light and creamy treats are great for breakfast or brunch. Use the batter as soon as possible so cakes will rise properly.

Makes about twenty 3-inch pancakes

4 eggs, separated, room temperature
1 cup ricotta cheese
¹/₃ cup sour cream
¹/₄ cup sugar
²/₃ cup all purpose flour
2 teaspoons baking powder

¹/₈ teaspoon salt
³/₄ cup milk
2 cups fresh blueberries
Pinch of cream of tartar

Melted butter
Blueberry Syrup*

Thoroughly combine yolks, ricotta, sour cream and sugar in large bowl. Sift flour with baking powder and salt over cheese mixture and stir until smooth. Mix in milk. Fold in blueberries. Beat whites with cream of tartar until stiff but not dry. Gently fold ¹/₄ of whites into batter. Fold in remainder.

Heat griddle or heavy large skillet over medium heat; brush lightly with melted butter. Ladle batter onto griddle by 3 tablespoonfuls. Cook until bubbles begin to appear on surface of pancakes, 2 to 3 minutes. Turn and cook until bottoms are golden brown and pancakes are cooked through, 1 to 1¹/₂ minutes.

Transfer to heated platter. Repeat with remaining batter, brushing griddle occasionally with melted butter. Divide pancakes among plates. Serve immediately accompanied with warm Blueberry Syrup.

*Blueberry Syrup

Makes about 1³/₄ cups

2 cups fresh blueberries	1 teaspoon fresh lemon juice
¹/₂ cup sugar	¹/₈ teaspoon vanilla
¹/₂ cup water	Melted butter

Cook 1 cup berries, sugar, water, lemon juice and vanilla in heavy medium saucepan, stirring until sugar dissolves. Increase heat and bring to boil. Reduce heat and simmer until mixture thickens to syrup, stirring occasionally. Add remaining 1 cup blueberries and cook until soft, stirring occasionally, about 5 minutes. (*Can be prepared 2 days ahead. Reheat before serving.*)

Macadamia Nut Waffles with Papaya and Strawberries

4 servings

1¹/₂ cups cake flour	1 teaspoon vanilla
2 tablespoons light brown sugar	
2¹/₂ teaspoons baking powder	¹/₃ cup ground toasted macadamia nuts
¹/₄ teaspoon salt	
1¹/₄ cups unsweetened coconut milk, room temperature	1 papaya, peeled, seeded and sliced
3 eggs, separated, room temperature	1 pint strawberries, hulled and quartered
5 tablespoons unsalted butter, melted	Orange-flavored Honey* or maple syrup

Sift flour, sugar, baking powder and salt into large bowl. Make well in center. Mix coconut milk, yolks, butter and vanilla in another bowl and pour into well. Whisk into dry ingredients until just blended.

Preheat Belgian waffle iron (medium heat). Beat whites in another bowl to medium peaks. Gently fold into batter with nuts (several lumps may remain). Ladle 1 cup batter onto center of waffle iron and cook until golden brown. Transfer to heated plate. Repeat with remaining batter. Garnish waffles with papaya and strawberries. Serve, passing honey separately.

*Orange-flavored Honey

Makes 1 cup

1 cup orange blossom honey	2 teaspoons julienne of orange peel

Combine honey and peel in heavy medium saucepan over low heat. Cook until warmed through, about 2 minutes.

6 ❦ Desserts

Americana, it seems, is the prevailing theme for desserts in this collection of recipes from 1987. Wholesome, homey desserts—like grandma used to make—seems to describe a number of them, such as Plum Hazelnut Crisp (page 82), Steamed Pumpkin Pudding (page 87), Orange, Date and Walnut Buttermilk Layer Cake (page 97) and Peanut Butter Blondies (page 112). All-American ingredients like peanuts, pumpkin, maple syrup and even spirits like bourbon and Southern Comfort are showcased in treats such as Southern Comfort Peanut Praline Ice Cream (page 88), festive Pumpkin Peanut Butter Pie (page 91) and sinfully rich Bourbon Butter Pecan Cheesecake (page 105).

Cookies, the staple of every busy cook's dessert repertoire, are more appealing than ever. We offer some new renditions of old favorites, including Yankee Clippers (page 107), mounds of spicy gingerbread; the aptly named Gobs of Chocolate (page 108), huge brownie drops filled with bittersweet and white chocolate chunks; and Grandmother Cookies (page 107), buttery brown sugar rounds decorated with dabs of jam or cinnamon-sugar "thumbprints."

But along with the plain and simple, there is still plenty of room for the kind of desserts for which *Bon Appétit* is famous—wonderfully rich, beautifully presented and worth every calorie. Among the year's best: heavenly Chocolate and Orange Marmalade Soufflé (page 84), almond-crusted Espresso and Chocolate Cheesecake (page 106) and Strawberry Surprise Cake (page 98), a moist poppy seed cake layered with strawberry buttercream and coated with a glossy chocolate glaze.

🍎 *Fruit Desserts*

Fruit with Salem Sauce

The rum-laced sauce is great over almost any combination of fruit. Serve this dessert with cinnamon- or jam-filled Grandmother Cookies (see page 107).

6 to 8 servings

1/2 cup firmly packed dark brown sugar
1 egg yolk
1 tablespoon dark rum
1 1/2 teaspoons vanilla
1 cup well-chilled whipping cream

1 pint strawberries, hulled and halved
1 pint blueberries
5 large peaches, peeled and sliced

Mix sugar, yolk, rum and vanilla in processor until smooth. Beat cream until stiff peaks form. Blend in sugar mixture. (*Can be prepared 6 hours ahead and refrigerated. Stir before using.*)

Combine berries and peaches. Divide among bowls. Spoon sauce over.

Plum Hazelnut Crisp

This down-home dessert shows off early summer plums at their best.

6 servings

Plums
3 pound red plums, pitted and cut into 3/4-inch-thick slices
9 tablespoons sugar
1 1/2 tablespoons all purpose flour
3/4 teaspoon vanilla
1/8 to 1/4 teaspoon cinnamon

Topping
3/4 cup rolled oats
2/3 cup firmly packed light brown sugar

1/2 cup all purpose flour
1/4 teaspoon cinnamon
Pinch of salt
1/2 cup (1 stick) well-chilled unsalted butter, cut into small pieces
1/2 cup very lightly toasted hazelnuts

Rich vanilla ice cream

For plums: Mix all ingredients in medium bowl. Let mixture stand for 30 minutes, stirring occasionally.

For topping: Combine first 5 ingredients in processor. Cut in butter using on/off turns until mixture resembles coarse meal. Add hazelnuts and chop coarsely using on/off turns.

Position rack in center of oven and preheat to 375°F. Butter one 2- to 2 1/2-quart baking dish with 3-inch sides or six 1 1/2- to 2-cup soufflé dishes. Stir plum mixture. Spoon into prepared dish. Sprinkle with topping. Bake until golden brown and bubbly, about 45 minutes. Cool at least 20 minutes. Serve Plum Hazelnut Crisp warm with ice cream.

Chocolate Crepes with Tangerines and Chocolate-Orange Sauce

This is the perfect finale to an elegant meal. Both the crepes and tangerines can be prepared ahead. Use a little of the tangerine marinade in the sauce.

Makes about ten 5-inch crepes

3 tablespoons unsalted butter
1 ounce bittersweet (not unsweetened) or semisweet chocolate, chopped
1/3 cup all purpose flour
1/4 cup sugar
2 tablespoons unsweetened cocoa powder (preferably Dutch process)
  Pinch of salt
2 eggs, room temperature

3/4 cup milk, room temperature
1 teaspoon vanilla

6 small seedless tangerines or oranges
2 tablespoons Grand Marnier or other orange liqueur

Melted butter

Chocolate-Orange Sauce*

Melt butter and chocolate in top of double boiler over barely simmering water. Stir until smooth. Cool slightly. Sift flour, sugar, cocoa and salt into large bowl. Make well in center and add eggs. Mix until smooth. Whisk in milk, melted chocolate and vanilla. Cover and refrigerate 3 hours.

Remove peel and white pith from tangerines. Working over large bowl to catch juice, cut between membranes with small sharp knife to release segments. Add to juices. Mix in liqueur. Cover and refrigerate at least 3 hours. (*Can be prepared 1 day ahead.*)

Stir batter gently. Heat crepe pan with 5-inch-diameter bottom over medium-high heat. Brush lightly with melted butter. Remove pan from heat. Stir batter and ladle 3 tablespoons into corner of pan, tilting so batter just coats bottom. Cook crepe until bottom is brown, about 1 minute. Turn crepe and cook until second side is speckled brown, about 30 seconds. Slide out onto plate. Repeat with remaining batter, stirring occasionally. Adjust heat and add more butter to pan as necessary. (*Chocolate Crepes can be prepared 2 days ahead. Wrap in foil and refrigerate.*)

Reheat crepes 1 at a time in crepe pan over low heat 5 seconds per side. Spoon sauce onto each plate. Fold crepes in fourths and arrange 2 crepes on each plate. Drain tangerines and place alongside. Serve immediately.

*Chocolate-Orange Sauce

Makes about 1 cup

3 ounces bittersweet (not unsweetened) or semisweet chocolate, coarsely chopped
1 cup (or more) whipping cream

1 tablespoon tangerine marinade (from recipe above)
1 teaspoon grated orange peel

Melt chocolate in top of double boiler over barely simmering water. Stir until smooth. Gradually mix in cream, tangerine marinade and orange peel. Stir until heated through. Thin with more cream if desired. (*Can be prepared 1 day ahead. Cover and refrigerate. Rewarm sauce over low heat before serving.*)

🍒 Mousses, Puddings and Soufflés

Chocolate Custard with Champagne Zabaglione

8 servings

2 cups whipping cream
1 cinnamon stick
8 egg yolks
⅓ cup sugar
1 tablespoon coffee liqueur or brandy
1 teaspoon vanilla

4 ounces bittersweet (not unsweetened) or semisweet chocolate, finely chopped

Champagne Zabaglione*
1 ounce semisweet chocolate, grated

Lightly oil eight 4-ounce custard cups. Line bottoms with parchment. Bring cream and cinnamon stick to simmer in heavy medium saucepan. Using electric mixer, beat yolks with sugar, liqueur and vanilla until pale yellow and slowly dissolving ribbon forms when beaters are lifted. Beat ½ cup hot cream into yolk mixture. Stir chopped chocolate into remaining hot cream until smooth. Whisk chocolate mixture into yolk mixture. Strain; discard cinnamon stick. Divide custard evenly among prepared cups. Place cups in large baking dish. Transfer to oven. Pour 1 inch warm water into baking dish. Bake until custards are just set, about 30 minutes. Remove custards from water bath and let stand at room temperature 30 minutes. Cover and refrigerate at least 4 hours or overnight.

Dip bottoms of cups in hot water. Run hot knife around sides of cups. Invert onto plates; peel off parchment. Spoon zabaglione over custards. Sprinkle with grated chocolate. Serve immediately.

*Champagne Zabaglione

Makes about 2½ cups

½ cup dry Champagne
⅓ cup sugar

4 egg yolks
½ cup well-chilled whipping cream

Combine Champagne, sugar and yolks in medium metal bowl. Set bowl over pan of simmering water and whisk until mixture triples in volume and mounds when spooned, about 5 minutes; do not let water boil or yolks will curdle. Remove from over water. Set bowl over larger bowl filled with ice water. Using electric mixer, beat mixture until cool. In another bowl, beat cream to soft peaks. Fold cream into zabaglione. Remove from over ice water. (*Can be prepared 2 hours ahead, covered and chilled.*)

Chocolate and Orange Marmalade Soufflé

4 servings

½ cup whipping cream
6 ounces bittersweet (not unsweetened) or semisweet chocolate, coarsely chopped
3 tablespoons orange marmalade
3 egg yolks
2 teaspoons Triple Sec or Grand Marnier

Sugar
5 egg whites, room temperature
¼ teaspoon cream of tartar
1 tablespoon sugar
Powdered sugar
Whipped cream

Combine cream, chocolate and marmalade in heavy medium saucepan over low heat. Stir until chocolate and marmalade melt and mixture is smooth. Remove from heat and beat in yolks 1 at a time. Mix in Triple Sec. Cool to tepid. (*Can be prepared 4 hours ahead. Press piece of plastic onto surface and let stand at room temperature. Stir over low heat until tepid before continuing.*)

Preheat oven to 425°F. Butter 2-quart soufflé dish. Sprinkle generously with sugar. Beat whites and cream of tartar in large bowl until stiff but not dry. Beat in 1 tablespoon sugar. Fold ¼ of whites into chocolate. Gently fold into remaining whites. Transfer to prepared dish. Bake until soufflé rises but center is not firm when touched, about 20 minutes. Dust top with powdered sugar. Serve immediately, passing whipped cream separately.

Individual Cappuccino Soufflés

6 servings

1 cup milk
½ large or 1 medium vanilla bean, split lengthwise

2 tablespoons plus 1 teaspoon instant espresso powder
2 tablespoons plus 1 teaspoon very hot water

3 egg yolks, room temperature
3 tablespoons sugar
¼ cup all purpose flour

1 ounce semisweet chocolate, finely chopped

5 egg whites, room temperature
Pinch of cream of tartar
2 tablespoons sugar

1 teaspoon unsweetened cocoa powder
1 teaspoon powdered sugar
½ teaspoon cinnamon
Sweetened whipped cream

Bring milk to boil with vanilla bean in heavy small saucepan. Remove from heat, cover and let steep 30 minutes.

Meanwhile, dissolve espresso in hot water. Cool to room temperature.

Remove vanilla bean from milk; reserve for another use. Return milk to boil. Remove from heat. Whisk yolks and 3 tablespoons sugar in medium bowl until creamy, about 1 minute. Add flour to yolks and whisk until just blended. Gradually whisk in hot milk. Return mixture to saucepan. Whisk over medium-low heat until very thick, about 3 minutes. Remove custard from heat. Add chocolate and whisk until melted. Gradually whisk in espresso. Scrape custard down and inward from sides of pan. Cool until just warm to touch. (*Can be prepared 1 day ahead. Press piece of plastic onto surface of custard. Refrigerate if making more than 4 hours ahead. Before continuing with recipe, whisk custard over low heat until barely warm. Do not boil.*)

Position rack in center of oven and preheat to 400°F. Generously butter six 1-cup soufflé dishes. Coat with sugar. Using electric mixer, beat whites with cream of tartar to soft peaks. Gradually add 2 tablespoons sugar and beat until stiff but not dry. Whisk custard until smooth. Fold ¼ of whites into custard to lighten; gently pour custard over remaining whites and fold together. Spoon into prepared dishes, spreading evenly. Bake until puffed and brown and almost firm to touch, about 15 minutes.

Combine cocoa, powdered sugar and cinnamon and sift over tops of soufflés. Serve immediately with cream.

Torta Mascarpone

Mascarpone, a fresh triple cream cheese, lends texture and richness to this simple layered dessert.

6 servings

1 cup mascarpone cheese*
1/2 cup powdered sugar, sifted
1/3 cup dry Marsala
1 teaspoon vanilla
3 ounces bittersweet (not unsweetened) or semisweet chocolate, grated

1 cup well-chilled whipping cream
2 egg whites, room temperature
20 amaretti (Italian macaroons), crushed
Fresh strawberries or raspberries (optional)

Beat mascarpone in large bowl until smooth. Stir in sugar, Marsala and vanilla. Fold in chocolate.

Beat cream in medium bowl until soft peaks form. Using clean dry beaters, beat whites in another bowl until stiff but not dry. Gently fold cream into mascarpone mixture, then fold in whites. Divide 1/3 of mascarpone mixture evenly among 6 goblets. Sprinkle with 1/3 of crushed amaretti. Top with 1/3 of mascarpone mixture. Sprinkle with 1/3 of amaretti. Top with remaining mascarpone mixture. Sprinkle with remaining amaretti. Cover and chill 3 to 24 hours. Top with berries.

*Italian cream cheese available at Italian markets. If unavailable, blend 3/4 pound cream cheese with 6 tablespoons whipping cream and 1/4 cup sour cream. Measure 1 cup to use in recipe. Reserve remainder for another use.

Ozark Apple Pudding

6 servings

1 cup pecans, toasted
14 ounces unpeeled Jonathan apples, cored and cut into 1-inch pieces
1 cup sugar
1/3 cup unbleached all purpose flour
2 eggs
1 tablespoon baking powder

1 tablespoon vanilla
1 teaspoon cinnamon
1 teaspoon grated lemon peel (yellow part only)
1/4 teaspoon salt

Vanilla ice cream

Position rack in center of oven; preheat to 325°F. Butter 9-inch square ovenproof glass or ceramic baking dish.

Coarsely chop pecans in processor using 4 to 5 on/off turns. Remove from work bowl. Chop apple pieces in 3 batches until uniformly coarse, using 4 to 5 on/off turns. Return all apples to work bowl. Add pecans, sugar, flour, eggs, baking powder, vanilla, cinnamon, lemon peel and salt and mix 5 seconds. Run spatula around inside of bowl. Blend until just combined using 1 to 2 on/off turns; do not overprocess.

Transfer mixture to prepared dish, spreading evenly. Bake until pudding is golden brown and center is set, about 37 minutes. (*Can be prepared 6 hours ahead. Rewarm in 300°F oven for 15 minutes.*) Serve warm with ice cream.

Bread Pudding with Maple Pecan Sauce

This French toast is dressed up for dessert.

8 servings

³/₄ pound challah or other egg bread (untrimmed), cut into 1-inch cubes
3¹/₂ cups half and half
1 cup plus 2 tablespoons sugar
3 eggs
2¹/₂ teaspoons grated lemon peel
2 teaspoons vanilla
1 teaspoon freshly grated nutmeg
¹/₂ teaspoon salt
³/₄ cup golden raisins
Maple Pecan Sauce*

Combine bread and half and half in large bowl. Let stand 45 minutes, turning occasionally with rubber spatula.

Preheat oven to 325°F. Generously butter 2¹/₂- to 3-quart baking dish. Whisk sugar, eggs, lemon peel, vanilla, nutmeg and salt to blend in small bowl. Using rubber spatula, fold egg mixture into bread. Fold in raisins. Turn into prepared dish. Bake until puffed and knife inserted in center comes out clean, about 80 minutes for deep dish or 50 minutes for shallow. Serve warm with sauce.

*Maple Pecan Sauce

Makes about 1¹/₂ cups

1 cup pure maple syrup
1 teaspoon grated lemon peel
¹/₂ teaspoon freshly grated nutmeg
2 tablespoons (¹/₄ stick) butter, cut into 4 pieces
¹/₂ cup toasted pecans, chopped

Cook first 3 ingredients in heavy small saucepan until very hot; do not boil. Remove from heat and whisk in butter. Add pecans. Serve warm.

Steamed Pumpkin Pudding

Delicious topped with crème fraîche or brandy-spiked whipped cream.

8 servings

1¹/₂ cups all purpose flour
1 teaspoon baking powder
1 teaspoon cinnamon
³/₄ teaspoon (scant) salt
¹/₂ teaspoon baking soda
¹/₂ teaspoon freshly grated nutmeg
¹/₂ teaspoon ground ginger
¹/₄ teaspoon ground cloves
1 cup canned solid pack pumpkin
¹/₃ cup light molasses
¹/₃ cup fresh orange juice
1 teaspoon finely grated orange peel
¹/₂ cup (1 stick) unsalted butter, room temperature
¹/₂ cup sugar
¹/₃ cup firmly packed light brown sugar
2 eggs
²/₃ cup toasted pecans, finely chopped

Generously butter 2-quart pudding mold with center tube. Whisk first 8 ingredients in medium bowl to blend. Combine pumpkin, molasses, orange juice and peel in small bowl and blend thoroughly. Using electric mixer, cream butter and ¹/₂ cup sugar until light and fluffy. Add brown sugar and beat until light. Beat in eggs 1 at a time. Mix in dry ingredients alternately with pumpkin mixture, beginning and ending with dry ingredients. Fold in pecans. Pour batter into prepared mold. Cover top with waxed paper and foil, crimping edges to seal. Cover with lid if available.

Place rack in bottom of large pot. Set pudding mold on rack. Pour enough boiling water into pot to come ⅓ up sides of mold. Bring water to gentle boil. Cover pot and steam pudding until tester inserted in center comes out clean and pudding begins to pull away from sides of mold, adding more boiling water to pot as necessary, about 2½ hours. Remove pudding mold from pot. Cool pudding 15 minutes. Discard foil and paper. Invert pudding onto platter. Serve warm.

❦ Frozen Desserts

Southern Comfort Peanut Praline Ice Cream

Makes about 2 quarts

1¼ cups sugar
1 cup roasted and husked unsalted peanuts

4 egg yolks

3 cups half and half
1 cup whipping cream
¼ cup Southern Comfort
1 teaspoon vanilla

Lightly butter baking sheet. Stir ¾ cup sugar in heavy small saucepan over low heat until sugar dissolves. Increase heat to medium and cook until golden brown, stirring frequently, about 5 minutes. Mix in nuts. Pour onto prepared sheet. Cool until firm. Break praline into 2-inch pieces. Coarsely chop in processor. (*Can be prepared 1 month ahead. Refrigerate in airtight container.*)

Whisk remaining ½ cup sugar and yolks in medium bowl. Bring half and half and cream to boil in heavy medium saucepan. Gradually whisk hot cream into yolks. Return mixture to saucepan and stir over low heat until custard thickens and leaves path on back of spoon when finger is drawn across, about 4 minutes; do not boil. Strain into large bowl. Stir in Southern Comfort and vanilla. Cover and refrigerate until well chilled. (*Can be prepared 2 days ahead.*)

Transfer custard to ice cream maker and process according to manufacturer's instructions, adding praline when ice cream is almost firm. Freeze in covered container several hours to mellow flavors. (*Can be prepared 1 day ahead.*) If frozen solid, soften slightly in refrigerator before serving.

Rum Coconut Ice Cream

A tropical treat that's easy to do—an ice cream maker is not necessary.

Makes about 1½ quarts

¾ cup half and half
¾ cup unsweetened fresh or canned coconut milk
½ cup dark rum
¾ cup sugar
¼ cup all purpose flour

¼ teaspoon salt
2 eggs

2 cups whipping cream
2 teaspoons vanilla

Shaved fresh coconut

Scald half and half and coconut milk in heavy medium saucepan. Blend in rum. Combine sugar, flour and salt in another heavy medium saucepan. Whisk in rum mixture and stir over low heat until thickened, about 5 minutes. Beat eggs in small bowl until pale. Whisk in ¼ cup rum mixture. Whisk back into saucepan

Irwin Horowitz

*Roast Tenderloin of Beef
with Pancetta, Marjoram
and Red Wine; Herbed
Turnips Dauphinois;
Tomato Bruschetta;
Radicchio, Endive and
Fennel Salad.*

Clockwise from right: Tamale Spinach
Roll with Corn, Chili and Tomato Sauce;
Texcoco-style Green Mole Chicken;
Mestizo Gaspacho

Irwin Horowitz

Paul Elledge

Grilled Pizza with Grilled
Peppers "Agrodolce"; Grilled
Pizza with Gorgonzola; Grilled
Pizza with Bitter Greens

Top: Clockwise from top: Salmon Ravioli with Tomato-Vodka Sauce; Artichoke-filled Half-Moon Pasta with Green Tomato Sauce; Pasta Daisies with Radicchio in Saffron Sauce

Bottom: Bean-filled Pasta with Two Sauces

Clockwise from top right: Jambalaya Stuffing; turkey pan juices; Creole Roast Turkey; Molded Cranberry Salad with Honey Mayonnaise; Baby Carrots and Brussels Sprouts Glazed with Brown Sugar and Pepper; Sweet Potato Corn Sticks

Clockwise from top left: Schümli;
Chocolate Fruitcake; Basler Bruns;
Chestnuts; Florentine Cookies

and cook until thick, stirring occasionally, about 2 minutes. Press plastic on surface to prevent skin from forming. Refrigerate custard until well chilled.

Transfer custard to bowl. Add cream and vanilla. Using electric mixer, beat until frothy. Pour into shallow bowl or ice cube tray. Freeze until custard begins to set, about 3 hours. Beat custard again to incorporate air. Freeze until firm, at least 5 hours or overnight.

Just before serving, spoon into bowls. Top with coconut.

The Sophisticated Hot Fudge Sundae

The ice cream and sauce are terrific individually, so mix and match them with your own favorites to create other tasty combinations. The framboise in both recipes can be omitted, or replaced with raspberry or cranberry juice.

6 servings

Vanilla Bean Ice Cream
- 4 cups half and half
- 2 7-inch vanilla beans, split lengthwise
- 6 egg yolks
- 1 cup sugar
- 5 tablespoons framboise (raspberry eau-de-vie)

Framboise Fudge Sauce
- 5 ounces extra-bittersweet (not unsweetened) or semisweet chocolate, coarsely chopped
- 1 ounce unsweetened chocolate, coarsely chopped

- 1/2 cup plus 2 tablespoons seedless raspberry preserves
- 1 teaspoon instant espresso powder
- 6 tablespoons (or more) whipping cream
- 1/4 cup framboise (raspberry eau-de-vie)

- 1 cup well-chilled whipping cream
- 1 1/2 tablespoons sugar
- 1 tablespoon framboise (raspberry eau-de-vie)
- 3 cups raspberries
- 6 tablespoons lightly toasted sliced almonds

For ice cream: Place half and half in heavy medium saucepan. Scrape in seeds from vanilla beans; add vanilla pods. Scald half and half. Remove from heat and let mixture steep 15 minutes.

Whisk yolks and sugar to blend in medium bowl. Reheat half and half. Gradually whisk 2 cups into yolks. Return to saucepan. Stir over medium-low heat until mixture thickens and leaves path on back of spoon when finger is drawn across, about 3 minutes; do not boil. Strain into medium bowl. Whisk 1 minute to cool. Stir in framboise. Cover and refrigerate custard until well chilled (or chill over ice water, whisking occasionally).

Transfer custard to ice cream maker and process according to manufacturer's instructions. Freeze in covered container several hours or overnight.

For sauce: Melt chocolates and preserves with espresso in top of double boiler over simmering water, stirring occasionally. Blend in 6 tablespoons cream and 1/4 cup framboise and heat through. (*Can be prepared 1 week ahead and refrigerated. Rewarm over barely simmering water, stirring occasionally.*) Add more cream if necessary to thin to pourable consistency. Cool slightly.

Beat 1 cup cream with sugar and 1 tablespoon framboise until soft peaks form. Scoop well-chilled ice cream (do not soften in refrigerator) into glass bowls. Spoon sauce over. Top with raspberries, then whipped cream. Sprinkle with almonds and serve.

Ice Cream Crunch Pie

16 servings

2 cups all purpose flour
1 cup chopped walnuts
1 cup (2 sticks) butter, room temperature
½ cup firmly packed light brown sugar

1 18-ounce jar hot fudge ice cream topping
1 ½-gallon carton vanilla ice cream, softened

Preheat oven to 375°F. Using electric mixer, blend first 4 ingredients in medium bowl at low speed until just crumbly, 3 to 4 minutes. Transfer to 11 × 17-inch jelly roll pan. Bake until light brown, stirring occasionally, 15 to 20 minutes. Cool crumb mixture slightly.

Sprinkle half of crumb mixture in 9 × 13-inch baking dish. Drizzle half of hot fudge topping over. Spoon ice cream over. Drizzle with remaining topping. Sprinkle with remaining crumbs. Cover and freeze until firm, at least 2 hours. Soften slightly in refrigerator before serving.

🍎 *Pies, Tarts and Pastries*

Dutch Double-Apple Brown Sack Pie

This pie cooks to perfection enclosed in a brown grocery bag—a popular Pennsylvania Dutch technique. Be sure to use a bag made from unglazed, nonrecycled paper.

8 to 10 servings

Crust
2½ cups unbleached all purpose flour
2 teaspoons sugar
½ teaspoon salt
½ teaspoon cinnamon
⅔ cup well-chilled solid vegetable shortening
6 tablespoons (¾ stick) well-chilled unsalted butter
¼ cup (about) ice water

Filling
2¾ pounds Granny Smith or other tart green apples, peeled, cored and thinly sliced
1¼ pounds Rome Beauty or Golden Delicious apples, peeled, cored and thinly sliced

⅓ cup sugar
⅓ cup firmly packed light brown sugar
3 tablespoons unbleached all purpose flour
¾ teaspoon cinnamon
½ teaspoon freshly grated nutmeg
⅛ teaspoon ground coriander
⅛ teaspoon salt

2 tablespoons (¼ stick) well-chilled unsalted butter, cut into small pieces
¼ cup whipping cream
Cinnamon

2 cups whipping cream
2 tablespoons powdered sugar
1½ teaspoons vanilla

For crust: Combine flour, sugar, salt and cinnamon in large bowl. Cut in shortening and butter until mixture resembles coarse meal. Mix in just enough water to bind dough. Gather into ball; flatten to disc. Wrap tightly and refrigerate at least 3 hours. (*Can be prepared 1 day ahead.*)

For filling: Position rack in center of oven and preheat to 425°F. Combine apples in large bowl. Mix next 7 ingredients in another bowl. Pour over apples and toss well.

Let pastry soften slightly at room temperature. Roll out on lightly floured surface to 13-inch round. Transfer to 9-inch pie dish, gently pressing into shape;

do not trim overhang. Mound filling in crust. Distribute butter over surface. Pour in ¼ cup cream. Sprinkle lightly with cinnamon. Gently fold pastry overhang over filling, pleating slightly; do not press down. Slide pie into heavy unglazed brown paper bag. Fold open end over several times to seal completely.

Place bag on baking sheet. Bake pie 20 minutes. Reduce heat to 400°F and bake 20 more minutes. Slash paper bag and fold back to expose pie completely. Continue baking until pastry is deep golden brown, about 35 minutes. Cool pie on rack until just warm.

Whip 2 cups cream with powdered sugar and vanilla until peaks begin to form. Serve pie warm with cream.

Pumpkin Peanut Butter Pie

Serve this big, bright orange and utterly old fashioned-tasting pie with a big scoop of Southern Comfort Peanut Praline Ice Cream (see page 88). The pastry leaf decoration is optional.

8 servings

Crust and Pastry Leaves
2½ cups unbleached all purpose flour
¼ teaspoon salt
10 tablespoons (1¼ sticks) well-chilled unsalted butter, cut into small pieces
5 tablespoons well-chilled solid vegetable shortening, cut into small pieces
6 tablespoons (about) ice water

Filling
1 16-ounce can solid pack pumpkin
¾ cup firmly packed light brown sugar
½ cup creamy peanut butter
3 eggs
1¼ cups half and half
¼ cup Southern Comfort
2 teaspoons vanilla
½ teaspoon freshly grated nutmeg
¼ teaspoon salt

1 egg yolk, beaten with 2 teaspoons whipping cream (glaze)

For crust: Mix flour and salt in processor. Cut in butter and shortening using on/off turns until mixture resembles coarse meal. With machine running, blend in water 1 tablespoon at a time until dough just starts to come together (do not form ball). Turn dough out onto lightly floured surface. Gather together. Cut off ¼ of dough. Form each piece into ball; flatten into discs. Wrap in plastic and refrigerate at least 30 minutes. (*Can be prepared 2 days ahead.*)

Roll large dough piece out on lightly floured surface into ⅛-inch-thick round. Transfer dough to 10-inch glass pie pan, leaving ½-inch overhang. Crimp edges, forming ½-inch-high decorative border. Refrigerate 30 minutes. (*Can be prepared 1 day ahead. Cover tightly.*)

For pastry leaves: Roll out small dough piece between 1/16 and ⅛ inch thick on lightly floured surface. Cut out leaves using leaf-shaped cookie cutters. Transfer leaves to baking sheet using metal spatula. Refrigerate 30 minutes. (*Can be prepared 1 day ahead. Cover tightly.*)

For filling: Mix first 3 ingredients in large bowl. Blend in eggs 1 at a time. Stir in half and half, Southern Comfort, vanilla, nutmeg and salt. (*Can be prepared 1 day ahead. Refrigerate.*)

Position rack in lower third of oven and preheat to 425°F. Pour filling into prepared shell. Bake 20 minutes. Reduce temperature to 350°F. Continue baking until filling is set and uniformly puffed, about 50 minutes. Transfer to rack. Brush glaze over pastry leaves. Bake until puffed and tops are golden brown, about 6 minutes. Transfer leaves to rack. Cool pie and pastry leaves completely. (Pie will fall in center as it cools.) (*Can be prepared 8 hours ahead.*) Arrange pastry leaves decoratively atop pie before serving.

Lime Soufflé Pie

This light and refreshing pie can be made a day ahead and topped with whipped cream and garnish at the last minute.

8 servings

6 eggs, separated
1/2 cup plus 6 tablespoons sweetened condensed milk
3/4 cup fresh lime juice
1 teaspoon finely grated lime peel
1/4 teaspoon salt
1 drop green food coloring

1 teaspoon unflavored gelatin
2 tablespoons water

1/2 cup sugar
1 baked 10-inch pie crust

1 1/2 cups whipping cream
1 1/2 tablespoons powdered sugar
Candied or fresh violets

Whisk egg yolks with 1/2 cup condensed milk and lime juice in top of double boiler over simmering water. Cook until mixture heavily coats back of spoon, about 10 minutes. Remove from over hot water. Stir in peel, salt and green food coloring. Set mixture aside.

Combine gelatin and water in small heatproof bowl. Let stand 5 minutes to soften. Mix in remaining condensed milk. Set bowl in pan of simmering water. Stir until gelatin dissolves. Add gelatin to yolks.

Preheat oven to 350°F. Beat egg whites until soft peaks form. Add 1/2 cup sugar 1 tablespoon at a time and continue beating until stiff but not dry. Carefully fold 1/4 of whites into yolk mixture. Fold in remaining whites. Spoon filling into crust.

Bake pie until edges of meringue are firm and begin to brown, about 13 minutes. Cool to room temperature. (*Can be prepared 1 day ahead and refrigerated.*) Whip cream with powdered sugar. Spread half of cream over top. Spoon remaining cream into pastry bag fitted with star tip. Pipe lattice pattern over pie. Garnish with candied or fresh violets before serving.

Chocolate-glazed Caramel Macadamia Torte

A terrific do-ahead dessert. Amaretto-plumped raisins highlight the rich caramel and macadamia nut filling.

8 servings

Pastry
3 cups sifted all purpose flour
1/4 cup sugar
3/4 teaspoon salt
1 cup (2 sticks) well-chilled unsalted butter, cut into small pieces
2 egg yolks
1/2 teaspoon vanilla
4 to 6 tablespoons ice water

Filling
1/2 cup raisins
1/4 cup amaretto liqueur

1 1/2 cups sugar
1 cup water

1 cup whipping cream, room temperature
14 tablespoons (1 3/4 sticks) unsalted butter, room temperature
1/3 cup honey

3 cups macadamia nuts, coarsely chopped

Glaze
8 ounces semisweet chocolate, coarsely chopped
6 tablespoons (3/4 stick) butter
2 teaspoons vegetable oil

10 macadamia nuts, half of each dipped in melted chocolate

For pastry: Combine flour, sugar and salt in processor. Add butter, yolks and vanilla and blend until mixture resembles coarse meal. With machine running, add enough water through feed tube so dough just begins to come together; do not form ball. Gather dough pieces together; flatten into disc. Wrap in plastic and chill at least 2 hours. (*Can be prepared 1 day ahead.*)

For filling: Combine raisins and amaretto and let stand for at least 30 minutes or until ready to use.

Cook sugar and water in heavy large saucepan over low heat until sugar dissolves, swirling pan occasionally. Increase heat and boil until syrup is thick and caramel-colored, swirling pan occasionally, about 15 minutes. Remove caramel from heat. Add cream, butter and honey and stir until smooth. Return caramel to medium heat and stir for 15 minutes.

Cut off ²/₃ of dough. Roll out on lightly floured surface to thickness of ¹/₈ inch. Fit into 11-inch tart pan with removable bottom. Trim edges, leaving ¹/₂-inch overhang. Roll remaining ¹/₃ of dough out into 11-inch round.

Preheat oven to 400°F. Fold nuts and undrained raisins into caramel mixture; filling will be very thick. Pour into tart shell. Brush dough overhang with water. Place dough round atop filling. Fold overhang onto round, pressing edge to seal. Trim off excess dough; do not overtrim. Cut slit in center. Bake until pastry is golden brown and filling is heated through, about 45 minutes, covering top with foil if necessary. Cool on rack 2 hours.

For glaze: Melt chocolate and butter in double boiler over gently simmering water, stirring frequently. Blend in oil. Cool completely, stirring occasionally.

Set rack on sheet of waxed paper. Remove torte from pan and invert onto rack. Pour glaze over. Spread evenly over top and sides. Decorate with chocolate-dipped nuts. Refrigerate until glaze is firm. Serve at room temperature. (*Can be prepared 1 day ahead.*)

Tangerine Marmalade Tartlets

This recipe can be easily doubled. Enjoy any leftover marmalade at breakfast or tea time.

Makes 12 tartlets

Pastry
¹/₂ cup all purpose flour
1¹/₂ teaspoons sugar
   Pinch of salt
¹/₄ cup (¹/₂ stick) well-chilled unsalted butter, cut into pieces
1¹/₂ teaspoons cold water

Frangipane
¹/₄ cup finely ground blanched almonds (about 1 ounce)

2 tablespoons (¹/₄ stick) unsalted butter, room temperature
2 tablespoons sugar
1 teaspoon all purpose flour

6 tablespoons Tangerine Marmalade*

For pastry: Blend flour, sugar and salt in medium bowl. Cut in butter until mixture resembles coarse meal. Add water and mix just until dough comes together. Shape dough into ball; flatten into disc. Wrap in plastic and refrigerate at least 20 minutes. (*Can be prepared 4 days ahead.*)

Roll dough out on lightly floured surface to thickness of ¹/₈ inch. Cut out 3¹/₂-inch rounds using cookie cutter. Gather scraps, reroll and cut additional rounds if necessary. Fit rounds into twelve 2-inch round, ¹/₂-inch-high fluted tartlet molds; trim edges. Transfer to baking sheet.

For frangipane: Preheat oven to 375°F. Blend first 4 ingredients in small bowl.

Place 1 teaspoon frangipane in center of each tartlet, pressing gently to even. Bake until frangipane and pastry are golden brown, about 15 minutes. Cool completely on rack. Unmold. (*Can be prepared 2 days ahead. Store at room temperature in airtight container between layers of waxed paper.*)

Soften marmalade over low heat, stirring constantly. Spoon 1¹/₂ teaspoons marmalade into each tartlet. Cool completely. (*Can be prepared 3 hours ahead.*)

*Tangerine Marmalade

Makes about 1¹/₂ cups

³/₄ **pound tangerines (about 3 large)**

1¹/₂ **cups sugar**
¹/₂ **cup water**

Pierce tangerines all over using fork. Bring large saucepan of water to boil. Add tangerines. Reduce heat and simmer until skin is just tender, about 45 minutes.

Drain tangerines. Refresh under cold water. Pat dry. Cut tangerines in half. Remove seeds. Cut peel and pulp into ¹/₄-inch dice. Transfer to heavy medium saucepan. Mix in sugar and ¹/₂ cup water. Cook over low heat, stirring until sugar dissolves. Increase heat and boil until candy thermometer registers 210°F,** stirring constantly, about 10 minutes. Transfer marmalade to bowl. (*Can be prepared 1 week ahead, covered and refrigerated or 1 month ahead, sealed in clean hot canning jar and refrigerated.*)

**Marmalade can also be tested for doneness by filling chilled spoon with marmalade. Slowly pour marmalade back into pan; last 2 drops should merge and sheet off spoon. One tablespoon ladled onto chilled plate and frozen 2 minutes should wrinkle when pushed with finger.

Blueberry Cassis Tartlets

Several different shapes of tart pans can be used for a nice presentation.

Makes about 12

Butter Crust Dough*

¹/₃ **cup black currant jelly, melted**

³/₄ **cup chilled whipping cream**
¹/₄ **cup crème de cassis**

1 **tablespoon sugar**
3 **cups blueberries**
Fresh mint leaves

Gather dough into ball; flatten to disc. Wrap in plastic and refrigerate 1 hour.

Roll dough out on lightly floured surface to thickness of ¹/₈ inch. Cut dough 1 inch larger than 2-inch tart pans. Transfer dough to pans, gently pressing to fit. Trim and finish edges. Place empty tart pan in each crust-lined pan (or line with foil and fill with pie weights or rice). Refrigerate at least 1 hour. (*Can be prepared to this point up to 1 day ahead.*)

Position rack in lower third of oven and preheat to 400°F. Bake tarts until crust is set, about 10 minutes. Remove upper pans (or weights and foil) and continue baking until crusts are brown, about 5 minutes. Cool.

Remove tarts from pans. Brush generously with currant jelly.

Whip cream with cassis and sugar until soft peaks form. Spoon into tart shells, filling to ¹/₄ inch from top. Arrange blueberries on top. (*Can be prepared 3 hours ahead and refrigerated.*) Garnish with mint leaves and serve.

*Butter Crust Dough

Makes enough for one 9¹/₂-inch tart or twelve 2-inch tartlets

1 **cup unbleached all purpose flour**
1 **tablespoon sugar**
¹/₈ **teaspoon salt**
¹/₂ **cup (1 stick) well-chilled unsalted butter, cut into ¹/₂-inch pieces**

1 **tablespoon ice water**
¹/₂ **teaspoon vanilla**

Combine flour, sugar and salt in processor. Cut in butter until mixture resembles coarse meal, using on/off turns. Add water and vanilla and mix until dough begins to gather together, using on/off turns; do not form ball.

Black Walnut Wagon Wheels

Individual "wagon wheels" fashioned from nut meringues and buttercream.

10 servings

Meringue
 ²/₃ cup hazelnuts (about 3¹/₂ ounces)
 ²/₃ cup sugar
  4 egg whites, room temperature
 ¹/₄ teaspoon salt
    Pinch of cream of tartar

Black Walnut Buttercream
  2 cups (4 sticks) unsalted butter, room temperature
  2 tablespoons dark molasses
 ¹/₂ cup plus 2 teaspoons sugar
 ¹/₄ cup water

  8 egg yolks
  1 cup finely ground black walnuts (about 4 ounces)

  1 cup finely chopped black walnuts (about 4 ounces)

Ganache
  2 tablespoons whipping cream
  4 ounces bittersweet (not unsweetened) or semisweet chocolate, finely chopped
 ¹/₂ teaspoon vanilla
 10 black walnut halves

For meringue: Preheat oven to 300°F. Line large baking sheets with parchment. Draw one 3-inch-diameter round in center of ¹/₄-inch-thick, 4-inch cardboard or styrofoam square. Cut out round and discard, forming stencil. Finely grind hazelnuts with ¹/₃ cup sugar in processor. Using electric mixer, beat whites with salt and cream of tartar until soft peaks form. Gradually add remaining ¹/₃ cup sugar and beat until stiff and shiny. Fold in ground hazelnut mixture.

Set stencil on prepared sheet. Spoon 2 tablespoons meringue into center. Smooth top with long narrow spatula. Carefully lift stencil. Repeat with remaining meringue, forming 30 meringue rounds and spacing 2 inches apart. Bake until brown, about 1 hour. (Meringues will crisp as they cool.) Cool meringues on rack. Turn parchment over. Gently pull parchment off meringues. (*Can be prepared 1 day ahead. Store between layers of waxed paper in airtight container.*)

For buttercream: Using electric mixer, beat butter and molasses in bowl until light and fluffy. Heat sugar and water in heavy small saucepan over low heat, swirling pan occasionally, until sugar dissolves. Increase heat and boil until syrup registers 238°F (soft-ball stage) on candy thermometer.

Meanwhile, using electric mixer, beat yolks until pale yellow and slowly dissolving ribbon forms when beaters are lifted. Gradually beat hot syrup into yolks in slow steady stream. Continue beating until cool and thick. Add butter in 2 batches, blending well after each addition. Mix in ground walnuts.

Spread 1 cup buttercream in thin layer on baking sheet. Spread 2 table-spoons buttercream onto 1 meringue. Top with another meringue. Spread with 2 tablespoons buttercream. Top with another meringue, forming 3-layered round. Repeat with remaining buttercream and meringues. Roll sides of each set of rounds (like a wheel) through buttercream on baking sheet, then through finely chopped walnuts. Set rounds on another baking sheet.

For ganache: Bring cream to boil in heavy medium saucepan. Remove pan from heat. Add chocolate and stir until melted and smooth. Blend in vanilla. Cool until firm enough to pipe.

Spoon ganache into parchment cone with fine opening. Pipe atop meringue rounds in 4 lines, crossing in center, dividing each into 8 wedges. Pipe dot in center of each round. Press walnut onto each dot. (*Can be prepared 8 hours ahead. Cover and refrigerate. Bring to room temperature before serving.*)

Lemon Honey Fritters with Apricots Poached in Vanilla Syrup

This makes a perfect finale to a brunch or a lovely addition to afternoon tea. The apricots are delectable alone as a breakfast treat.

4 servings

Apricots
1½ cups water
½ cup plus 2 tablespoons sugar
1 4-inch vanilla bean, split lengthwise
1 lemon slice
1 pound apricots, peeled, halved and pitted

Whipped Sour Cream
⅓ cup well-chilled whipping cream
4 teaspoons sugar
¼ teaspoon vanilla
½ cup sour cream
1½ teaspoons Cognac or brandy (optional)

Fritters
½ cup water
3 tablespoons unsalted butter, cut into small pieces
1½ tablespoons honey
½ teaspoon grated lemon peel
¼ teaspoon salt
¼ teaspoon freshly grated nutmeg
½ cup sifted all purpose flour
2 eggs
¼ teaspoon vanilla

Vegetable oil (for deep frying)
Powdered sugar

For apricots: Cook water, sugar, vanilla and lemon in heavy medium saucepan over low heat until sugar dissolves, swirling pan occasionally. Increase heat and simmer gently 10 minutes. Adjust heat so liquid barely shimmers. Add apricots and cook until just tender, about 5 minutes. Transfer apricots to glass bowl using slotted spoon. Boil syrup until reduced to ¾ cup (returning juices that accumulate in apricot bowl), about 12 minutes. Pour over apricots. Cover and refrigerate. (*Can be prepared 3 days ahead.*)

For sour cream: Beat cream, sugar and vanilla until soft peaks form. Add sour cream and Cognac if desired and beat until soft peaks form again. Cover and chill. (*Can be prepared 1 day ahead.*)

For fritters: Cook water, butter, honey, lemon peel, salt and nutmeg in heavy medium saucepan until butter melts and water boils. Remove from heat. Immediately add flour. Beat with wooden spoon until thick mass forms. Set pan over medium-high heat and stir until dough pulls away from sides of pan and leaves film on bottom, about 1 minute. Transfer to processor and cool 5 minutes. Add eggs 1 at a time, mixing until just incorporated. Blend vanilla into batter.

Meanwhile, pour oil into wide saucepan to depth of 2 inches. Heat to 350°F to 360°F. Using spoon dipped in hot oil, add batter to oil by heaping teaspoonfuls (in batches; do not crowd). Cook until fritters are golden brown and cooked through, turning occasionally, about 5 minutes. Remove using slotted spoon; drain on paper towels. Dust with powdered sugar. Serve with apricots and cream.

Sweet Fritters from Crete

6 servings

Sugar Syrup
3 cups water
2 cups sugar
2 thin lemon slices
1 cinnamon stick

Pastry
1 egg
1 cup sifted all purpose flour

1 tablespoon melted unsalted butter, cooled
Pinch of salt

Vegetable oil (for deep frying)
1 cup finely chopped walnuts
¼ teaspoon cinnamon

For syrup: Cook water, sugar, lemon and cinnamon stick in heavy large saucepan over low heat until sugar dissolves, swirling pan occasionally. Bring to boil and cook until white bubbles appear, syrup coats back of spoon and candy thermometer registers 220°F, about 15 minutes. Maintain syrup at simmer.

For pastry: Whisk egg to blend in medium bowl. Stir in flour, butter and salt. Knead dough in bowl until smooth and elastic, adding up to 2 tablespoons warm water if dough is too dry. Turn dough out onto lightly floured surface. Divide in half. Roll each half out to thickness of dime, sprinkling with water if dough is dry. Cut dough into ³⁄₄ × 12-inch strips. Immediately tie dough strips into bows, knots or any other desired shapes.

Heat oil in heavy large skillet to 375°F. Fry dough shapes (in batches; do not crowd) until crisp and golden brown, about 2 minutes. Remove using slotted utensil and drain on paper towels. Dip fritters immediately into sugar syrup. Set on platter. Combine walnuts and cinnamon. Sprinkle over fritters.

❦ Cakes

Orange, Date and Walnut Buttermilk Layer Cake

A terrific old-fashioned molasses spice cake.

10 to 12 servings

2 cups plus 3 tablespoons sifted unbleached all purpose flour
2¹⁄₂ teaspoons baking powder
1 teaspoon baking soda
1 teaspoon ground cloves
³⁄₄ teaspoon salt
³⁄₄ teaspoon cinnamon
1 cup (2 sticks) unsalted butter, room temperature
³⁄₄ cup sugar

2 eggs
10 tablespoons light molasses
2¹⁄₂ tablespoons grated orange peel
1 teaspoon vanilla
³⁄₄ cup buttermilk
²⁄₃ cup pitted dates, chopped
²⁄₃ cup coarsely chopped walnuts

Orange Molasses Icing*
Walnut halves

Preheat oven to 350°F. Butter two 9-inch round cake pans. Line bottoms with parchment. Butter parchment; dust with flour. Sift first 6 ingredients into medium bowl. Using electric mixer, cream butter and sugar in another bowl until light and fluffy. Beat in eggs 1 at a time. Add molasses, orange peel and vanilla and beat 3 minutes. Mix in dry ingredients alternately with buttermilk, beginning and ending with dry ingredients. Fold in dates and chopped walnuts. Divide batter between pans. Bake until cakes begin to pull away from sides, about 30 minutes. Cool in pans on rack 5 minutes. Invert cakes onto racks. Peel off paper. Cool cakes completely.

Set 1 cake layer on platter, flat side down. Spread with some of icing. Top with second layer, flat side up. Spread icing over tops and sides of cake. Arrange walnut halves around edges. Serve at room temperature. (*Can be prepared 1 day ahead. Wrap and chill. Bring to room temperature before serving.*)

*Orange Molasses Icing

Makes about 3³⁄₄ cups

8 ounces cream cheese, room temperature
¹⁄₂ cup (1 stick) unsalted butter, room temperature
2 tablespoons grated orange peel

1 teaspoon vanilla
4 cups (or more) powdered sugar, sifted
¹⁄₄ cup light molasses

Using electric mixer, beat cream cheese and butter until smooth. Blend in orange peel and vanilla. Gradually beat in 4 cups powdered sugar. Mix in molasses. Beat in more powdered sugar if icing is too thin to spread.

Strawberry Surprise Cake

6 to 8 servings

Poppy Seed Cake
- 1/4 cup poppy seeds
- 1/3 cup milk
- Butter
- All purpose flour
- 1 cup all purpose flour
- 1 1/4 teaspoons baking powder
- 1/4 teaspoon salt
- 1/4 cup (1/2 stick) unsalted butter, room temperature
- 3/4 cup sugar
- 2 eggs, room temperature
- 1 teaspoon grated orange peel
- 1/2 teaspoon vanilla

Buttercream
- 1 cup (2 sticks) unsalted butter, room temperature
- 5 egg yolks, room temperature
- 1/2 cup sugar

- 1/3 cup water
- 1 teaspoon vanilla

- 8 tablespoons orange liqueur
- 1/2 teaspoon finely grated lemon peel
- 1 cup sliced strawberries, well drained

Ganache
- 3/4 pound semisweet chocolate, chopped
- 3/4 cup whipping cream

For cake: Soak poppy seeds in milk 1 hour. Position rack in center of oven and preheat to 325°F. Line 7 × 3-inch round cake pan with parchment; butter and flour paper. Sift together flour, baking powder and salt and set aside. Using electric mixer, cream 1/4 cup butter with 3/4 cup sugar in large bowl until light and fluffy. Beat in eggs 1 at a time. Sift flour mixture into butter in 3 batches, alternating with poppy seed mixture in 2 batches and blending well after each addition. Stir in orange peel and vanilla. Pour batter into prepared pan. Bake until cake pulls away from sides of pan and top feels springy to touch, about 65 minutes. Cool in pan on rack 30 minutes. Invert onto rack and cool completely. Slice off puffed dome in center of cake.

For buttercream: Cream butter to consistency of mayonnaise. Using electric mixer, beat yolks in large bowl until pale yellow and creamy. Heat sugar and water in heavy small saucepan over low heat, swirling pan occasionally, until sugar dissolves. Increase heat and boil until candy thermometer registers 234°F (soft-ball stage). Add syrup to yolks in thin stream, beating at medium speed. Increase speed to high and beat until mixture is completely cool, 10 to 15 minutes. Reduce speed to low. Blend in vanilla. Gradually beat in creamed butter. Set buttercream aside.

Cut out 7-inch cardboard round. Cut cake into 3 layers using serrated knife. Reserve 1/2 cup buttercream. Blend 2 tablespoons liqueur and lemon peel into remaining buttercream. Fold in sliced strawberries. Place 1 layer on cardboard. Brush with 3 tablespoons liqueur. Spread with half of strawberry buttercream. Top with second layer. Brush with 3 tablespoons liqueur. Spread with remaining strawberry buttercream. Top with third layer. Frost top and sides with reserved buttercream. Refrigerate cake 10 minutes, then smooth top and sides with warm spatula. Refrigerate.

For ganache: Melt chocolate in double boiler over gently simmering water; stir until smooth. Warm cream in heavy medium saucepan over medium heat. Remove from heat. Stir in melted chocolate. Cool until just room temperature; do not allow to set.

Place cake on rack over pan. Pour ganache over, tilting cake back and forth so glaze coats sides. Refrigerate cake until glaze sets. Let cake stand at room temperature 1 hour before serving.

Orange-Raisin Cake

A light cake combining many favorite Italian ingredients: raisins, pine nuts, oranges and Marsala.

8 servings

3/4 cup raisins
1/4 cup dry Marsala

2 cups sifted cake flour
3 tablespoons pine nuts, toasted
1 1/2 teaspoons grated orange peel
1/2 cup fresh orange juice
1 teaspoon vanilla
2 teaspoons baking powder
1/4 teaspoon salt

1/2 cup (1 stick) unsalted butter, room temperature
1 cup sugar
3 eggs, room temperature, beaten to blend

Honey Syrup*
Orange peel julienne
Sweetened whipped cream or crème fraîche (optional)

Combine raisins and Marsala in small bowl. Let stand 30 minutes.

Position rack in lower third of oven and preheat to 350°F. Butter and flour 9-inch round cake pan. Drain raisins, reserving Marsala. Combine raisins, 1 tablespoon cake flour, pine nuts and orange peel in small bowl. Mix reserved Marsala with orange juice and vanilla in another small bowl. Sift remaining flour, baking powder and salt into large bowl. Set aside.

Using electric mixer, cream butter with sugar in another large bowl until light and fluffy. Add eggs and beat until smooth. Carefully blend in dry ingredients alternately with orange juice mixture beginning and ending with dry ingredients; do not overmix. Fold in raisin mixture. Pour batter into pan.

Bake until cake is golden brown and pulls away from sides of pan, 35 to 40 minutes. Cool in pan on rack 10 minutes. Invert onto rack. Brush top and sides of warm cake with warm syrup. Cool completely. (*Can be prepared 1 day ahead. Wrap tightly and store at room temperature.*) Sprinkle top with orange peel. Serve with sweetened whipped cream or crème fraîche, if desired.

*Honey Syrup

Makes 3 tablespoons

2 tablespoons honey   1 tablespoon fresh orange juice

Cook honey and orange juice in heavy small saucepan over low heat until heated through, stirring frequently.

Pineapple Ginger Upside-down Cake with Pineapple Bourbon Ice Cream

8 servings

Pineapple
1   4- to 4¹/₂-pound pineapple, peeled, halved and cored
¹/₂   cup firmly packed light brown sugar
¹/₂   cup bourbon

Ice Cream
1   cup whipping cream
1   cup half and half
1   6-inch vanilla bean, split lengthwise

4   egg yolks
¹/₂   cup sugar
3   quarter-size slices fresh ginger

Cake
1¹/₄   cups firmly packed dark brown sugar
¹/₂   cup (1 stick) unsalted butter
2   tablespoons bourbon
¹/₃   cup minced crystallized ginger

1   cup all purpose flour
¹/₂   teaspoon baking soda
¹/₂   teaspoon baking powder
¹/₈   teaspoon salt
2   eggs, room temperature
1   teaspoon vanilla
¹/₃   cup sour cream

For pineapple: Cut half of pineapple into ³/₈-inch-thick slices. Cover and refrigerate. Finely chop enough of remaining pineapple to measure 2¹/₂ cups. Combine 2 cups (refrigerate remaining ¹/₂ cup) with sugar and bourbon in heavy medium saucepan and boil over medium-high heat until almost all liquid evaporates, stirring often at end, about 18 minutes. Cool completely.

For ice cream: Combine cream and half and half in heavy medium saucepan. Scrape in seeds from vanilla bean; add pod. Scald cream mixture. Remove from heat and let steep 15 minutes.

Whisk yolks and sugar to blend in small bowl. Bring cream mixture to simmer. Gradually whisk half of cream mixture into yolks; return to saucepan. Stir over medium-low heat until mixture thickens and leaves path on back of spoon when finger is drawn across, about 3 minutes. Strain custard into medium bowl. Whisk 1 minute to cool. Press ginger 1 slice at a time through garlic press into custard; discard pulp. Cover and refrigerate custard until well chilled (or chill over ice water, whisking occasionally).

Transfer custard to ice cream maker and process according to manufacturer's instructions until almost frozen. Add 2 cups chopped pineapple-bourbon mixture and process until frozen. Freeze in covered containers several hours or overnight to mellow flavors.

For cake: Preheat oven to 350°F. Generously butter 9-inch round cake pan with 3-inch sides. Stir ³/₄ cup brown sugar with ¹/₄ cup butter in heavy small saucepan over low heat until sugar dissolves and mixture is smooth. Remove from heat. Stir in bourbon. Pour into prepared pan, spreading evenly. Sprinkle ginger over. Drain reserved pineapple slices and remaining ¹/₂ cup chopped pineapple; keep separate. Cut 1 slice into ³/₄-inch pieces. Arrange in center of pan. Arrange remaining slices in pan radiating from center toward edge, leaving small space between each slice.

Sift flour, baking soda, baking powder and salt into small bowl. Using electric mixer, cream remaining ¹/₄ cup butter until light and fluffy. Add remaining ¹/₂ cup sugar and beat until light. Beat in eggs 1 at a time. Blend in vanilla. Mix in dry ingredients and sour cream alternately, beginning and ending with dry ingredients. Fold in remaining ¹/₂ cup chopped pineapple. Spoon batter over pineapple in pan, spreading evenly. Bake until tester inserted in center comes out clean, about 40 minutes. Let cake cool in pan 3 minutes. Invert onto platter and cool at least 25 minutes.

Chilled Espresso Charlotte

This elegant dessert show-cases some traditional end-of-meal flavors in a delightful new guise.

8 servings

Sponge Cake
- ¹/₂ cup cake flour, sifted
- ²/₃ cup powdered sugar
- Pinch of salt
- 3 eggs, separated, room temperature
- ¹/₂ teaspoon orange liqueur
- ¹/₂ teaspoon vanilla

Powdered sugar

Filling
- 8 ounces bittersweet (not unsweetened) or semisweet chocolate, chopped
- ¹/₂ cup (1 stick) unsalted butter
- ¹/₂ cup sugar
- 2¹/₂ tablespoons instant espresso powder dissolved in ¹/₄ cup hot water

- 3 eggs, separated, room temperature
- ¹/₄ cup orange liqueur
- ¹/₄ cup coffee liqueur
- ³/₄ cup chilled whipping cream, beaten to soft peaks

Topping
- ³/₄ cup whipping cream
- 2 tablespoons powdered sugar
- 1 tablespoon orange liqueur
- 1 tablespoon coffee liqueur

Shaved bittersweet (not unsweetened) or semisweet chocolate

For cake: Preheat oven to 350°F. Trace 2 circles on sheet of parchment, 1 the size of top and 1 the size of bottom of 6-cup charlotte mold, using mold as guide. Invert paper on large baking sheet. Line another baking sheet with parchment. Sift flour, ¹/₃ cup sugar and salt together 3 times. Using electric mixer, beat whites until soft peaks form. Gradually add ¹/₃ cup sugar, beating until stiff but not dry. Beat yolks in another bowl until pale yellow and slowly dissolving ribbon forms when beaters are lifted. Mix in liqueur and vanilla. Fold ¹/₄ of whites into yolks to lighten; gently fold in remaining whites. Gradually sift flour mixture over eggs, gently folding in.

Spoon batter into pastry bag fitted with ¹/₂-inch plain tip. Pipe batter in ¹/₂-inch-thick spiral over each circle, covering completely. Pipe remaining batter on second prepared sheet in ³/₄ × 4-inch ladyfingers, spacing 1¹/₂ inches apart. Dust cakes with powdered sugar. Bake until golden brown, 12 to 15 minutes. Transfer cakes on paper to racks and cool.

Lightly butter 6-cup charlotte mold; dust with sugar. Line bottom with smaller cake round, discarding paper. Line sides with ladyfingers, rounded side toward pan sides.

For filling: Melt chocolate and butter with sugar and dissolved espresso in top of double boiler over barely simmering water, stirring until smooth. Cool. Using electric mixer, beat yolks to blend. Blend in chocolate mixture and li-queurs. Using clean dry beater, beat whites until stiff but not dry. Fold ¹/₄ of whites into chocolate mixture to lighten; gently fold in remaining whites. Gently fold in whipped cream.

Spoon filling into cake-lined mold. Cover with large cake round, pressing gently. Refrigerate at least 6 hours. (*Can be prepared 1 day ahead.*)

For topping: Whip cream with sugar and liqueurs until peaks form.

Just before serving, unmold dessert onto platter. Spread some topping over sides and top. Spoon remainder into pastry bag fitted with star tip. Pipe rosettes of cream around top of dessert. Sprinkle with shaved chocolate.

Gâteau Nougatine

Layers of dense almond cake are filled with chocolate ganache and topped with cookie wedges.

12 servings

Frangipane
- 2 cups almond paste
- 1 cup (2 sticks) unsalted butter, room temperature
- 4 eggs, room temperature
- 4 egg whites, room temperature
- 2 cups all purpose flour

Ganache Filling
- 1¹/₂ cups whipping cream
- 2 tablespoons (¹/₄ stick) unsalted butter, room temperature
- 1¹/₄ pounds bittersweet (not unsweetened) or semisweet chocolate, finely chopped
- 2 tablespoons brandy

Florentine
- ³/₄ cup sugar
- ¹/₂ cup whipping cream
- 1 cup sliced blanched almonds (about 4 ounces)
- ¹/₄ cup plus 1¹/₂ teaspoons chopped candied orange peel
- ¹/₄ cup plus 1¹/₂ teaspoons chopped candied citron
- 3 tablespoons all purpose flour
- 1 tablespoon unsalted butter

- 1 cup toasted sliced almonds (about 4 ounces)

For frangipane: Preheat oven to 350°F. Grease and flour two 9-inch round springform pans. Using electric mixer, blend first 3 ingredients in large bowl. Add egg whites 1 at a time, blending well after each addition. Beat until mixture is very smooth and light, about 5 minutes. Fold in flour. Divide batter among prepared pans. Smooth top. Bake until toothpick inserted in centers comes out clean, about 25 minutes. Cool completely on rack. (*Can be prepared 1 day ahead. Wrap tightly and store at room temperature.*)

For ganache: Bring cream and butter to boil in heavy medium saucepan. Pour into medium bowl. Add chocolate and stir until smooth. Stir in brandy. Refrigerate until ganache is almost firm.

For florentine: Preheat oven to 350°F. Line large baking sheet with parchment. Draw 9-inch round on sheet. Turn parchment over, drawing side down. Stir sugar and cream in heavy medium saucepan over medium-low heat until sugar dissolves. Increase heat and bring to boil. Add blanched almonds, orange peel, citron, flour and butter and stir 2 minutes. Pour mixture onto center of circle, spreading into 9-inch round. Bake until edges are light brown, 15 to 17 minutes. Mixture will spread during baking. While florentine is still warm, push edges back to reform 9-inch round, using metal spatula. Cool slightly on pan. Cut into 12 wedges. Cool completely. (*Florentine can be prepared 1 day ahead. Store in airtight container.*)

To assemble: Using electric mixer, beat ganache until light and fluffy. Spoon ³/₄ cup ganache into pastry bag fitted with star tip. Set 1 cake layer on platter. Spread with half of remaining ganache. Top with second cake layer. Spread top and sides of cake with remaining ganache. Press toasted almonds onto sides of cake. Arrange florentine wedges atop cake, points facing toward center. Pipe 1 rosette on outside center edge of each wedge. (*Can be prepared 2 hours ahead and refrigerated.*) Cut into wedges to serve.

Divine Madness

Bittersweet chocolate and walnut praline are featured in this rich flourless cake.

9 servings

1 pound bittersweet (not unsweetened) or semisweet chocolate, finely chopped
3/4 cup (1 1/2 sticks) unsalted butter
1/2 cup Praline Paste*
1/2 cup whipping cream

6 eggs, separated, room temperature
1/4 teaspoon cream of tartar
1/3 cup sugar
1 cup toasted walnuts (about 3 3/4 ounces), finely ground

2 tablespoons powdered sugar

Preheat oven to 350°F. Grease 9-inch square pan with removable bottom. Line bottom with parchment. Dust pan with flour; tap out excess. Melt chocolate, butter and Praline Paste in top of double boiler over hot water, stirring until melted. Blend in cream. Remove from over water.

Using electric mixer, beat yolks until pale yellow and slowly dissolving ribbon forms when beaters are lifted. Using clean dry beaters, beat whites and cream of tartar in another bowl until soft peaks form. Gradually add 1/3 cup sugar and beat until almost stiff but not dry. Add yolk mixture to whites and beat until well blended. Fold 1/2 of lukewarm chocolate mixture and 1/2 of ground nuts into egg mixture. Fold in remaining chocolate mixture and remaining nuts.

Pour batter into prepared pan. Bake until tester inserted in center of cake comes out clean, about 50 minutes. Cool cake in pan on rack. Cover and refrigerate until well chilled. (*Can be prepared 1 day ahead.*)

Run knife around edge of cake to loosen. Invert cake onto platter. Remove pan sides and bottom. Peel off parchment. Sift powdered sugar over cake. Serve at room temperature.

*Praline Paste

Makes about 1 cup

1 cup sugar
1 1/4 cups water

1 cup chopped toasted walnuts (about 3 3/4 ounces)

Butter baking sheet. Cook sugar and water in heavy small saucepan over low heat, swirling pan occasionally, until sugar dissolves. Increase heat and boil until syrup turns caramel color. Mix in nuts. Pour onto prepared sheet. Cool completely. Break into 2-inch pieces. Transfer to processor and blend until smooth paste forms, about 5 minutes. (*Can be prepared 1 month ahead and refrigerated.*)

Chocolate Fruitcake

Start the fruitcake several days ahead to allow flavors to blend and mellow.

10 servings

1 cup Grand Marnier or other orange liqueur
1 cup 1/2-inch wedges candied pineapple
3/4 cup 1/2-inch pieces dried apricots
3/4 cup raisins

All purpose flour
1/2 cup plus 2 tablespoons all purpose flour

1/4 cup plus 2 tablespoons unsweetened cocoa powder (preferably Dutch process)
1/2 teaspoon baking powder
1 cup chopped walnuts (about 4 1/2 ounces)
1/2 cup (1 stick) unsalted butter, room temperature
2/3 cup sugar
3 eggs, room temperature

Combine first 4 ingredients in medium bowl. Cover and let stand 2 days to let flavors blend, stirring occasionally.

Drain liquid and fruit through fine sieve, pressing gently to extract liquid; reserve liquid. Transfer fruit to medium bowl.

Preheat oven to 325°F. Butter and flour 8½ × 4½ × 2½-inch loaf pan. Sift flour, cocoa powder and baking powder into small bowl. Mix in walnuts. Using electric mixer, cream butter with sugar in large bowl until light and fluffy. Add eggs 1 at a time, blending well after each addition. Gently fold in flour mixture, then fruit. Spoon batter into prepared pan. Bake until tester inserted in center comes out clean, about 50 minutes.

Brush top of warm cake with ¼ cup reserved soaking liquid. Cool cake completely in pan on rack. Unmold cake. Wrap in plastic and store in airtight container. Let mellow 6 days before serving. (*Can be prepared 1 month ahead stored at room temperature or 3 months ahead and frozen.*)

Apricot Chocolate Soufflé Cake

An elegant flourless cake garnished with chocolate-dipped apricots.

10 servings

½ cup dried apricots

Cake
   Butter
¾ cup (1½ sticks) unsalted butter, room temperature
¾ cup sugar
10 eggs, separated, room temperature
6 ounces bittersweet (not unsweetened) or semisweet chocolate, melted and cooled to lukewarm
1 tablespoon instant coffee granules dissolved in 1½ teaspoons water
¼ cup chopped walnuts (about 1½ ounces)

6 ounces bittersweet (not unsweetened) or semisweet chocolate, finely chopped
7 dried apricots

Cream Topping
2 cups whipping cream
2 tablespoons sugar
1 teaspoon vanilla

   Semisweet chocolate shavings
7 walnut halves
   Powdered sugar

   Chocolate Mocha Sauce*

Soak apricots in hot water to cover 30 minutes. Drain; coarsely chop.

For cake: Preheat oven to 350°F. Butter 8-inch round cake pan with 2-inch-high sides. Line bottom with parchment. Using electric mixer, cream ¾ cup butter with ¼ cup plus 2 tablespoons sugar in large bowl until light and fluffy. Add yolks 1 at a time, blending well after each addition. Blend in 6 ounces melted chocolate and coffee. Stir in chopped apricots and walnuts. Using clean dry beaters, beat whites until peaks begin to form. Gradually add remaining ¼ cup plus 2 tablespoons sugar and beat until soft peaks form. Gently fold whites into chocolate mixture in 2 additions. Pour batter into prepared pan. Bake cake until tester inserted in center comes out clean, approximately 1 hour. (Cake will form crust and crack.)

Cool cake completely in pan. (Cake will fall as it cools.) Run sharp knife around edge of cake. Invert onto 8-inch cardboard round. (*Can be prepared 1 day ahead. Cover and chill.*)

Line baking sheet with waxed paper. Melt 6 ounces chopped chocolate in top of double boiler over barely simmering water, stirring until chocolate registers 115°F on candy thermometer. Dip 1 apricot halfway into chocolate. Shake off excess chocolate. Set apricot on prepared sheet. Repeat with remaining apricots. Refrigerate until chocolate sets, about 30 minutes.

For topping: Whip cream, sugar and vanilla in bowl until soft peaks form.

Spread half of cream atop cake. Spoon remaining cream into pastry bag fitted with star tip. Pipe 7 rosettes around edge of cake. Sprinkle chocolate shavings in center of cake. Arrange 1 walnut between each rosette. Dust cake with powdered sugar. Top each rosette with chocolate-dipped apricot. (*Can be prepared 2 hours ahead and refrigerated.*)

Cut cake into wedges and serve, passing warm chocolate sauce separately.

*Chocolate Mocha Sauce

Makes about 1 cup

1 tablespoon instant coffee granules
¼ cup hot water
6 ounces bittersweet (not unsweetened) or semisweet chocolate, finely chopped
¼ cup whipping cream

Dissolve coffee in hot water in medium bowl. Add chocolate. Bring cream to boil in heavy small saucepan. Reduce heat to low. Add chocolate mixture and whisk until smooth and melted. (*Can be prepared 2 days ahead. Cool, cover and refrigerate. Rewarm over low heat before serving, stirring occasionally.*) Serve warm.

Bourbon Butter Pecan Cheesecake

The rich pecan crust holds a smooth bourbon-spiked cream cheese filling.

10 servings

Crust
¾ cup finely ground graham cracker crumbs
¼ cup plus 2 tablespoons coarsely chopped pecans (about 2 ounces)
¼ cup firmly packed light brown sugar
¼ cup (½ stick) unsalted butter, melted

Filling
¼ cup sugar
2 tablespoons water

¼ cup plus 3 tablespoons whipping cream
1½ teaspoons unsalted butter
3 tablespoons bourbon

2 8-ounce packages cream cheese, room temperature
⅓ cup sugar
4 eggs

¾ cup whipping cream, whipped to soft peaks
10 whole pecans, toasted

For crust: Preheat oven to 350°F. Wrap foil around outside of 8-inch springform pan, bringing foil 1½ inches up sides. Finely grind cracker crumbs with pecans and sugar in processor. Blend in butter using on/off turns. Press mixture into bottom of pan. Bake 10 minutes. Set aside. Reduce oven temperature to 275°F.

For filling: Cook ¼ cup sugar and water in heavy small saucepan over low heat, swirling pan occasionally, until sugar dissolves. Increase heat and boil until syrup turns caramel color.

Meanwhile, bring ¼ cup cream to boil in another heavy small saucepan. Gradually whisk hot cream into caramel (mixture will bubble vigorously). Whisk in butter. Return mixture to boil. Remove from heat and let cool. Stir 3 tablespoons cream and bourbon into caramel.

Using electric mixer, beat cream cheese and ⅓ cup sugar in large bowl just until smooth, 1 to 2 minutes. Add eggs 1 at a time, blending just until combined and occasionally scraping down sides of bowl. Stir in caramel mixture. Pour filling into crust. Place cheesecake in large shallow baking pan. Add enough hot water to pan to come 1 inch up sides of cheesecake. Bake until center is firm, about 70 minutes. Remove from water and cool on rack. Chill overnight.

Remove pan sides from cheesecake. Set cake on platter. Spoon cream into pastry bag fitted with star tip. Pipe 10 rosettes around border. Place 1 pecan atop each rosette before serving.

Espresso and Chocolate Cheesecake

Easy to make and worth every calorie.

10 servings

Crust
1 cup finely ground chocolate wafer cookies
1 cup finely ground lightly toasted almonds
2 tablespoons sugar
5 tablespoons unsalted butter, melted

Filling
6 tablespoons finely ground espresso coffee beans
½ cup (about) water

16 ounces cream cheese, room temperature
1 cup sugar
3 ounces semisweet chocolate, melted
1¼ cups sour cream
4 eggs, beaten to blend

3 ounces semisweet chocolate, chopped

1 cup well-chilled whipping cream
Powdered sugar

For crust: Combine cookie crumbs, almonds and sugar in 9½-inch springform pan. Gradually mix in butter, using fork. Pat mixture over bottom and halfway up sides of pan. Refrigerate while preparing filling.

For filling: Preheat oven to 350°F. Brew espresso beans with ½ cup water. Add more water to brewed coffee if necessary to measure ⅓ cup. Using electric mixer, beat cream cheese to soften. Gradually blend in sugar and beat until smooth. Blend in coffee, then melted chocolate, mixing just until smooth. Beat in sour cream, then eggs. Pour mixture into crust-lined pan. Bake 45 minutes. Turn off heat and let cake cool 1 hour in oven with door slightly ajar. Refrigerate cheesecake at least 6 hours.

Melt 3 ounces chocolate in top of double boiler over barely simmering water. Stir until smooth. Spread in ⅛- to 1/16-inch-thick layer on baking sheet. Refrigerate until just firm, about 10 minutes. Cut out 8 to 10 decorative shapes. Refrigerate until very firm.

Whip cream until peaks form. Transfer to pastry bag fitted with large star tip. Pipe cream in decorative border around edge of cake. Garnish with chocolate shapes. Sprinkle center of cake with powdered sugar and serve.

🍏 *Cookies, Brownies and Confections*

Grandmother Cookies

These brown sugar "thumbprint" cookies are best served the same day they are baked.

Makes about 3 dozen

2 tablespoons sugar
³/₄ teaspoon cinnamon
1³/₄ cups plus 2 tablespoons sifted all purpose flour
³/₄ cup firmly packed dark brown sugar

¹/₄ teaspoon salt
1 cup (2 sticks) unsalted butter, room temperature
1 egg yolk
1¹/₂ teaspoons vanilla
Raspberry jam

Preheat oven to 350°F. Butter baking sheets. Mix 2 tablespoons sugar and cinnamon in small bowl. Combine flour, brown sugar and salt in bowl of electric mixer. Add butter, yolk and vanilla and beat until just combined. Form dough into 1-inch rounds, refrigerating dough briefly if too soft to form. Arrange rounds on prepared sheets, spacing 1 inch apart. Using fingers or handle of wooden spoon, make indentations in centers of half of rounds. Using small spoon, fill indentations with cinnamon sugar. Bake all rounds 5 minutes. Remove from oven. Make indentations in centers of remaining rounds. Fill indentations with jam. Return to oven and bake until cookies begin to color around edges, 8 to 10 minutes. Cool on rack.

Yankee Clippers

Big molasses softies reminiscent of a spice-filled gingerbread.

Makes about 16

2 cups sifted all purpose flour
1¹/₄ teaspoons ground allspice
1¹/₄ teaspoons cinnamon
³/₄ teaspoon salt
¹/₂ teaspoon baking soda
¹/₂ teaspoon finely ground pepper
¹/₄ teaspoon baking powder
¹/₄ teaspoon ground cardamom
10 tablespoons (1¹/₄ sticks) unsalted butter, room temperature

¹/₂ cup firmly packed dark brown sugar
²/₃ cup light molasses
1 egg, room temperature
2 tablespoons dark rum
2 teaspoons cider vinegar
1 teaspoon vanilla
1¹/₂ cups dried currants

Rum Icing* (optional)

Sift first 8 ingredients into medium bowl. Using electric mixer, cream butter with sugar in large bowl until light and fluffy. Blend in molasses, then egg, rum, vinegar, vanilla and dry ingredients. Mix in currants. Chill 4 hours. (*Can be prepared 1 day ahead.*)

Position rack in center of oven and preheat to 350°F. Invert heavy large baking sheets and cover with foil. Grease and flour foil; shake off excess. Trace 3-inch rounds on prepared sheets, spacing 2¹/₂ inches apart and using cookie cutter as guide. Line ¹/₄-cup measure with plastic wrap, extending plastic 2 inches beyond edges. Fill cup with dough; smooth top. Invert dough onto center of 1 round on prepared sheet, using plastic as aid. Peel off plastic. Using moistened fingertips, press dough to fill round evenly. Repeat with remaining dough.

Bake until cookies begin to firm, about 14 minutes. Slide foil with cookies onto counter. Cool until firm enough to move, 3 to 4 minutes. Transfer cookies to racks and cool. (*Can be prepared 2 days ahead. Store between layers of waxed paper in airtight container.*)

Spread cookies with rum icing just before serving if desired.

*Rum Icing

Makes about ³/₄ cup

1 cup powdered sugar	1 teaspoon dark rum
6 to 7 teaspoons whipping cream	

Blend sugar, 6 teaspoons cream and rum in small bowl. If icing is not thin enough to spread, add more cream.

Gobs of Chocolate

Rich, brownielike cookies that are studded with white chocolate. These are best the day they are made.

Makes about 12

1³/₄ cups sifted all purpose flour
²/₃ cup unsweetened cocoa powder
¹/₂ teaspoon salt
¹/₂ teaspoon baking soda
¹/₄ teaspoon baking powder
1¹/₄ cups firmly packed light brown sugar
¹/₂ cup (1 stick) unsalted butter, melted and cooled
2 eggs

¹/₄ teaspoon vanilla
2 3-ounce bittersweet (not unsweetened) chocolate bars, cut along lines into squares, squares halved
2 3-ounce white chocolate bars, cut along lines into squares, squares halved
1 3-ounce white chocolate bar, cut along lines into squares

Position rack in center of oven and preheat to 350°F. Line heavy large baking sheets with foil. Grease and flour foil; shake off excess. Sift first 5 ingredients into medium bowl. Using electric mixer, beat sugar, butter, eggs and vanilla in large bowl until light and fluffy. Gently mix in dry ingredients, then halved bittersweet and white chocolate squares.

Mound dough on prepared sheets, using ¹/₃ cup for each cookie and spacing 5 inches apart. Using moistened fingertips, flatten each dough mound into 3-inch round. Gently press 2 squares white chocolate onto each round. Bake until cookies are puffed and cracked, 12 to 14 minutes. Cool cookies on foil on racks.

Florentine Cookies

Thin, chewy cookies with candied orange peel, citron and almonds.

Makes about 40

¹/₂ cup plus 2 tablespoons sugar
¹/₂ cup whipping cream
1 cup plus 2 tablespoons sliced blanched almonds (about 4¹/₂ ounces)
¹/₄ cup finely chopped candied orange peel

¹/₄ cup finely chopped candied citron
3 tablespoons all purpose flour
1 tablespoon unsalted butter
8 ounces bittersweet (not unsweetened) or semisweet chocolate, finely chopped

Preheat oven to 350°F. Line heavy large baking sheets with parchment. Cook sugar and cream in heavy medium saucepan over medium-low heat, stirring until sugar dissolves. Bring to boil. Reduce heat and simmer 3 minutes. Add almonds, orange peel, citron, flour and butter and stir 3 minutes. Spoon mixture by teaspoonfuls onto prepared sheets, spacing 2½ inches apart. Bake until golden brown, 8 to 10 minutes (cookies will spread during baking). Reshape cookies by gently pressing edges in with 2-inch round cookie cutter. Cool completely on parchment set on rack.

Melt chocolate in double boiler over barely simmering water, stirring frequently, until smooth. Using long narrow spatula, spread bottom of 1 cookie with thin layer of chocolate. Immediately draw icing comb through chocolate in S pattern. Set cookie chocolate side up on baking sheet. Repeat with remaining cookies and chocolate. Let stand in cool dry place until chocolate sets. Store cookies in airtight container between sheets of waxed paper. (*Can be prepared 2 weeks ahead.*)

Basler Bruns

These chocolate-almond bell cookies are a Christmas tradition in Basel. Use a heavy-duty mixer for blending the ingredients. If the cookies harden after baking, soften them by storing in an airtight container with half an apple.

Makes about 20

1 cup almond paste
½ cup sugar
1 cup finely ground crustless dry white breadcrumbs (about 4 ounces)
¼ cup honey

3 ounces unsweetened chocolate, melted and cooled to lukewarm
2 tablespoons all purpose flour
1 tablespoon cinnamon
2 egg whites, room temperature

2 tablespoons (or more) sugar

Mix in first 2 ingredients in large bowl of heavy-duty mixer fitted with paddle attachment. Blend in ground breadcrumbs, honey, unsweetened chocolate, flour and cinnamon. Add egg whites 1 at a time, blending well after each addition. Let dough stand 30 minutes.

Position rack in upper third of oven and preheat to 400°F. Line baking sheets with parchment. Turn dough out onto lightly floured surface. Pat dough into square. Sprinkle with 2 tablespoons sugar. Roll dough out to thickness of ½ inch. Cut out cookies using 2-inch bell-shaped cookie cutter, dipping cutter in flour as necessary to prevent dough from sticking. Reroll scraps, sprinkle with more sugar and cut out additional cookies. Arrange cookies sugar side up on prepared sheet. Bake until sides are just set, about 6 minutes. Slide cookies on paper onto rack. Cool completely. (*Can be prepared 2 weeks ahead and stored in airtight container or 1 month ahead and frozen.*)

Almond Crisps with Amaretto-glazed Almonds

These thin, buttery cookies will keep for several weeks in an airtight container. The recipe doubles easily.

Makes about 30

Glazed Almonds
1½ teaspoons unsalted butter
¾ cup slivered almonds (about 3 ounces)
1½ tablespoons amaretto liqueur

Dough
1 cup all purpose flour
Pinch of salt

½ cup (1 stick) unsalted butter, room temperature
½ cup sugar
1 small egg, room temperature
2 teaspoons amaretto liqueur

Sugar

Powdered sugar (optional)

For almonds: Melt butter in heavy small skillet over medium heat. Add almonds and amaretto and stir until almonds are golden brown, about 5 minutes. Cool completely on paper towels.

For dough: Preheat oven to 350°F. Lightly grease 2 large baking sheets. Sift 1 cup flour with salt into small bowl. Using electric mixer, cream butter with ½ cup sugar in large bowl until light and fluffy. Blend in egg and amaretto. Add flour and mix until dough binds. (Dough will be sticky.)

Divide dough into 30 pieces. Roll each between palms into balls, dusting hands with flour if necessary. Set on baking sheets, spacing 2 inches apart.

Fill small bowl with water. Mound sugar on plate. Dip bottom of 2½-inch round glass into water and then into sugar. Press glass down onto 1 dough ball, flattening into 2½- to 3-inch round. Repeat with remaining dough. Sprinkle rounds lightly with sugar.

Gently press several glazed almond slivers into each round in flower pattern. Bake until edges of cookies are golden brown, 8 to 10 minutes. Cool on rack. Just before serving, dust cookies with powdered sugar if desired.

The Cosmic Apple Cookie

This enormous cookie, baked on a pizza pan, is fun for a children's party–but adults love it too.

Makes one 12½-inch round

1¼ cups coarsely chopped unsulfured dried apple slices (about 3½ ounces)
7 tablespoons defrosted frozen filtered apple juice concentrate
1 tablespoon fresh lemon juice
1 tablespoon grated lemon peel

1⅓ cups sifted all purpose flour
¾ cup sugar
1 tablespoon light brown sugar
½ teaspoon salt
½ teaspoon cinnamon
¼ teaspoon baking soda
   Generous pinch of ground cloves
   Generous pinch of ground ginger

5 tablespoons well-chilled unsalted butter, diced
3 tablespoons beaten egg (about 1)
1 teaspoon vanilla
1 generous cup coarsely chopped toasted walnuts
2 tablespoons raisins

Icing
5 tablespoons powdered sugar, sifted
1 tablespoon well-chilled whipping cream
¼ teaspoon (or more) strained fresh lemon juice

Combine apples, apple juice and lemon juice in heavy medium skillet over low heat. Cook 5 minutes, stirring twice. Increase heat to high. Add lemon peel and boil 15 minutes. Cover tightly. Cool completely.

Position rack in center of oven and preheat to 350°F. Lightly grease 12½-inch round pizza pan. Line with foil, leaving ½-inch overhang. Grease and flour foil; shake off excess. Blend flour, ¾ cup sugar, brown sugar, salt, cinnamon, baking soda, cloves and ginger in processor. Using on/off turns, cut in butter until mixture resembles coarse meal. Transfer mixture to large bowl. Stir egg and vanilla into apple mixture. Add apple mixture, walnuts and raisins to dry ingredients. Mix until well combined. Turn mixture into prepared pan. Cover with plastic and press dough to within ¼ inch of edge of pan. Peel off plastic. Bake until brown, about 30 minutes. Slide cookie and foil onto wire rack. Cool cookie 30 minutes.

Slide large knife between foil and cookie to loosen. Pull foil out from under cookie. Cool cookie completely.

For icing: Blend powdered sugar, cream and ¼ teaspoon lemon juice in small bowl. Thin with additional lemon juice if necessary to drizzle icing in 3-inch-long lines over cookie. Let cookie stand until glaze sets. Cut into wedges and serve. (*Can be prepared 1 day ahead. Cover tightly and store at room temperature.*)

Coconut Puddles

Moist macaroons with a hint of lemon

Makes about 11

4 cups sweetened shredded coconut
1/3 cup powdered sugar
6 egg whites
1 teaspoon fresh lemon juice
3/4 teaspoon minced lemon peel
1/4 teaspoon vanilla
12 drops of almond extract

2/3 cup sugar
1/4 cup finely chopped, lightly toasted sweetened shredded coconut

11 tablespoons (about) sweetened shredded coconut

Mince 4 cups coconut with powdered sugar in processor, stopping occasionally to scrape down sides of work bowl. Add 2 egg whites and blend until pasty mixture forms. Blend in remaining 4 whites, lemon juice, peel, vanilla and almond extract. Stir in 2/3 cup sugar. Transfer to bowl. Stir in toasted coconut. (*Dough can be prepared 1 day ahead. Cover and refrigerate.*)

Position rack in center of oven and preheat to 300°F. Invert heavy large baking sheets and cover with double thickness heavy-duty foil. Grease and flour foil; shake off excess. Trace 4-inch rounds on prepared sheets, spacing 3/4 inch apart and using bowl or large can as guide. Spoon 1/4 cup dough onto round. Spread evenly to edges of round using back of spoon. Repeat with remaining dough. Sprinkle top of each cookie with 1 tablespoon coconut. Bake 25 minutes. Reverse sheets and bake until cookie tops and edges are brown, about 30 minutes more. Transfer cookies to racks and cool completely. (*Can be prepared 2 days ahead. Store between layers of waxed paper in airtight container.*)

All-American Double Chocolate Brownies

Part truffle and part cake, these are best several hours after baking.

Makes 16

1 cup (2 sticks) unsalted butter
3 ounces unsweetened chocolate, coarsely chopped
1/2 cup plus 1 tablespoon all purpose flour, sifted
1/2 teaspoon baking soda
2 eggs, room temperature
1/4 teaspoon salt

1 cup sugar
2 tablespoons orange liqueur, such as Grand Marnier or Cointreau
1 teaspoon vanilla
1 6-ounce package semisweet chocolate chips
1 cup chopped walnuts
Sugar

Position rack in center of oven and preheat to 350°F. Grease 8-inch square baking pan. Line with parchment, extending paper 1 inch above pan sides. Grease paper generously; dust with sugar. Melt butter and unsweetened chocolate in top of double boiler over barely simmering water. Stir until smooth. Remove from over water. Sift flour and baking soda together. Using electric mixer, beat eggs and salt until lemon colored. Gradually add 1 cup sugar and beat until mixture is pale yellow and slowly dissolving ribbon forms when beaters are lifted. Blend in chocolate mixture, then liqueur and vanilla. Stir in flour. Fold in chocolate chips and walnuts. Pour batter into prepared pan, spreading evenly. Bake until top is firm but center is soft, 20 to 22 minutes. Sprinkle top with sugar. Cool in pan.

Remove brownies from baking pan using parchment as aid. Cut into 2-inch squares using serrated knife.

Peanut Butter Blondies

For best flavor and texture, these brown sugar-peanut butter brownies should be eaten the same day they are made.

Makes 9

Butter
All purpose flour
1/2 cup (1 stick) unsalted butter
1/2 cup super chunky peanut butter
1 tablespoon light molasses
1 tablespoon honey
1 teaspoon vanilla
1 cup sifted all purpose flour

Pinch of salt
1 egg
1 cup firmly packed light brown sugar

1/2 cup coarsely chopped roasted salted peanuts
1/2 cup peanut butter chips

Position rack in center of oven and preheat to 325°F. Butter and flour bottom of 9 × 9 × 2-inch baking pan. Melt 1/2 cup butter in heavy medium saucepan over low heat. Cool to lukewarm. Mix in peanut butter, then molasses, honey and vanilla. Combine 1 cup flour and salt in small bowl. Using electric mixer, beat egg with sugar in large bowl until thick and light colored. Fold in peanut butter mixture. Gently stir in flour just to combine.

Spread batter in prepared pan. Sprinkle top with peanuts and peanut butter chips. Bake until center is almost set, about 30 minutes. Cool in pan on rack. Cut into 9 squares to serve.

Chocolate-Almond Coconut Brownies with Bananas Gratinée

6 servings

Topping
1/4 cup sugar
3 egg yolks
1 cup well-chilled whipping cream

Chocolate-Almond Coconut Brownie
1 cup finely ground blanched almonds
2/3 cup sugar
1/2 cup (1 stick) unsalted butter, room temperature
2 eggs
4 ounces bittersweet (not unsweetened) chocolate, melted and cooled slightly

1 cup unsweetened coconut shavings*

3 bananas, sliced into rounds
1/4 cup dark rum

2 pints coconut or vanilla ice cream
Toasted sliced almonds

For topping: Stir sugar in heavy small saucepan over low heat until dissolved. Cook until candy thermometer registers 120°F. Using electric mixer, gradually beat hot syrup into yolks. Continue beating until pale yellow and slowly dissolving ribbon forms when beaters are lifted, about 5 minutes. Whip cream in another bowl to stiff peaks. Gently fold cream into yolks. Refrigerate 2 hours.

For brownie: Preheat oven to 350°F. Lightly butter 7 × 12-inch ovenproof glass baking dish and line with parchment paper. Butter paper. Sift ground almonds and sugar into large bowl. Add butter. Using electric mixer, beat butter with almond mixture until smooth. Beat in eggs 1 at a time. Gently fold in melted chocolate. Stir in coconut shavings. Pour batter into prepared pan, smoothing surface. Bake until tester inserted in center comes out clean, 10 to 15 minutes. Cool in pan on rack. Cut into six 3-inch rounds using cookie cutter.

Place 1 brownie in bottom of 6-inch broilerproof gratin dish. Arrange about 5 banana slices in spiral atop brownie. Sprinkle with 2 teaspoons dark rum.

Spoon 3 to 4 tablespoons topping over, covering completely. Repeat with remaining brownies, banana, rum and topping.

Preheat broiler. Broil brownies 2 inches from heat source until topping is puffy and brown, watching carefully, about 2 minutes. Top each with scoop of ice cream. Sprinkle with almonds and serve.

*Available at many natural foods stores and some supermarkets.

Schümli

Delicate chocolate meringues sandwiched with coffee buttercream.

Makes about 18

Meringues
- ¹/₄ cup sugar
- ¹/₄ cup water

- 2 egg whites, room temperature
  Pinch of cream of tartar
- 3 tablespoons powdered sugar
- 1 ounce unsweetened chocolate, melted and cooled to lukewarm

Buttercream
- 2 tablespoons instant coffee powder
- 2 teaspoons hot water
- 2 tablespoons coffee liqueur
- 1 cup (2 sticks) unsalted butter, room temperature
- ¹/₂ cup powdered sugar

For meringues: Preheat oven to 350°F. Cook ¹/₄ cup sugar and water in heavy small saucepan over low heat, swirling pan occasionally, until sugar dissolves. Increase heat to high. Cover and boil 30 seconds. Uncover and boil until syrup registers 234°F on candy thermometer.

Meanwhile, beat whites with cream of tartar in large bowl until soft peaks form. Gradually add powdered sugar and beat until stiff but not dry. Beat hot sugar syrup into whites in slow steady stream and continue beating until cool, about 5 minutes. Fold in chocolate. Spoon meringue into pastry bag fitted with large plain tip. Pipe 1-inch-diameter rounds on prepared sheets, mounding ¹/₂ inch high in center and spacing 1 inch apart. Bake until meringues are just set, about 12 minutes. Cool slightly. Carefully push in bottoms of warm meringues with thumb, forming hollow space. Cool completely. (*Can be prepared 1 day ahead. Store in airtight container.*)

For buttercream: Dissolve coffee in water. Stir in liqueur. Using electric mixer, beat butter in large bowl until light and fluffy. Blend in coffee mixture and powdered sugar. Spoon buttercream into pastry bag fitted with medium plain tip. Pipe buttercream into hollow portion of meringues, mounding slightly. Press flat sides of two meringues together, forming sandwich. Repeat with remaining meringues and buttercream. (*Can be prepared up to 2 hours ahead.*)

Chestnuts

A creamy trufflelike confection dipped in chocolate and decorated to resemble a chestnut. To temper chocolate—a technique that gives these treats their glossy finish—you'll need an accurate candy thermometer.

Makes 45

- ¹/₂ cup whipping cream
- 3 ounces canned unsweetened chestnut puree
- 1 tablespoon kirsch
- 1 tablespoon unsalted butter
- 17 ounces milk chocolate, finely chopped

- 1¹/₂ pounds bittersweet (not unsweetened) or semisweet chocolate, finely chopped

- 15 camellia, lemon or mint leaves

Bring first 4 ingredients to boil in heavy medium saucepan, stirring constantly. Remove pan from heat. Add 9 ounces milk chocolate and stir until smooth and melted. Cool completely.

Line large baking sheets with waxed paper. Stir chocolate mixture until thick enough to mound on spoon. Spoon mixture into pastry bag fitted with large plain tip. Pipe into 45 walnut-size mounds on prepared sheets. Chill until firm, about 1 hour.

Working in batches (keep remainder refrigerated), roll each mound into ball. Return to prepared sheet. Refrigerate until ready to dip.

Melt 6 ounces milk chocolate in double boiler over barely simmering water, stirring frequently until chocolate registers 110°F on candy thermometer. Remove from over water. Mix remaining 2 ounces milk chocolate into melted chocolate and stir until melted and chocolate registers 75°F. Place chocolate over barely simmering water and stir until chocolate is 91°F to 93°F. Pour some of chocolate into palm of hand. Roll 1 chestnut ball between palms to coat in chocolate. Set on another prepared sheet. Repeat with remaining chestnuts and chocolate, re-warming chocolate in double boiler if necessary, to maintain given temperature range. Chill until firm.

Prepare bittersweet chocolate for dipping following above instructions, melting 1 pound chocolate and stirring in ½ pound to cool. Drop 1 chestnut ball into chocolate and quickly turn from side to side, covering all but thin line of milk chocolate. Lifting chestnut ball up with index finger and thumb, remove from chocolate. Move hand from side to side, shaking excess chocolate back into pan. Set on another prepared sheet, milk chocolate line facing up. Repeat with remaining chestnut balls. Refrigerate until firm.

Spread some of bittersweet chocolate over veined side of camellia leaves, being careful not to drip on edges. Arrange on plate, chocolate sides up. Freeze until just firm, about 10 minutes. Starting at stem end, gently peel leaf away from chocolate, freezing briefly if too soft to work. Refrigerate.

Allow remaining chocolate in pan to thicken slightly. Spoon chocolate into parchment cone. Pipe small spikes of chocolate onto surface of chestnuts to give prickly appearance. (*Can also be done using tip of toothpick dipped in chocolate and applied to chestnut.*) Refrigerate until firm. (*Can be prepared 1 week ahead. Transfer chocolate chestnuts to airtight container and refrigerate.*)

Arrange chocolate leaves on platter. Set chestnuts on and around leaves. Serve chocolate chestnuts at room temperature.

❧ *Index*

Bon Appétit's

News '87

The Year of Food and Entertaining in Review

Trends & New Products

Foods & Info by Mail

Restaurants & People

Getaways

For the Kitchen & Table

Diet News

❧ Trends & New Products

A recent survey of Congress, conducted by a chocolate company, shows that 84 percent of all members of the House of Representatives love chocolate, with Republicans showing more fondness for the sweet than Democrats—87 percent to 80. In the Senate, the Republicans lead their Democratic counterparts by 2 percent. All this was revealed at the debut of Karina chocolate at the Potomac Restaurant in D.C. They obviously believe that you should "vote chocolate."

❧

Now that the American palate has gone "goat gourmet," Meyenberg Goat Milk by Jackson-Mitchell, Inc., of Santa Barbara, California, is gaining new popularity. Long this country's only producer of evaporated and powdered goat's milk, their line currently includes the fresh kind, which is higher in calcium and lower in cholesterol, as well as easier to digest, than cow's milk. For more information contact Jackson-Mitchell, Inc., P.O. Box 5425, Santa Barbara, CA 93150; telephone (805) 565-1538.

❧

Effie Marie's Sutton Cakes couldn't be better if you made them yourself. Meltingly delicious pound cakes in either rich chocolate or vanilla flavor, both with a rum-butter glaze, they are light and moist. The glaze serves as a natural preservative so the cakes stay fresh and remain sweetly rummy to the end. Refrigerated, they last for months. Named after the founder's grandmother, whose recipe started it all, a two-pound treat yields about ten slices. Available in fine food shops nationally for about $15.

❧

Nowadays it seems that everything is dipped in chocolate, from popcorn and potato chips to pretzels and—fortune cookies. These last, complete with fortunes and dubbed Divine Poetry in Chocolate, are sold in specialty foods stores nationwide. Then there are chocolate-dipped nut cookies, which come together as The Beverly Hills Confection Collection. Created by a husband-and-wife team, Carol and Shelly Dubow, each is immersed in one of three flavors of chocolate: dark, milk and white, also known as Sunset, Wilshire and Rodeo. Heavenly pink packages of a half-dozen, one and two dozen "confections" cost $5, $10 and $20, respectively, and are sold at gourmet food stores.

❧

Big, free-form hunks of chocolate are the specialty of CB Chocolates in Traverse City, Michigan. Made from high quality ingredients, Leelanau Chocolat Chocolate Gourmet Chocolate Chips come in half-pound and one-pound packages, plain or with macadamias, pecans or almonds. The chunk chips are about $4.50 and $8 in fancy foods shops and gourmet departments of grocery stores; or dial (616) 947-4533 for mail order information.

❧

It's a premium peanut butter for grown-ups—not at all sticky, just pleasantly buttery with a wonderful roasted nut flavor. Labeled P.B. and pronounced "quite simply . . . incomparable" by aficionado William F. Buckley, it has been dubbed the quintessential brand by many a peanut butter addict. It comes in creamy and crunchy versions in one-pound jars for about $3.50. Look for it in specialty foods shops, or dial (800) 654-5473 for a source in your area.

❧

Charming and thoroughly delicious is Crabtree & Evelyn's "Tea for Two." It contains tea *en sachet,* a drum of crunchy lemon cookies and liqueur-flavored preserves—all done up in a mock two-volume set of books titled *The Complete Picnic.* This, a thermos of hot, hot water and a bosky dell are all that's needed for a lazy summer afternoon. The package would also make a pretty hostess gift. At all Crabtree & Evelyn shops for about $12.50.

There's always room for a better cookie, and the Royal Court Cookie Company has a quartet of some of the finest we've ever tasted. A family company, it packages these delectables in half-pound bags at about $3.95 and in handsome 1¼-pound gift tins at $16.95. The cookies are handmade and contain no artificial ingredients or preservatives. They include the buttery Almond Crescents, crunchy Oatmeal Raisin, Cinnamon Raisin Twists and plump Chocolate Chip. These are sold in specialty foods stores, gourmet sections of leading department stores and through selected catalogs. For further information write the Royal Court Cookie Company, P.O. Box 723, Reseda, CA 91335.

The three main varieties of Indian tea are Darjeeling, Assam and Nilgiri. This last one, Nilgiri, makes the best of all possible iced teas—and with no fuss: Just sprinkle the leaves into a pitcher of cool water and refrigerate overnight for a crystal-clear and smoky-flavored beverage. Maya brand high-grown Nilgiri is available in attractive ¼-pound tin boxes for about $3 each at department stores throughout the country. Of course it is also fine hot, particularly when enhanced with a curl of orange peel.

The Vacu-Vin is what the wine world has been waiting for—an efficient as well as inexpensive way to preserve leftover wine. Invented by a Dutch oenophile, Bernd Schneider, the system keeps wine fresh tasting for two weeks. It is made up of a vacuum pump easily operated by hand and a stopper made of plastic that reseals the opened wine after air and bacteria are withdrawn. The pump is packed with two stoppers, and sells for about $19.95. Additional corks are approximately $1.50 each. Available at specialty foods stores, department stores and through catalogs.

Commemorative bottles are a new idea from vintners both here and abroad. Veuve Clicquot Champagne from France, for instance, issued a special cuvée saluting the 150th anniversary of Texas's independence from Mexico. Harvard University's 350th anniversary was joyously celebrated with special labels from California's Belvedere Winery—a 1985 Napa Valley Chardonnay and 1983 Lake County Cabernet Sauvignon. Alumni bought these by the case to lay down for their children to sip upon *their* hoped-for graduations from Harvard. And the Statue of Liberty celebration inspired handsome wine bottles carved and sandblasted with the Lady herself as decoration. A trend? What can we look forward to for the 200th anniversary of the Constitution?

Fast foods have hit the French right where they live with the opening of the second PARS Restaurants smack in the heart of Paris's Latin Quarter. PARS offers such fascinating—and speedy—international fare as Borani, creamed spinach and yogurt; Panir, feta cheese with shredded lettuce and walnuts; and a tangy lowfat fried chicken.

What is the least liked food in America? According to the surveyors at the Roper organization, it is tofu, with liver as runner-up and yogurt in third place. After that, brussels sprouts, lamb and prunes are close behind in the rankings.

Down on the bayou it all began; then a Mr. Paul Prudhomme picked it up and ran. Now blackened fish is everywhere. We've encountered blackened tilefish, monkfish, even blackened bluefish and sea bass. Currently it's catfish, thanks to Aquaculture Products, growers of Golden Pond farm-raised catfish in Greenwood, Mississippi. Enrobed with a hot and herbed Cajun blend that lends a "blackened" flavor, fillets ready for broiling, baking or microwaving are being delivered to restaurants right from the freezer. The result is a light, nonoily dish high in protein and low in calories, cholesterol and fat. Golden Pond Cajun Catfish is currently available in restaurants and soon to be in markets and specialty foods stores.

❧ *Foods & Info by Mail*

Fresh American foie gras is news, and it's one of several delicious products that are available now from D'Artagnan, a New Jersey company. They're working with Commonwealth Enterprises in upstate New York, who are raising Moulard ducks. This bird differs from the French Moulard in that it doesn't require force-feeding to fatten the liver.

The prime-quality raw foie gras sells for $45 per pound. Other cooked products, prepared under the watchful eyes of D'Artagnan partners George Faison and Ariane Daguin, the pioneering young daughter of famous French chef André Daguin, include terrines of foie gras, *confit de canard, magret fumé, jambon* and *saucisse de canard*. For further details, write D'Artagnan, Inc., 399-419 St. Paul Avenue, Jersey City, NJ 07306; (800) DARTAGNAN.

❧

There's natural and pure, but not always flavorful and delicious. The Gentleman Farmer in Erwinna, Pennsylvania, makes more than five thousand jars of jams, preserves, conserves, relishes and pickles in his kitchen—all natural, pure *and* delicious. The varieties are wonderfully varied and tempting, as only small-batch cookery can produce (he makes no more than eight pints at a time). The ingredients are limited to fruit, sugar and lemon juice with a touch of liqueur or brandy.

There are stunningly creative things here—pumpkin marmalade (great between layers of carrot cake), tomato basil jam, grapefruit lime marmalade with rum, apple butter with Port (a nice glaze for pork) and dozens more. Relishes and condiments are about $4.00. Jams with liqueurs are $4.50. Buy them at the 200-year-old River Road Farms, Route 32, Erwinna, PA 18920, or for mail order information call (215) 294-9763.

❧

Grandma Morgan's has done it again, this time with bagels by mail. And what bagels! Tender whole wheat ones with a touch of sweetness, they are light and perfect for toasting. Baked daily at a small bakery in Clackamas, Oregon, they are shipped right out of the oven on Mondays and Tuesdays. Packed with a 12-ounce jar of slightly tart marionberry preserves, a dozen plump bagels are $17.95 (including air shipment) from Grandma Morgan's Gourmet Kitchen, P.O. Box 972, Lake Oswego, OR 97034; (503) 761-4303.

❧

Clarified butter is one of the purest cooking agents you can use. A dairy product from which all the milk solids, curds and whey have been removed, it is perfect for cooking seafood, eggs, potatoes, steaks, chops and all kinds of vegetables. It is also wonderful for sauces. Now it is available by mail order. Natural and salt free, it doesn't even require refrigeration. A 16-ounce jar is $10 including shipping at Maison Glass, Inc., 52 East 58th Street, New York, NY 10022; (212) 755-3316.

❧

Pasta made to order is the specialty of European Noodles, Inc. Elena Quistini is the creator of these exotics. Among the choices are versions made with double-smoked salmon, hot chili pepper, basil, garlic and squid ink. Shipped fresh at $4 per pound, the pastas can be ordered in a single kind or assorted and can be frozen. Contact European Noodles, Inc., 1130 Caledonia Road, Unit 2, North York, Ontario M6A ZW5, Canada; (416) 78-PASTA.

Fruit juices in boxes, cocktails in cans, wine in spigoted four-liter containers and now smoked salmon and oysters in pouches. The trend toward easy storage, damage-free handling and lighter-weight transportation is leading to the demise of glass packaging. Pacific Select smoked oysters and salmon in gift-pack pouches not only travel well, but also make great party snacks. They can be shipped almost anywhere at $17.50 for an 8-

ounce pouch of oysters, $16.25 for an 8-ounce oyster/salmon combo pouch and $29.75 for 16 ounces of salmon. Contact Port Chatham, 632 N.W. 46th Street, Seattle, WA 98107.

Applesource is the company that ships delicious apple-tasting kits that will teach us to call our favorites by name. The tantalizing assortments are sent from late October through early January, and come two ways: the Sampler, one apple each of 12 different varieties at $18, or the Explorer with two each of 6 varieties for $15. These are postpaid (allow three weeks for delivery) and packed attractively enough to send as a gift. Here are some of the crispest, freshest apples you've ever tasted, wonderful old and new varieties, such as Blushing Golden, Empire, Esopus Spitzenburg, Fuji (the Japanese apple that was Applesource's most popular for 1986), Jonalicious, Newtown Pippin, Spigold and others. What about an apple-tasting party with cheese and wine for a fall get-together? Send for the apples or a free catalog by writing Applesource, Tom Vorbeck, Route One, Chapin, IL 62628.

The craze for Creole and Cajun foods continues with fervor. From the source of it all—Louisiana, of course—the hottest news is a trio of products right from the kitchens of one of New Orleans's most prestigious restaurants, Commander's Palace. They are called Commander's Creole Cravings. The flavorful combinations include Turtle Soup with fresh turtle from the Louisiana bayous, the award-winning Creole Mayonnaise, as well as the Creole Herb Mayonnaise. Available by mail from Commander's Creole Cravings, 1427 Washington Avenue, New Orleans, LA 70130; telephone (504) 891-4466.

If you're planning a big Cajun dinner party and lack the basics, then Cajun Cargo could be the answer for fresh Louisiana seafood, packaged to travel. Three popular gift packs are: Taste of New Orleans, at $42, with two servings of seafood gumbo, four boiled crabs and one pound of fresh Gulf shrimp; The Cajun Feast, at $58, including two fillets of fish, six boiled crabs and two pounds of fresh shrimp; and The Bayou Banquet, at $85.50, with a pound of peeled crawfish tails, one dozen boiled crabs, three pounds of fresh shrimp and two dozen shucked oysters. Prices include 24-hour delivery. Call (800) 99-CARGO.

Monterey Dry Jack is a superb all-purpose domestic cheese, and one of the best comes from Vella Cheese Company of Sonoma, California. This hard, pale yellow, slightly sweet, nutty product is made from California's beloved fresh Jack, but aged for seven to ten months. Sent anywhere in the continental United States by UPS, an eight-pound wheel costs about $31. To order, contact Vella Cheese Company, P.O. Box 191, Sonoma, CA 95476; (707) 938-3232.

The Ultimate Basket in Manhattan really does make baskets for any occasion. Their catalog includes fitness baskets, corporate executive ones and get-well baskets, with prices starting at $40. The Ultimate Basket, (212) 877-3291.

Los Angeles's answer to this unique gift-giving idea is Perfect Picnics . . . Specially Delivered, engineered by ex-*Bon Appétit* staffer Leslie Dame. Four complete menus are offered, from a country-fresh bagel and lox breakfast to a Mexican or hearty Italian meal. Each basket comes lined with a pretty, old-fashioned checked cloth, and includes glasses, cutlery and napery. For information and prices, call (213) 534-4447.

Booklets abound these days. One of the most interesting is *The President's Silver Award Pasta Gourmet Recipe Collection*. It's from The Prince Company and includes delicious recipes, using their line of dried gourmet pastas, from 17 of America's most distinguished chefs. Available free from Silver Award Recipe Collection, The Prince Co. Inc., P.O. Box 8549, Lowell, MA 01853.

Another collectible recipe booklet, *Caviar Lifestyle,* comes to us from Romanoff Caviar. It offers over two dozen recipes using caviar by such food mavens as Kit Snedaker, the Silver Palate chefs and Craig Claiborne. It is available for $1 from Caviar Lifestyle, Romanoff, 1200 Milik Street, Carteret, NJ 07008.

For those heading for the Sonoma Valley this harvest season, there is *A Guide Map to Sonoma Valley Wineries,* distinguished in its design and clarity. Free from Sonoma Valley Vintners, 453 First Street East, Sonoma, CA 95476.

Another lively no-cost booklet, titled *Beaujolais,* provides a short course in one of France's most versatile wines. It profiles the region's eight leading winemakers and includes recipes from the different family kitchens. Get this colorful 24-page booklet from Food and Wines from France, Dept. BW, 24 East 21st Street, New York, NY 10010.

Good old Mazola has produced a cookbook to celebrate its birthday. Called *75 Years of Good Eating,* it includes 50 recipes from past to present and will undoubtedly be a collector's treasure in years to come. For 50 cents postage and handling, you may have a copy from Mazola Anniversary Cookbook, Dept. MA-C, Box 307, Coventry, CT 06238.

Corning's newest four-color book, *Corning Microwave Cooking,* is available for just $3. Its nearly 100 recipes are perfect for year-round menu planning. For your copy, send to Microwave Cookbook Offer, Corning Glass Works, P.O. Box 375, Big Flats, NY 14814.

Polly-O, makers of ricotta and cottage cheeses, offers the *Cooking with Cheese Cookbook,* with 80 pages of magnificent recipes by cooking teacher and author Anna Theresa Callen, edited by Wilma G. deZanger. Beautiful color illustrations by noted photographer Ari deZanger are plentifully dispersed throughout this keepsake book. It is yours for $3 from Pollio Dairy Products Corporation, Dept. Q, 120 Mineola Boulevard, Mineola, NY 11501.

The classic cakes we love take the low-calorie route in the *Swans Down's Breakthrough Baking* booklet, with recipes that offer calorie reductions of 45 percent and more. Enjoy such treats as buttermilk cocoa cake with chocolate silk filling, which matches the taste and texture of its calorie-laden counterpart. To order a copy, send $1 to Swans Down Breakthrough Baking, P.O. Box 60296, New Orleans, LA 70160.

Thelma Pressman might indeed be called Madame Microwave, so well known is she for her pioneering uses of that miracle appliance. Now she has produced a helpful little book for Sybil Henderson Fresh Set Cookbooks, titled *Sybil's Guide to Microwaving Vegetables.* It is a compact gem. You need nothing more on the subject. Order it for $2 from Microwave Cooking Center, 17728 Marcello, Encino, CA 91316. California residents should add sales tax.

Hoppin' John's is the name of "the Southeast's only bookstore devoted exclusively to the world of food." The property of John M. Taylor, the store boasts more than three thousand new and out-of-print books, antique food prints, handcrafted knives and more. The energetic proprietor also cranks out a newsletter and an occasional art show focusing on food. His hand-tinted greeting cards, printed from nineteenth-century fruit and vegetable illustrations, are available by mail. Boxed in sets of eight, they are $13.75 including shipping. Contact Hoppin' John's, 30 Pinckney Street, Charleston, SC 29401.

❦ *Restaurants & People*

New look, new menu—and three new stars from Bryan Miller, Manhattan's most severe restaurant critic. That's what's happened at The Sign of the Dove, owner Dr. Joseph Santo's brainchild, which just celebrated its 25th anniversary. Never has the French-influenced fare been so delightful as under the aegis of young chef Andrew D'Amico. And never has the setting been more romantic, with its masses of flowers, soft lighting, silk-clouded skylight and rosy brick arches that allow for sequestered dining. This enduring fine dining establishment is indeed having a glorious renaissance.

The inspired menu offers a sweet onion and ham tartlet or oysters and caviar with quail eggs and sour cream, as a tasteful opener. For a main course you might try medallions of veal with wild mushrooms and a light sweet garlic custard or some grilled venison with polenta, red currants and Zinfandel. Desserts are truly devastating. "The chocolate plate" embraces all the Dove's fabulous chocolate desserts in a single dégustation. The Sign of the Dove, 1110 Third Avenue at 65th Street, New York, NY; (212) 861-8080.

❦

Darbar is the ongoing darling of Manhattan's Indian food aficionados. It is a romantic and serene restaurant with a bill of fare that is both alluring and affordable. Here you may indulge in a parade of North Indian selections from a colorful menu that explains each item. For instance, you will learn that *hyderabadi murgh shorba* is a soup of chicken, potatoes, coconut and lemon.

Of course, there are also classic dishes, cooked in the clay tandoori oven. A collection of *vindaloo* combines the fiery and the subtle. And the appetizers are almost endless—*anguri samosa,* crisp vegetable pastries; cumin-seasoned and batter-fried *onion bhajia*; *murgh pakoras,* tender chicken bits marinated in yogurt and Indian spices and batter fried; and wonderfully savory vegetable fritters. The tandoori shrimp are a main-course treat, and for vegetarians there is a special vegetarian *thali* with appetizer, chutneys and dessert. Add to all this the soothing warmth of terra-cotta–colored walls discreetly decorated with woven silks, carved wooden panels, flattering globe lamps and hammered copper and brass art. Darbar, which means "palace court," is located at 44 W. 56th Street, New York; (212) 432-7227.

❦

Manhattanites are going to the Foucher Cafe these days for breakfast, lunch, dinner, even tea. This chip off the chocolate shop and cafe in Paris is filled with handmade chocolates packaged in shiny red and gold boxes. The cafe serves wonderful breakfasts with bite-size raspberry pastries and French *café au lait* or espresso, brunches of caviar and blinis with crème fraîche, light lunches, and delightful dinners. Find this quaint spot at 789 Lexington Avenue.

❦

The ghosts of presidents past may whisper over your table at the painstakingly restored Willard Room in the historic Willard Inter-Continental in Washington, D.C. Once chef Brent Holleman's culinary masterpieces begin to appear, there is delight at such perfectly prepared courses as roast young New Zealand venison, American foie gras, Maryland crab in many guises and a score of other great American dishes. Breakfast is the tour de force of head pastry chef Dominique Leborgne–the walnut-studded rolls are an absolute triumph and the warm, buttery croissants are the best to be had this side of Paris.

The 1850 hotel and the restaurant are the "in" places on newly spruced-up Pennsylvania Avenue. If you plan a stay, ask for a room that offers a view of both the Washington Monument and the Lincoln Memorial. (The Willard Inter-Continental, 1401 Pennsylvania Ave., N.W., Washington, DC 20004; 202/628-9100. Willard Room, 202/637-7440.)

People are talking about Amérique, a new-age bistro in the trendy River North area of Chicago. They are taken with the postmodern, neo-Grecian decor and the innovative cuisine of chefs Jennifer Newbury and Dennis Terczak (formerly of Avanzare). The restaurant offers such entrées as squid *agrodolce* (a sweet and sour sauce), duck and juniper berry ravioli, salmon cured with basil and chilies, and pork with cabbage and garlic sausage. (Amérique, 312/943-6341.)

If you find yourself in Milwaukee—and hungry—try John Byron's. With its view of Lake Michigan, top-rated wine list and distinctive cuisine, it has a far-reaching reputation for excellence. Chef Sanford D'Amato, a classically trained hometown boy, shows off the best of the state's bounty in such dishes as smoked baby trout with herbed mayonnaise and veal with endive and chanterelles. (John Byron's, First Wisconsin Center, 777 East Michigan Street, Milwaukee, WI 53202; 414/291-5220.)

Saint-Emilion, a charming French country restaurant in a rustic A-frame at the edge of town, is the talk of Fort Worth. This small and friendly establishment is named for the village in southwest France near Bordeaux. Its owner, Bernard Tronche, grew up there, so his knowledge of the region's wines and cooking came right from the source. Now he is packing sophisticated Texans into his beam-ceilinged dining room with its open kitchen. The grill and rotisserie are kept active with fragrant lamb kebabs, pheasant, duck, fish and shrimp.

Tronche and chef Jean-Claude Rosset also serve up fresh lamb sausages, light goat cheese croquettes, Basque omelets and an exquisite stuffed boneless quail with Belgian endive. A first for Fort Worth, this convivial spot may well nudge a few rib joints and chili places out as favorites. (Saint-Emilion, 3617 West Seventh Street, Fort Worth, TX 76107; 817/737-2781.)

Out in Texas, where taste buds typically tingle with the hot and zesty foods of southwestern cooking, a truly stylish restaurant blossoms with the unusual and inviting flavors of Hunan. Decorated with priceless Chinese porcelain, Dong Ting offers such rarities as ground pork and crabmeat balls with Chinese cabbage and black mushrooms; frog legs in hot garlic; and spicy squid, wok-fried with garlic and ginger in a fiery red sauce. One of our experts on oriental culinary matters, Ken Hom, dined there with great pleasure and reported back: "Owner San Hwang and his wife have brought delicious and innovative Chinese food to the Southwest. Their Eggplant Peppercorn is a wonderfully different dish of cold eggplant in a pungent peppercorn-scallion sauce. Not to be missed are the Hunan smoked dishes, Lah Gee, smoked chicken, and Lah Rou, stir-fried smoked pork." (Dong Ting Restaurant, 611 Stuart, Houston, TX 77006; 713/527-0005.)

That celebrated chef who endowed Vincent's—the Scottsdale restaurant—with his name has moved on to open his very own place in Phoenix. It's called Vincent Guerithault on Camelback. He is still up to his high standards of cuisine, with emphasis on freshness. The menu includes mesquite-grilled lobster and veal chops with parsnip puree, in addition to other southwestern dishes with a French accent. And for dessert, there are deliciously light hot raspberry-blueberry tarts with sorbets. The address is 3930 East Camelback Road, Phoenix, AZ 85018; (602) 224-0225.

Michel Richard, one of the best-known chefs in Los Angeles and erstwhile proprietor of two popular local patisseries, may have found his dream-come-true in the ultra-chic, ultra-hip restaurant called Citrus. He is the proud master of a huge stainless steel kitchen with marble counters and the last word in gleaming contemporary equipment. The restaurant is a true California-style retreat, with color as far as the eye can see, from the lovely flowers and a counter resplendent with some of the most tempting desserts from the master's own hand. The largest area of the restaurant is a canopied patio with giant white canvas umbrellas—a bustling space where assorted power brokers and aspiring moguls can see and be seen.

Richard changes the menu frequently. Typical goodies include a crab "cole slaw" (crab salad wrapped in a single pretty green cabbage leaf and served with a tomato mayonnaise); scallops with sweet Maui onion rings and fresh thyme sauce (the chef's herb garden is back of the patio); an appetizer of baby lettuce with crisp sweetbreads in balsamic vinaigrette; a pretty eggplant and tomato terrine; and a colorful sautéed salmon with a seemingly improbable but wonderfully complementary red beet sauce and cucumber "spaghetti." The sauces are kind to the waistline, too, with very little cream or butter used. (Citrus, 6703 Melrose Avenue, Los Angeles, CA 90038; 213/857-0034.)

Barbara Tropp is one of the West Coast's most knowledgeable persons in the realm of Chinese cooking, and now she brings both Western and Eastern techniques and tastes to her new China Moon Cafe in San Francisco. It is located in an old 1930s luncheonette that has been changed very little except for a coat of paint, a deco polish and modern chairs. From either the long bar or the cozy booths, you can watch some of the cooking at the front of the restaurant.

The dinner menu lists several "foods to make the wine go down," among them Szechwan cucumber fans and cold-tossed asparagus with sesame vinaigrette. Appetizers include an East-West dish of crisp spring rolls stuffed with chicken and serrano chilies. Gingery fish-ball soup with lemongrass and glass noodles is a winner, as are such entrées as hoisin-explosion sparerib nuggets in a sand pot with pine nut fried rice and pot-browned noodle pillow with hot and sour chicken. All this might be followed by a fabulous assortment of cookies of good fortune or a chocolate rum torte with kumquat ice cream. (China Moon Cafe, 639 Post St., San Francisco, CA 94109; 415/775-4789.)

The James Beard House in New York plans to restore and expand Mr. B.'s original research library, which was dispersed upon his death. Historical and contemporary cookbooks, food and wine references, booklets, wine labels, magazines and menus are all being sought, and the public is invited to contribute. Query the foundation first by sending a list of your proposed offering and an estimated value of its worth to Mrs. Christine Schefman, The James Beard House, 167 West 12th Street, New York, NY 10011.

 Getaways

For a fabulous culinary adventure on your next trip abroad, consider these many fine programs:

Celebrated author, teacher and television personality Madeleine Kamman retains her teaching facilities in Annecy, France, and now offers guided cultural and gastronomic tours of "The France of the French." Private excursions can also be arranged. Write to Madeleine Kamman, Inc., P.O. Box 363, Bartlett, NH 03812, for more information.

The famed cooking school La Varenne in Burgundy will sponsor one-week-long gastronomic courses at the Château du Fëy, located in the northern Burgundian town of Villecien. Each will be presented by a different personality, with the assistance of La Varenne chefs and a bilingual support staff. For complete details, contact La Varenne in Burgundy, P.O. Box 25574, Washington, DC 20007; telephone (202) 337-0073.

Les Etapes des Gourmets in Lyons, France, allows you to live the life of a French *cuisinier* or *pâtissier*. Program participants spend a working week in one of 88 world-famous restaurants. Write M. Michel Dreyfus, Les Etapes des Gourmets, 47, rue Rabelais, 69003 Lyons, France, for additional details or call Jebb Curelop, (212) 753-6018.

❦

In Italy, the International Academy of Italian Food and Wine holds classes at the magnificent Villa Ranuzzi Cospi in Bologna. There are 8- to 10-day courses beginning May 3 and featuring excursions and wine tastings. For information, call Mary Beth Clark, (212) 755-8938, or Bob Bruno, (718) 816-4490.

❦

And, of course, there is Giuliano Bugialli's famous series, Cooking in Florence. Classes begin in May and continue through October. A special dine-and-travel program to Sardinia is also being offered. For details, contact Audrey Berman, 2830 Gordon Street, Allentown, PA 18104; (215) 435-2451.

❦

Learning from the top is the thrust of Robert Noah's food tours, called Paris en Cuisine. A dozen years old, this highly acclaimed gastronomic tour organization provides top-level cooking classes and tours throughout Paris and the French provinces. Groups are small as they tour the finest restaurants and food shops, whose chefs and owners are the professors. Fall classes include Cooking in Les Baux-de-Provence, Cooking with Michel Guérard and Cooking with the Troisgros. For information, write Paris en Cuisine, 1221 Locust, Suite 405, St. Louis, MO 63103; (314) 436-2002.

❦

At Tenth and Main in Boise, Idaho, the Idanha Hotel reared its French château corner turrets, opened its canopied doors in 1901 and proceeded to entertain a series of presidents. Fully restored in 1977, its grandeur and luxury continue. Within, just off the lobby (with its art deco chandelier from the celebrated Astor Hotel in New York), is Peter Schott's Continental Restaurant. The serene atmosphere is a perfect setting for executive chef Peter Schott's interpretations of classic French and his native Austrian cuisine. Using local specialties—trout, wild mushrooms, game, salmon and the potatoes that made the state famous—Schott has created a distinguished menu that has led many food critics to pronounce the restaurant the best in Idaho. Some of the offerings include ham spaetzle with Gruyère cheese and smoked pork loin with veal sauce. (Idanha Hotel, 928 Main St., Boise, ID 83702; 208/342-3611.)

❦

Lim Cuisine, an innovation of Gary L. Jackson, offers a new way to see the sights and dine in style while in the Phoenix/Scottsdale area. The service combines the comforts and prestige of a limousine with the ambience of one of that region's finest restaurants, Vincent Guerithault on Camelback. Jackson offers customers French-Southwestern meals in his elaborate automobiles as they are driven from one scenic desert spot to another. A four-hour excursion, for instance, includes a sunset toast atop Camelback Mountain and a grand finale of moon watching on Sahauro Lake. Vintage Champagne is chilled in silver ice buckets and recessed tables are set with elegant napery, crystal and silver. The food is arranged on hot plates at the restaurant and kept warm in an oven in the car. The tab for two is about $300. (Lim Cuisine, 6526 North 24th Lane, Phoenix, AZ 85015; 602/242-5567.)

❦

Off the beaten path and far from the madding crowd is a small, elegant hotel that offers comfort and charm after the pleasures of Paris nightlife. Convenient to the hub of activity, yet removed from the sound and fury, the Hotel Balzac has been completely remodeled. It provides comfortable rooms and a lobby area with an inviting sitting room and friendly bar. Located just off the Champs Elysées, it is at 6, rue de Balzac, 75008 Paris; (1)45.61.97.22.

❦

When in Paris, for those determined to dine with the locals, hail a cab or hop on the *métro* and head for Au Pupillin, a lively neighborhood wine bar-restaurant run by brothers Yves and François

Vidonne. Here you will often find a line of the BCBG *(bon chic, bon genre),* the city's young, hip urban professionals, waiting to get in. The innovative and delicious light fare includes a salad of apples, fruit and avocados; crispy Chinese chicken dumplings with ginger sauce; and salmon *rillettes* on bread from the fabled Poilâne bakery. There are also chicken with black mushrooms and salmon steamed in Thai banana leaves, as well as brochettes of pork with coconut and curry. Be sure to leave room to splurge on such fantastic desserts as terrine of two chocolates and preserved oranges, warm pear tart and sorbet "Kalamansi" made from wild lemons and vodka.

It all adds up to the best of East and West, served by a very cheerful staff. The wine list is full of outstanding selections, including those from the Jura, in eastern France. Reservations are advised. (Au Pupillin, 19, rue Notre Dame de Lorette, 75009 Paris.)

For a meal to remember, dine outdoors in the arched arcade of La Guirlande de Julie across from the park on the historic place des Vosges in Paris. You can enjoy the classic French food proffered by young chef Christian Bochaton: Sip a cool Meursault with, say, a delicious *terrine de lotte et saumon à l'estragon.* It will be a long, leisurely dinner (the French don't bolt their food) as you watch the passing parade. If it's too cool outside, switch to La Guirlande's indoor dining room, which has all the feeling of a country pavilion. The fare is absolutely delicious and beautifully presented. This spot could be the perfect ending of your vacation or simply the climax of a long, busy day. Restaurant La Guirlande de Julie is at 25, place des Vosges, 75003, Paris; (1)48.87.94.07.

Graues Haus, or "Gray House," is anything but gray, with its three floors of stone walls crossed with warm wooden beams, softly lit through arched Romanesque windows with clear views of the Rhine and steep Rheingau vineyards. Located in Oestrich-Winkel, near Wiesbaden, and believed to be the oldest stone house in Germany (circa A.D. 800), Graues Haus is venerated not so much for its age but for the food and wine

served at Count Matuschka Greiffenclau's restaurant and popular *Weinschmeckerlokal* ("wine-tasting bar"), a showcase for the fine Rheingau wines.

Meals to harmonize with these local bottlings, characterized by their low alcohol content, are the charge of chef Egbert Englehardt, who came to Graues Haus "to get away from goose liver and truffles." Here he draws on such local products as nettles, wild mushrooms and mirabelles, goat, rabbits and suckling pigs. Each day, with these ingredients at his command, he prepares regional menus, employing lighter, creative cooking techniques and older fast-disappearing traditions such as *Schmoren* ("stewing"). (Graues Haus, Graugasse 10, 6227 Oestrich-Winkel 2; [06723] 2619.)

A few miles northeast of Siena, just over the border of the Chianti Classico region, you'll find a perfect example of the new-style Italian country restaurant, called Il Molino delle Bagnaie. One glance at the 400-year-old stone mill in the flower-dotted meadow and you might expect to find a white-aproned *mamma* in the kitchen serving up hearty rustic food, but Il Molino, opened two years ago by a group of young Sienese, has a city sophistication.

The metal gears and housings of the old millstones look like modern sculpture against the white stucco walls of the main room, and a glass panel reveals the paddle wheel that drove the mill until the mid-1960s. The menu features local game, including grilled pheasant and hare. Their spicy Tuscan prosciutto is coated with salt and red and black pepper. And for dessert, the *tiramisù* is a standout, assembled from creamy mascarpone, chocolate and sponge cake.

As befits the restaurant's location, the list of Chiantis is a wine lover's dream, with a dozen or so outstanding selections, most under $10. Co-owner George Ceccarelli greets patrons in the perfect English he learned at his American mother's knee. Il Molino delle Bagnaie is located northeast of Siena, north of Pianella on Highway 408.

❦ For the Kitchen & Table

Alessi, the famous Italian housewares company, commissioned designer Richard Sapper to create a cookware set with the help of such top chefs as Pierre and Michel Troisgros, Gualtiero Marchesi and Roger Vergé, among others. The result is a 23-piece line called The Orion Belt. It took seven years to move from the drawing board to the marketplace and sells for a cool $4,000.

Each piece is made for an individual function and each is a work of art in itself. A big oval cast iron Dutch oven (cocotte), stainless steel faitout or casserole, copper sauteuse and handsome stainless steel stand with a copper flambé pan are just a few of the items. Cast iron pans are intended for slow cooking, black steel for frying or omelets, copper for quick heating and stainless for boiling.

Each chef contributed the idea for the equipment used in his specialty: Vergé, the fish poacher; Marchesi, casseroles and a stock pot; the Troisgroses, the frying pans; Angelo Paracucchi, the flambé; Raymond Thuilier, the cocotte; and from Alain Chapel, the sauteuse. For information and sources, write Markuse Corporation, 10 Wheeling Avenue, Woburn, MA 01801.

❦

Those ingenious Australians have done it yet again: this time with a series of self-sharpening knives. A Melbourne company, McPherson's Ltd., conceived this unique patented cutlery that resharpens itself every time it is removed from its specially designed sheath. Sold here through the U.S.-based subsidiary, Wiltshire International, Inc., the sets range from those for sportsmen to utility and kitchen types. Called the 1500 Series, these tools are forged with full tang construction, stainless steel bolsters and rivets, and tapered and hardened stainless steel blades. The housing units can be wall mounted. Available in stores and through mail-order catalogs nationally, the knives range from about $22 to $100. For additional information, write Customer Service Dept., Wiltshire International, P.O. Box 219, Farmingdale, NY 11735; telephone (800) 872-3343.

❦

Truly trendy is owning a Traulsen refrigerator right from that company's commercial line, with models now modified for residential use. The Traulsen Ultra Model URS 48 DT is a side-by-side refrigerator/freezer that has everything a cook might desire. It is stainless steel inside and out, with a glass door available, a precision temperature monitoring system, vinyl magnetic door gaskets (for silent opening and closing), chrome-plated shelves, door bins, pullout drawers with removable anodized aluminum pans and, of course, an automatic ice maker. This dream fridge costs in the neighborhood of a cool $3,500, and is available through dealers nationwide. For one in your area, call (800) 542-4022, or write Traulsen & Co., Inc., 114-02 15th Avenue, College Point, NY 11356.

❦

Some of the smartest designer kitchens these days are black—with black ranges, countertops, fridges, freezers and so on. Now Cuisinart's food processors can blend with the trend. Both the compact model and the Superpro model are available in a sleek jet black.

❦

A decorative 17x24-inch chart, laminated for easy cleaning and eyeletted for convenient hanging, is just what the pantry door needs for quick reference on food storage and handling data. Refrigerator, shelf and freezer storage times and packing details are clearly itemized. There is also a column of safety tips. It is $8 postpaid from Beam Enterprises, Department E-25, 19812 Acre Street, Northridge, CA 91324.

❦

Brown Bag Cookie Art offers one of the best selections of cookie molds in the country, with teddy bears and woolly lambs, piglets, Victorian hearts and rocking horses. The ceramic molds make attractive wall hangings, so are great gifts in their own right. Each costs $12 plus shipping. A special collection of 21 recipes called *The Gourmet Cookie Book* is also available at $2.95. To order, write A Hill Design Company, Route 3A, Hill, NH 03243; telephone (800) 228-4488.

Wonder where those demitasse spoons, tea balls and cake decorating tips disappear to in your dishwasher? Avoid such losses (and washer repairs) with a blessed little gadget called Wee Washbasket, a "cage" for all your tiny oddments. It costs $11.95; order it from Just An Idea, 25605 Willow Bend, El Toro, CA 92630; telephone (714) 586-6468.

Quicker than a squirrel and twice as neat, the Texan "York" Nut Sheller can produce perfect whole nutmeats for your next pecan pie. Looking like high tech pliers, its heavy steel razor-sharp serrated jaws simply snip off the ends and sides of each nutshell and the nut can be plucked out whole. It also shells almonds, Brazil nuts, walnuts and hazelnuts, as well as cracking both lobster and crab claws. A protective shield over the blades deflects shell pieces, thus eliminating the mess nutcrackers usually make. It is available for $9.95 from Texan Nut Sheller Co., Inc., P.O. Box 2900, San Angelo, TX 76902.

From trencher to salad or luncheon size, the new Wilton Armetale scallop shell plates are perfect for year-round entertaining. In a cool bicolor design, the plates are rimmed with raised shells that are scored with the color of coral. With the gleam of fine new pewter, this ever-shiny alloy requires no polishing. Part of the "Shell" line, these are available in china and housewares departments throughout the country. Prices for the plates range from about $25 to $50. Also available are a wine bottle coaster, goblets and serving tray.

The Russian samovar, that traditional urn used to boil water for tea, may have to take a back seat to Mr. Tea, a modernized beverage heater. Except for the once-necessary charcoal, the new Mr. Tea is a line-for-line replica of the samovar that works even more efficiently for serving up to 24 cups of mulled wine or other cold-weather favorites. Manufactured by Beem Royal of West Germany, it comes in gold plate for $590, silver plate for $440, chrome for $295 and stainless steel for $250. Each is packed in a handsome gift box with a matching teapot, instructions in four languages and a one-year warranty. Imported by the Beem California Corporation, Mr. Tea is available nationally, or write the company for more information at P.O. Box 2001, Glendale, CA 91209.

It seems that someone somewhere is always coming up with yet another way to extract a recalcitrant cork from its wine bottle. One more implement has debuted this year, which would make a great present for your favorite wine buff. The Wine Key is a cordless electric affair that is totally automatic, requiring no twisting or turning. Simply press a button, and the screw is driven into the cork. Press again, and the stopper is withdrawn. Press one more time, and the cork is released. A conversation piece, yes, but it works. Available for about $35 in fine stores everywhere, or order it from Meyer Corporation, U.S., 700 Forbes Boulevard, South San Francisco, CA 94080; (415) 871-2444.

The Verkade Corporation puts it all together in a solid oak and chromed steel free-form carrier that displays (or transports) up to four bottles of wine and four to six glasses. It can be placed on counters or tables, and easily taken poolside, or wherever needed. This new wine and stemware display rack is perfect for the high-tech home. It is available for $29.95 plus $3.50 shipping from Verkade Corporation, P.O. Box 3402, Grand Rapids, MI 49501.

❦ Diet News

Light, lean—what do these words mean? The American Meat Institute (AMI), which represents all segments of the meat industry, offers suggested guidelines in the use of these words to clarify their meaning for the consumer. These could well serve the entire food and beverage industry. First off, they say, the use of *lite, light* or *lightly, lean, leaner, lower fat* or *reduced fat* should require a uniform minimum standard of a 25 percent reduction in the total amount of the fat, calories, sodium, sugar, breading, etc., in the food item in question. And, when used, these terms should be explained on the label. There are more suggested guidelines. This is a great beginning.

❦

Just exactly what are cruciferous vegetables? Said to be beneficial in warding off cancer, they are members of the botanical mustard family, the Cruciferae. The family includes such healthy things as mustard greens, horseradish, cabbage, turnips, watercress, radishes, broccoli and cabbage. Flowers of these plants are cross shaped, hence the name.

❦

If your cholesterol is up, bring it down by using olive oil in place of other fats. Bertolli's Extra Light Olive Oil—a new one—is extremely light in flavor and aroma. Those who tend not to like the taste of more intense olive oils may well take kindly to this one.

❦

New salt-free notes include Mrs. Dash's all-natural Crispy Coating Mix for chicken or pork, a zesty blend of herbs and spices. Also from Mrs. Dash is a "Low pepper–No garlic" seasoning blend. With both, those who must can throw away the salt shaker.

❦

Parsley Patch in Windsor, California, is adding more savory healthwise spice blends to their line. They include a seasoned saltless popcorn blend, garlic saltless and seafood saltless.

Reed's Dairy in Idaho Falls, Idaho, offers a smooth, rich ice cream that's sugar free, natural and 20 to 50 percent lower in calories than regular ice cream. Among its listed ingredients are Idaho's number one product—potatoes! Look for Al & Reed's All Natural Ice Cream.

❦

Vitari is another low-calorie delight, a creamy, frozen fruit, soft-serve product with the taste and texture of soft ice cream. In delicious fresh fruit flavors, it is 99 percent fruit and fruit juice. A 3½-ounce serving has just 63 calories.

❦

Beef-alternative burgers started off with Alaska's popular salmonburger. Made with Alaska canned salmon, they offer calcium and omega-3 fatty acids. They've been served at the Space Needle in Seattle and appeared on menus at Spat's in Nashville, Old Ebbitt Grill in Washington, D.C., and Great State Fare in Chicago. We've even heard of prawnburgers in Denmark. Can crabburgers and soleburgers be far behind?

❦

For sodium watchers, there's SPA, both sparkling and still waters. Regulated by the Institut Henrijean in Belgium (the source), SPA waters are virtually salt free, pure, light and the least mineralized of today's bottled waters. Perfect for both drinking and cooking, these natural waters are derived from melting snow and rainwater. Look for them in specialty and natural foods stores.

❦

Here's a summer drink for calorie counters, currently popular both at the bar and at the table: Half fill a tall glass or a goblet with sparkling water or club soda. Add a half-dozen healthy dashes of bitters, fill with cracked ice and enjoy.

Calories are low and vitamins are high in a 4-ounce flute of Chandon Napa Valley Brut. The count is just 88 calories and the vitamins are A, C, D and E. The sparkler is produced by Domaine Chandon, America's first French-owned winery.

❦

Dr. Thomas B. Turner, president of Hopkins Alcoholic Beverage Medical Research Foundation at Johns Hopkins University, reports that his study of 17,000 Canadians reveals that moderate wine and Champagne drinkers suffer 25 percent fewer illnesses than nondrinkers or those who drink hard liquor.

❦

The new Santé de-alcoholized white wine has about half the calories of regular whites, with a three-ounce serving coming in at just 36 calories. This new breed is 99.51 percent alcohol free. Blended with French Colombard, Chenin Blanc and dry white wines, it is a fine pale yellow with a rich fragrance and taste, lightly sparkling and very refreshing. Santé has been acknowledged by several wine authorities as one of the best-tasting of all nonalcoholic wines.

❦

The hottest spot for "spaing" right now is the Cal-a-Vie in Vista, California. Chef Michel Stroot is dishing up these diet delectables: paillard of turkey with lemon and rosemary, watercress gazpacho, spicy ratatouille and raw vegetable salads. Michel calls his style of cooking "cuisine fraîche" and shows each guest how to plan menus and purchase ingredients sensibly and healthfully.

❦

Abigail Kirsch's famous catering company in New York City and Bedford Hills, New York, is offering low-calorie party fare in "Dining without Guilt" menus. One delightful meal that tops up at 782 calories includes hors d'oeuvres of halibut scallops, vegetables Provençal in crepe, and crudités with herbed dipping sauce. There is a swordfish appetizer served with saffron yogurt sauce, followed by Cornish hen with wild mushrooms, baby spring vegetables and wild and brown rice. A salad of radicchio, Bibb, endive and sprouts is accompanied by an herbed French crisp (for those who must have bread). Dessert

is beautiful: ripe strawberries and blackberries in an almond tuile with fresh fruit *coulis*. A glorious feast for so few calories. Dial (212) 696-4076 for details.

❦

In New Orleans, where dieting is a hush-hush subject, there is a popular and pretty restaurant called Flagons, A Wine Bar & Bistro. The first of its kind in the Crescent City, the alternative lunch menu was planned with the aid of Covert Bailey's Fit-or-Fat System and offers delicious original entrées with complete nutritional breakdowns. (Flagons, 3222 Magazine St., New Orleans, LA 70115; 504/895-6471.)

❦

An ample supply of foods containing risk-reducing fibers in our diets is highly recommended by the National Cancer Institute. To help you find your way among the various fiber-containing foods, including those served at breakfast time, the Kellogg Company offers an informative free booklet called "A Step-by-Step Guide to a High Fiber Diet." It includes everything from charts, recipes and tips on ways to achieve a wholesome diet to a calorie/fiber counter for the most common food categories. For a copy write the Kellogg Company, 1 Kellogg Square, Dept. Q-7, P.O. Box 3599, Battle Creek, MI 49016.

❦

Campbell's Soup's new pamphlet, "The Working Person's Diet," is a freebie full of nutritious menu ideas and helpful tips for eating on the run with a balanced diet in mind. Fast, easy breakfasts, lunches and dinners using quick-cooking frozen foods do the trick here for workaholics. Take a look. Order by sending a stamped, self-addressed envelope to Working Person's Diet, P.O. Box 1232, Adams Avenue, Bensalem, PA 19020.

❦

One of the new and worthy books for high-blood-pressure sufferers is *The Control Your High Blood Pressure Cookbook* (Doubleday, 1987) by Cleaves M. Bennett, M.D., and Cristine Newport. It tells how to shop for and prepare over two hundred healthy and innovative recipes using low-sodium, low-cholesterol and low-priced ingredients without sacrificing taste. There are also tips on how to hew to the program when traveling and when dining out.

❦ *Credits and Acknowledgments*

The following people contributed the recipes included in this book:

Leslie Balick
Nancy Verde Barr
Lula Bertram
Beth Carlson
Virgil Carrington
Courtney Carswell
Casa Madrona Restaurant, Sausalito,
  California
Diane Castelli
Ginger Chang
Linda Chrisey
John and Polly Clingerman
CoCo La Fleur, Carmel Valley,
  California
Colette, Beverly Hills, California
Marion Cunningham
Karen Danielson
Mimi and Robert Del Grande
Harriet and Randy Derwingson
Emilio's Restaurant, Hollywood,
  California
George Germon
Rick Guldan
Kathy Gunst

Patti Hardy
Ruedi Hauser
Patricia Hopkins
John Hudspeth
Michael Hutchings
Jenny's, Lahaska, Pennsylvania
Karen Kaplan
Barrie Kavasch
Kristine Kidd
Johanne Killeen
Skippy Krohn
La Villa, Tucson, Arizona
Julianne Lansing
Sofi Konstantinidis
Faye Levy
Judy Lew
Portia Little
Abby Mandel
Gerard Maras
Carol and Ian McHarg
Michael McLaughlin
Jefferson and Jinx Morgan
Selma Morrow
Peter Mow

Donna Nordin
Beatrice Ojakangas
Consuelo Peña
Rapallo, Oakland, California
Betty Rosbottom
David Rosengarten
Julie Sahni
Richard Sax
Sebanton, Longmont, Colorado
Piero Selvaggio
Edena Sheldon
Patricia Silva
Marie Simmons
Aletha Soule
Frank Stitt
Sylvia's Good Food, Red Lodge,
  Montana
Trader Vic's, San Francisco, California
John and Meredith Whiting
Lin and Rex Young
Yum Cha Dim Sum Cafe & Market,
  Santa Monica, California
Alan Zeman
Socorrito Diego de Zorrilla

"News '87" text was supplied by:
  Zack Hanle.

Special thanks to:

Editorial Staff:
  William J. Garry
  Barbara Fairchild
  Angeline Vogl
  MaryJane Bescoby

Graphics Staff:
  Bernard Rotondo
  Gloriane Harris

Rights and Permissions:
  Karen Legier

Indexer:
  Rose Grant

The Knapp Press
is a wholly owned subsidiary of
KNAPP COMMUNICATIONS CORPORATION

Composition by Andresen's Tucson Typographic Service, Inc., Tucson, Arizona

This book is set in Sabon, a face designed by Jan Teischold in 1967
and based on early fonts engraved by Garamond and Granjon.